Peacemaking and the Challenge of Violence in World Religions

Peacemaking and the Challenge of Violence in World Religions

Edited by

Irfan A. Omar and Michael K. Duffey

WILEY Blackwell

This edition first published 2015
© 2015 John Wiley & Sons, Ltd.

Registered Office
John Wiley & Sons, Ltd, The Atrium, Southern Gate, Chichester, West Sussex, PO19 8SQ, UK

Editorial Offices
350 Main Street, Malden, MA 02148-5020, USA
9600 Garsington Road, Oxford, OX4 2DQ, UK
The Atrium, Southern Gate, Chichester, West Sussex, PO19 8SQ, UK

For details of our global editorial offices, for customer services, and for information about how
to apply for permission to reuse the copyright material in this book please see our website at
www.wiley.com/wiley-blackwell.

The right of Irfan A. Omar and Michael K. Duffey to be identified as the authors of the editorial
material in this work has been asserted in accordance with the UK Copyright, Designs and Patents
Act 1988.

Library of Congress Cataloging-in-Publication Data applied for.

Hardback ISBN: 9781118953433
Paperback ISBN: 9781118953426

A catalogue record for this book is available from the British Library.

Cover image: © ussr/ iStockphoto

Set in in 10/12pt Minion by SPi Publisher Services, Pondicherry, India

1   2015

(IAO) To Farah for her unfailing support

(MKD) To Mary Beth and our four children, my teachers all

Contents

Acknowledgments

This book is the result of a joint project between the Marquette University Center for Peacemaking and the Department of Theology. In conjunction with planning this book, the editors collaborated with the Office of the Provost to organize a one-day symposium on the topic of "Peacemaking and Nonviolence in World Religions" held at Marquette University on October 3, 2013. The Associate Provost for Diversity and Inclusion, Dr William Welburn, generously provided funding for the symposium for which we are very grateful. The Center for Peacemaking provided additional funds to host the visiting scholars. The symposium was partially funded by a grant from the United States Institute of Peace, and by the Edward D. Simmons Religious Commitment Fund from Marquette University Office of Mission and Ministry. The staff of the Center for Peacemaking, Patrick Kennelly (director), Carole Poth (associate director), and Chris Jeske (office associate) gave their invaluable assistance in planning and organizing the day-long event. Other Marquette colleagues who participated as session chairs include Abderrahman Atifi, Pranavkumar Achar, Sarah Bond, Bronwyn Finnigan, Duane Loynes, Mark Thiel, and Jing Zhai; we are deeply grateful to each for their contribution.

We would like to acknowledge additional support given by the Vice Provost for Research and Dean of the Graduate School Dr Jeanne Hossenlopp. Special thanks are due to Dr Rick Holz, Dean of the Klingler College of Arts and Sciences, for his opening remarks at the symposium and for his overall enthusiasm for the project. Numerous members of the greater Milwaukee community were in attendance at the symposium to whom we are in debt both for their physical presence and questions and comments. As we subsequently discovered, this collaboration between academics and community leaders and peace activists was immensely inspiring to many of the undergraduate students present at the event.

We are enormously grateful to each of the authors for putting so much effort into this project and for keeping to the deadlines. They not only graciously accepted our invitation to write a chapter on the topic from the perspective of their tradition, and present a summary version at the symposium, they also gave freely of their time to make revisions and offer suggestions for improvement. We thank the reviewers of the manuscript that were assigned by Wiley for their valuable comments and questions, which helped us frame the issues better. Several Marquette students helped at various stages of the editorial process; we would like to acknowledge the assistance given by Jakob Rinderknecht and Marisola Xhelili. Finally, we are deeply grateful to the folks at Wiley, Georgina Coleby, Lisa Sharp, and Ben Thatcher for their professionalism and for entertaining our numerous queries to each of which they replied promptly and graciously. Thanks to Camille Bramall and Sherleena Sandou for shepherding the manuscript through the final stages before printing. We also thank Rebecca Harkin for her willingness to consider our initial proposal and for accepting it, thus making this book possible.

Introduction

Irfan A. Omar and Michael K. Duffey

For several years we have sought a book like this one for our courses in comparative religion and peace studies. We wanted a book that would introduce the teachings on peace, violence, and contemporary peacemaking in world religions. We combed the literature, but no book met this need. We found articles that did deal with aspects of religious violence and peacemaking. Studies of religious violence vastly outnumbered those of religious peacemaking.[1] The tragic fact of our times is pervasive violence. The troubling reality is that so much research focuses on the relationship between religion and violence. There is no end to the claim that religion fosters violence. Religion has become the whipping boy for much of the world's violence. But one finds hardly a word about religions' aspirations for peace and engagement in peace activism.

This book does not ignore violence committed in the name of religion. Analyses of case studies of seeming religious violence often conclude that violence is strongly driven by ethnic animosities. In Northern Ireland, Protestants and Catholics attacked each other for economic and political reasons: Protestants possessed the wealth and wanted to be part of Great Britain; Catholics wanted to be part of the Republic of Ireland. Sunnis and Shi'as in Iraq feud over control of the state. At the time of India's struggle for independence, some Muslims feared being overrun by "Hindu" rule and demanded a separate nation, Pakistan. All of these were about economic and political control, often initiated by and for the benefit of the political and economic elite, having more to do with ethnic rather than religious identity. In some situations politicians invoked a "threat to religion" card to galvanize support.

The claim is often made that religion incites violence. Some lay the blame for violence at the feet of religion, while others argue that it arises due to particular interpretations of sacred texts. From the perspective of the former, religions employ violence to protect the integrity of their faith and to punish those who they believe threaten their faith. Indeed, religious institutions have engaged in deadly

Peacemaking and the Challenge of Violence in World Religions, First Edition.
Edited by Irfan A. Omar and Michael K. Duffey.
© 2015 John Wiley & Sons, Ltd. Published 2015 by John Wiley & Sons, Ltd.

violence and people continue to do so in the name of religious teachings and institutions. The historical records and narratives of religious traditions are tainted with blood. Arvind Sharma describes the salutary role of religion, observing that since the Enlightenment there has been a "neglect of the emotional and transcendental dimensions of life" (Sharma 2010, xii). He describes religious authority as "seek[ing] to reclaim religion in the public square." But Sharma also speaks of the corruption of religion as manifested in forms of fundamentalism. For fundamentalists, sacred texts are the literal word of God and their authority is "absolute." Fanatics go further, convinced that those who do not share their religious views must be eliminated (Sharma 2010, xii). No religion is immune from fundamentalism and fanaticism, but in the present, some have displayed fanaticism more than others. In religions tied to textual authority this is especially dangerous.

This book is motivated by the need to place the meaning of peace, violence, nonviolence, and peacemaking in particular religious contexts. We focus on seven religions: Buddhism, Christianity, Confucianism, Hinduism, Islam, Judaism, and the Native American Osage Nation.[2] The book offers a wealth of information to readers from a variety of backgrounds and levels – from undergraduates to the general public reader who want to understand the role of religion in this violent age. We have carefully crafted the book, with each chapter unfolding in a similar fashion:

- a description of religious texts;
- an introduction to the religion;
- a description of the meaning and development of the concept of peace;
- the involvement in violence and war;
- the practices and disciplines, organizations and individuals that play important roles in peacemaking;
- questions for discussion;
- a glossary of terms.

We have assembled a group of scholars who have plumbed their religious traditions to describe peace, peacemaking, and violence. They include (in alphabetical order) Joshua Ezra Burns (Marquette University), assistant professor of Hebrew Bible; Sin Yee Chan (University of Vermont), associate professor of Chinese philosophy and Confucianism; Michael K. Duffey (Marquette University), associate professor of Christian ethics; Kalpana R. Mohanty (Gandhigram Rural University, India), a scholar of Hinduism, an educator and social justice activist; Irfan A. Omar (Marquette University), associate professor of Islam and interreligious dialogue; Eleanor Rosch (University of California-Berkeley), professor of Buddhist psychology, and Tink Tinker (Iliff School of Theology), professor of American Indian cultures and religious traditions, and an enrolled member and traditional spiritual leader of the Osage Nation in the United States. The order of essays in the book does not follow the usual historical/chronological arrangement. Instead, we have chosen to proceed in the reverse order, starting with Islam and ending with the Native American tradition. This order made sense due to the oft-argued point that the explicitly text-based Western religions are often grounded within a dogmatic theological and historical framework that makes them more prone to sacralized violence (Ellens 2003; Hoffman 2006). At the same time, it seems fitting that the chapter on Native American tradition appears last as it raises critical questions regarding the very categories that sustain the notion of world religions. The Native traditions are neither text-bound nor do they claim the kind of universality deemed intrinsic to the religions generally assembled under the banner of world religions. We hope that reading this chapter last will help the reader see things through a wider lens.

Below are the summary introductions from each of the seven chapters.

Irfan Omar's study of peacemaking and the challenge of violence in Islam has led him to believe that peace is at the heart of Islam. The word "Islam" means surrender in peace to the will of God. Since the Islamic tradition has been generally characterized as violent in Western/Christian accounts, in Chapter 1, he examines the charge that the Qur'an promotes violence. His admonition is that texts must be read without ideological agendas in order for them to be efficacious to a reader in achieving basic objectives of faith. This leads him to a careful analysis of jihad in the Qur'an and Islamic history, explaining its various meanings and applications. Omar argues that it does not make sense to understand jihad as a violent enterprise, as the Qur'an sees it primarily as spiritual struggle. Even justified armed struggle or "just war" – at least from the quranic perspective – may not be termed a jihad. He questions the wisdom of religious extremists being given a "loudspeaker" by the media, in the form of excessive coverage of their views and activities. The extremist groups welcome this attention and are eager to take advantage of the air time and print space to broadcast their message of violence and hate. The chapter also treats readers to a very rich examination of quranic teachings on the attributes of peacemakers: reconciliation, forgiveness, patience, and nonviolence. The challenge is to recognize that violence – even when it is "permitted" by the Qur'an for self-defense only and as a last resort – is increasingly unnecessary and even counterproductive in achieving peace.

In Chapter 2 on Christianity, Michael Duffey connects the New Testament texts and the early churches' teachings and practices to argue that Christians are called to live nonviolently. However, Christian history has been another matter. Once Christianity became the established religion of the Roman Empire, Christian churches used their political power to justify war, protect orthodoxy, and evangelize by force. Institutional Christianity was often on the wrong side of history, but peace churches (Mennonites, Quakers, *et al.*) arose in the sixteenth century that were committed to nonviolence. Only in the twentieth century did most other Christian churches begin to promote justice and peace nonviolently. Duffey describes some of the current Christian peacemaking initiatives. He concludes with the challenges of structural violence that Christian communities must still address.

In Chapter 3 on Jewish peacemaking, Joshua Ezra Burns discusses the religious ideologies behind the values of peace and peacemaking as well as key prospects and problems in their implementation. Exploring the classical concepts of peace (*shalom*) and social justice (*tikkun olam*), he shows how Jewish interpreters through the ages have pursued these moral objectives to the common benefit of their own people and the world at large. Finally, Burns discusses the Israeli–Palestinian conflict, a longstanding political impasse, which has served both to complicate and impassion Jewish peacemaking efforts in the Middle East and across the globe. Assessing the dilemma from multiple perspectives, he stresses negotiation and mutual compromise as necessary preconditions for the achievement of a lasting peace agreeable to both parties of the conflict as well as their international supporters.

Confucianism arose as a result of the teachings of Confucius, who lived approximately 2500 years ago in China. With his disciples, he taught the importance of personal moral cultivation of the virtues of love and benevolence. In Chapter 4 Sin Yee Chan explores the Confucian texts that stress social harmony beginning in the family and moving outward to include all human beings. She writes that duties and responsibilities exercised in a hierarchy of right relationships are designed "to pre-empt human conflicts and social chaos by coordinating and regulating people's desires." Her chapter explores how Confucian teachers responded to the use of state violence in different periods of imperial China. A strong theme has always been the need for a virtuous leader—an "inner sage/outer king." As have all the authors, Chan also describes the contributions of Confucianism to peace.

Eleanor Rosch's chapter on Buddhism informs us that the goal of Buddhism is liberation from suffering through insight into the nature of the world and actions that would sustain experience. Her chapter includes much about the evolution of Buddhism and its relationship to peace that may be surprising to many readers. Unusual for a religion, Buddhism contains a detailed psychology of aggression, including an account of why people continue to perform acts of greed and violence even when their religion or other values tell them not to. Rosch explains a wide range of meditative, contemplative, and compassion practices to bring about the personal and social transformations through which peace and nonviolence can flow. Rosch's chapter ends with an account of seven specifically Buddhist principles of peacemaking, one of which is that the peacemaker him/herself must "be peace" and must have empathy and compassion for all sides in a conflict, and must remain committed to nonblame and nonretribution.

Hinduism, the oldest of the world's religions, in the Sanskrit language is called Sanatana Dharma or "eternal"/everlasting path. In Chapter 6 Kalpana Mohanty describes the purpose of Hinduism as achieving union of the human soul and *Brahman*, the Ultimate Reality. Since at the highest level of realization, there is no division between the Real and the manifest, reverence for all life is an important element in Hinduism. Mohanty observes that the Hindu tradition in its true sense has welcomed people of all races and religions to Bharat, presently known as India.

Accepting all and "blending diverse cultures into one" is a nonviolent aspect of the Hindu tradition. "Our tradition," she writes, "accepts that the entire world is one family." This concept originates in the Vedic scriptures, the oldest scriptures of Hinduism. Mohanty's chapter includes a discussion of Gandhi's spirituality and his strategies for making peace, which exemplified the principles of Hinduism and the aspirations of the unity of the human family.

In Chapter 7 on the Native American vision of peace, Tink Tinker deconstructs the dichotomies that permeate discussion of peace and violence. He argues that the "cosmic/holistic harmony and balance [is] the ultimate ideal or goal of all human activity – rather than an ideal of competitive achievement (which presumes various kinds of violence)". Native American ceremonies reflect cosmic relationships. For native peoples, morality is not founded on dualism of good versus evil, but on balance. This discourages viewing others as evil and doing violence to them. The popular portrayal of Indians as violent savages stands in sharp contrast to the savagery of European conquerors. Tinker's chapter challenges people of other faiths, Christians most notably, providing a critique of their worldviews and their understanding of peace, nonviolence, and violence. The missionary zeal of Christians has done great violence to indigenous peoples, most conspicuously to the peoples of the Americas and of Africa. The manner in which Euro-centric peoples have viewed the world contradicts what is sacred to native peoples: the earth itself.

An important feature of the book is that each chapter is written by a practitioner-scholar with a deeper understanding of the subject than a mere theoretical expertise. These are lived traditions that they both sympathize with and criticize. We also wanted the book to be a conversation among the authors, almost unheard of in anthologies. The authors began this conversation as part of the symposium held at Marquette University where they presented summaries of their chapters and invited comments and criticism from the audience, which largely consisted of members of the wider community in Milwaukee. Each author/participant in the symposium was also asked to be an "outsider" for two other religious traditions and prepare a brief formal response to each of the two religions. Our objective in asking for these responses was to replicate (in print) examples of the cross-cultural and inter-religious conversation we hope to stimulate among the readers. The rationale that guided this schedule was to have each religion experience a response from one religion that is "close" and another that is "distant" based on the notion of the family of religions. Here is how the religious traditions were matched:

- The author of the *Buddhism* chapter provided a response to *Christianity* and *Confucianism*.
- The author of the *Christianity* chapter provided a response to *Hinduism* and *Judaism*.
- The author of the *Confucianism* chapter provided a response to *Islam* and *Native North American*.

- The author of the *Hinduism* chapter provided a response to *Buddhism* and *Native American*.
- The author of the *Islam* chapter provided a response to *Christianity* and *Hinduism*.
- The author of the *Judaism* chapter provided a response to *Confucianism* and *Islam*.
- The author of the *Native American* chapter provided a response to *Buddhism* and *Judaism*.

These outsider responses have been included alongside the chapter on which they comment.[3] We hope that they provide a starting point for comparative discussions on peacemaking and nonviolence. Every attempt was made to provide a forum where each respondent would be able to represent his/her assigned tradition's interrelationship with other traditions. This is an opening for rich dialogue, a dialogue that recognizes similarities, appreciates differences, admires insights and practices, and seeks to overcome barriers. Different scholars responded to different points in their colleagues' chapters; however, they were asked to be specific in drawing those items that attended to the goal identified above. This freedom in constructing responses allowed for creativity and depth, however, it also meant that the responses were not always in sync with respect to key elements in their colleague's chapter. For example, some responses are heavy on identifying similarities between the traditions, while others sought to highlight the differences. Some focused on theological possibilities of dialogue, while others noted the phenomenological parallels. Some responses posed direct questions to their inter-locutor in order to draw out his or her thought process, while others challenged his or her assumptions and/or conclusions.

Each author remained careful and judicious in his/her response, as it can be tempting to compare *teachings* of one religion with *acts* of a few groups or individuals in another religion. This is in fact, one of the persistent problems of history – one that causes misrepresentation and fear of the "other." In his recent work *Abraham's Curse: The Roots of Violence in Judaism, Christianity, and Islam*, Bruce Chilton noted that,

> Even Islam's fiercest critics estimate that Muslim militants account for only between 10 and 15 percent of the faithful, a lower proportion than [Christian] Fundamentalists in America, voters from the far right in France 2002, or Jewish Israelis who believe Arabs should be expelled from Israel. Yet many observers evaluate Islam according to its most extreme expressions rather than according to its classic teaching or the behavior of the majority of believers. (Chilton 2008, 146)[4]

Communities/individuals often compare the "best" in their own faith tradition with the "worst" in other's religion. This warrants a mention of an important prac-tice in the dialogue of religions; that is, we should avoid associating ideals and teachings with actions of the faithful. Ideals are ideals. Realities are realities. Here is a book that seeks to emulate that practice by providing a balanced perspective.

What we find most hopeful in the chapters and responses that follow is that the aspirations for peace and active peacemaking are evident across religions. Many have peace fellowships that muster support for peace and justice work in local communities. Others have organizations to rally support for peace and to teach peacemaking skills. Others have what may be termed "peace brigades," whose mission is to intervene in conflict zones. Many religious leaders mediate conflicts and shape opinion.

One of the possible etymologies of the word "religion" is to "bind fast." To what are we bound? We are bound to the transcendent. We are also bound to each other, called to live in harmony across all religious lines. We hope that readers will discover this in *Peacemaking and the Challenge of Violence in World Religions* and that learning about these seven religions will foster a deeper appreciation for the centrality of peace. This is a unique book to help us do just that. Its authors share a common purpose of opening the teachings of their faiths and in doing so illuminating pathways to peace. It is hoped that this conversation can continue to move us to recognize our common search for the Ultimate by the way we search for peace today.

Notes

1 For example, see the following: Desjardins (1997), Ellens (2003), Kepel (1994), McTernan (2003), and Partner (1998).
2 We regret that space considerations did not allow the inclusion of Daoism, Jainism, Shintoism, and Sikhism, all of which have important contributions to make to our topic.
3 Since the original authors were not accorded the opportunity to "reply" to the responses, we have edited the response slightly and removed passages that seemed to warrant a reply and/or those items that addressed topics that were deemed secondary to the original project's main focus. In some instances respondents raised questions that would seem to help the reader in understanding the broader context; we have left those untouched. We hope readers will reflect on these and theorize their own "response" to the chapters as well as the author responses.
4 Unfortunately the continued violence in Iraq, Syria, Nigeria, Somalia, and other hot spots does not help in countering the overall view regarding the Muslim share in religiously inspired violence.

References

Chilton, Bruce. 2008. *Abraham's Curse: The Roots of Violence in Judaism, Christianity, and Islam*. New York: Doubleday.
Desjardin, Michel. 1997. *Peace, Violence and the New Testament*. Sheffield: Sheffield Academic Press.

Ellens, Harold, ed. 2003. *The Destructive Power of Religion: Violence in Judaism, Christianity, and Islam*. Four volumes. Westport, CT: Praeger Publishers.

Hoffmann, R. Joseph, ed. 2006. *The Just War and Jihad: Violence in Judaism, Christianity, and Islam*. Amherst, NY: Prometheus Books.

Kepel, Gilles. 1994. *The Revenge of God: The Resurgence of Islam, Christianity and Judaism in the Modern World*. University Park, PA: Pennsylvania State University Press.

McTernan, Oliver. 2003. *Violence in God's Name. Religion in an Age of Conflict*. Maryknoll, NY: Orbis Books.

Partner, Peter. 1998. *God of Battles: Holy Wars of Christianity and Islam*. Princeton, NJ: Princeton University Press.

Sharma, Arvind. 2010. *The World's Religions: A Contemporary Reader*. Minneapolis, MN: Fortress Press.

1

Jihad and Nonviolence in the Islamic Tradition

Irfan A. Omar

The most excellent jihad is speaking a word of truth to a tyrant.
A Hadith of Prophet Muhammad (Hasan 1984)

Islam's Sacred Texts

The Qur'an: the compilation of revelations received by Muhammad over the period of 23 years (from 610–632 C.E.). The Qur'an contains 114 chapters (chapter is a loose translation of the word *sura*) with topics ranging from announcing God's compassion and proximity to creation as well as his judgment and transcendence. The Qur'an also places great emphasis on human responsibility to nourish righteousness and promote justice on earth. One of the key themes in the Qur'an is to remind the reader of an enduring life after death.

The Hadith: the collection of sayings of Muhammad and reports of actions as observed by his companions. These were compiled by scholars and theologians roughly around two centuries after his death. There are six different collections that are recognized as authoritative.

The Shari'a: this is generally translated as "law." However, in its fundamental sense, it is a succinct version of the guidelines to live a life of faith distilled from the Qur'an and the Hadith. *Shari'a* is based on the ethical and legal injunctions presented in a language of faith. It is formulated through the use of reason and by consensus of religious scholars. Every application of *shari'a* guidelines is an act of interpretation based on specific context. A large part of the *shari'a* deals with aspects concerning inheritance, marriage, divorce, and the practice of faith.

Peacemaking and the Challenge of Violence in World Religions, First Edition.
Edited by Irfan A. Omar and Michael K. Duffey.
© 2015 John Wiley & Sons, Ltd. Published 2015 by John Wiley & Sons, Ltd.

Creedal Statement – "the Shahadah": *There is no divinity except God (Allah), Muhammad is the messenger of God.* Practicing Muslims recite the *shahadah* as a sign of their remembrance of God and their commitment to the practice of faith taught by Prophet Muhammad. It is recited in the ears of a newborn child as a symbolic gesture of her/his reception into the Muslim community.

This chapter provides a concise description of Islam's position on violence, non-violence, and peacemaking. Although analysis is not entirely absent, the emphasis is placed on explaining the ideas on the subject found in the primary texts of Islam. First, I include a brief introduction to the faith tradition, its founder, Muhammad, and beliefs and practices most Muslims hold. The following section deals with ways of understanding violence and contextualizing "religious" violence. Here I have outlined the way the Qur'an speaks of and condemns violence while permitting it in exceptional circumstances as a last resort. The section on jihad considers the quranic understanding of this much misunderstood notion, and its subsequent ever-expanding meanings. The next section provides select sources for peace and nonviolence in the Qur'an and the Prophetic tradition. And finally, I have included a brief discussion of key Muslim thinkers and their contributions to Islamic non-violence including their role in creating the discourse and providing models for nonviolent activism in the way of peace.

Overview of the Islamic Tradition

Islam is a monotheistic religion that arose in Arabia in the early seventh century as a movement for social and spiritual reform. It began with Muhammad (571–632 C.E.), whom Muslims regard as a prophet who received revelations from God (*Allah* in Arabic) through the Archangel Gabriel. Muhammad, son of Abdullah, was born in Mecca and was brought up by his mother and grandfather, both of whom died while he was still young. His father had died just before Muhammad was born, thus his childhood was marred by the tragic experiences of the loss of these immediate relations. Muhammad's uncle Abu Talib, a respected elder of the community, became his protector until the latter's death in circa 620 C.E. These were some of the most difficult years for Muhammad, as the Meccan leaders were opposed to his preaching the message of monotheism. Hence besides the shock of experiencing a personal loss, the lack of his uncle's patronage was deeply felt by Muhammad. In a tribal system, support of a tribal leader/elder was essential for an individual's survival and success. Muhammad's struggles as a prophet and as an activist for justice became even more difficult when, in the same year, he also lost his wife Khadijah, the mother of their only daughter, Fatima.

In the year 610 C.E., when Muhammad was 40, he received the call of prophet-hood as he meditated in seclusion inside a cave on Mount Hira. This call came in the form of his first divine revelations, which were given to him through the Archangel Gabriel, who would continue to serve as an intermediary between God and Prophet Muhammad throughout his ministry. This experience of an encounter with God mediated by the presence of Gabriel was traumatic for Muhammad, who at first was unsure and fearful. Through the confirmation he received from his wife, Khadija, and her Christian cousin, the aged priest Waraqa bin Nawfal, Muhammad gradually became confident that this was indeed a divine call for him to be the messenger of Allah.[1]

Prophet Muhammad continued to receive revelations for over 22 years until his death in 632 C.E. These revelations were recited and memorized by his followers and were also written down during his lifetime. In the decades that followed, the revela-tions, which were already bound together, were copied and made available widely in Muslim communities. The Qur'an, as it is known, is the most widely read and revered book in the Muslim world. Muslims believe it to be the "final" and perfectly "preserved" revelation from God. The Qur'an is central to Islam and thus is some-times compared with Christ as the embodiment of the divine Word. Thus it has been said that the Qur'an is to Islam what Christ is to Christianity (Ayoub 1984).

Even though the Qur'an is central in Islam, it reached Muslims through Muhammad since he was the first to receive these words. Thus Muhammad's interpretation and application of the principles and teachings of the Qur'an are of great significance and value. For practicing Muslims, Prophet Muhammad provides an example for a simple and spiritual way of life. His actions and his relationships with others embody the ethics outlined in the Qur'an. For Muslims, he embodies the best practice of Islam as taught by the Qur'an. His words (excluding those which he recited saying "this is the revelation") are preserved in what is known as the Hadith and are consulted for guidance on issues not found in the Qur'an.

Based on the teachings of the Qur'an, Muslims believe that human beings are born "pure" without any sin. The evil aspects of the world are the result of worldly influences and distractions acquired as part of becoming a person. These aspects include vices such as greed, lust for power, and jealousy, and can be removed by following universal ethical guidelines – the Islamic versions of which are presented in the Qur'an and the Hadith. These vices eventually lead human beings to com-mit violence against another and oneself. To protect oneself from these "unnat-ural" tendencies one must strive (do jihad) to resist the temporary appeal of self-centered existence. Islamic guidelines for a life of faith lived in awareness of God and through peaceful relations with others are found in the literature broadly known as the *shari'a*, or "Islamic law."

Islamic theology, in trying to balance between the notions of predestination and free will, informs us that in the end only God decides who will be able to resist the temptations and trials of this world and who will succumb to them. Thus what matters most in Islam is not mere beliefs but one's sincere practice of faith. Etymologically Islam means "peaceful submission" or "commitment" to God, and a Muslim is one who acknowledges the need of such a submission and commits to required practices identified as the "Five Pillars" or acts of faith. The Five Pillars include the creedal statement, which acknowledges the one God (creator and sustainer of all) and recognizes Muhammad as a prophet of God (*shahadah*), ritual prayer five times a day (*salah*), fasting during Ramadan – the ninth month of the Islamic calendar (*sawm*), almsgiving (*zakat*) according to one's ability, and pilgrimage to Mecca (*hajj*) if one's resources permit.

In Islam, God has no material representation, although the practice of making calligraphic imagery of the many names (also known as attributes) of God is fairly common and can be seen in mosques and in Muslim homes. Islam does not prescribe priesthood and there is no official clergy in Sunni Islam. However some of the roles that clergy play in some Christian denominations may be viewed as equivalent to the role played by the *'ulama* (religious scholars) in Muslim societies. The primary role of the *'ulama* is to strive (implies doing jihad) to understand, interpret, and teach the Qur'an (sacred scripture), the Hadith (reports of the words and actions of Prophet Muhammad), and *shari'a* to others. The majority of Muslims in the world are Sunni but a smaller percentage belong to the second major branch of Islam known as Shi'ism, which has a variety of leadership roles within the category of *'ulama*.

Muslims believe that the revelations God sent to Muhammad were in essence not unlike those that were sent to countless others throughout human existence. Muhammad, as he received these revelations, recited them to his followers many of whom memorized these verses. Later these were collected into one document (*mushaf*) and canonized as the sacred Qur'an (or "recitation"). Islam sees itself as a continuation of the Judeo-Christian heritage, leading some to argue that it would be better to regard this as a "Judeo-Christian-Islamic" heritage (Esposito 2002). Thus viewed through its original sources (the Qur'an and the Hadith), Islam does not regard itself as a "new" religion. It openly claims to continue in the path of earlier religious traditions, notably the Jewish and the Christian traditions. Muslims regard the Qur'an to be the final and definitive revelation given by God to his messenger, Muhammad, whom the Qur'an identifies as the "seal" of the prophets.

God is at the center of Islam, not Muhammad. Muslims believe in and pray to "the one true God" who is the Source of all as well as the final destination for all. In the Qur'an, God is said to be the creator and the final judge of all creation including human beings. The Islamic sacred story (including Creation and the destiny of human beings) is similar to the one found in Judaism and Christianity, with notable exceptions with regards to how some events are described and interpreted (Kaltner 2003). Islam also shares the notion of monotheism with Judaism and Christianity; that is, the idea of one God who is both transcendent and immanent; however, it rejects Christianity's notion of the Trinity. Muslims regard Jesus Christ ('Isa) as one of the most important prophets appointed by God for the guidance of humankind. They believe in the notion of Jesus' virgin birth, and uphold the holiness and the sanctity ascribed to Mary, the mother of Jesus. Here, as in the case of monotheism, the Qur'an has a distinct viewpoint; while the reverence for Jesus and Mary are clearly manifest in the Qur'an, it rejects the divinity of Jesus. Thus Islam maintains a rather complex relationship with Christianity. There are both similarities and differences in its worldview and its view of the afterlife.

The figure of Abraham (Ibrahim) is another major connection between the three monotheistic faiths (Hinze and Omar 2005). Abraham is seen as instrumental in bringing humanity back toward the direction of ethical monotheism. Muslims regard him as one of the most influential figures (a major prophet from God) who helped guide humanity to the "right path." The Qur'an suggests that there have been numerous prophets (c. 124 000) since the beginning of the creation of human beings. Like Abraham, a messenger or prophet was appointed (or a succession of them) to every human community who came from within and spoke their language. A typical role of such prophets was to "warn" people of dangers that arise due to deviation from the path of ethical monotheism (belief in one God followed by a firm commitment to universal ethical principles). Along with Abraham, Noah, Moses, Jesus, and Muhammad were all important prophets (due to the seminal civilizational changes they brought). Based on the Qur'an Muslims see Muhammad as the "seal" of the line of prophet-hood understood in the sense of him being the last prophet.

Ways of Understanding Violence and Nonviolence

Two main questions are addressed in this chapter. First, how to understand violence carried out in the name of religion from an Islamic perspective? Second, what role might the Islamic religious tradition, its texts, and those who interpret these texts play in "transforming" the societies we live in, both locally and globally by producing, adopting, and promoting other legitimate ways of understanding?

One of the questions that is implicit in this kind of inquiry is to ask whether, because sacred texts include violence and the followers of faith traditions have historically (and/or are presently) engaged in violence, we should simply discard these traditions or perhaps explore the possibilities – inherent within these traditions – to "rethink" the ways of articulating and practicing them. This in fact is key to the argument for the relevance (or otherwise) of religious traditions in the twenty-first century. Evidently the very existence of this anthology gives away the positive biases of the editors and authors; they wish to not only address the question but respond to it as honestly as possible with the help of their traditions' texts and historical application of meanings. Acknowledgement of the presence of violence in texts and in history is a step in the right direction. However the focus of inquiry here is not the past per se but the present and the future. This chapter seeks to show that the primary sources of the Islamic tradition are primarily concerned with peace and peacemaking. While many examples of religiously inspired violence can be found in Muslim history and in the present, one can also find examples of peacemaking and practice of nonviolent spirituality as well as an acknowledgment of common humanity. The Islamic tradition, based on the Qur'an and the prophetic example, contains ample sources for peacemaking and nonviolent activism for justice.

Although not focusing on the past, many events from history may be cited to support the enormous potential for religious peacemaking. Furthermore, like any sacred text, the Qur'an, can be, and indeed has been, interpreted in a number of ways. The problem of violence is less that of the text comprising or containing violence and more that of an interpretation of the text. More often than not, religiously inspired violence is forced upon the text rather than the other way around. In other words, texts give us meaning as they are interpreted; hence the role of the interpreter is critical. Any interpreter's own historical, cultural, and social context will inevitably be visible in the meanings drawn from the text. Since each interpreter is bound by such influences despite claims to objectivity, no interpretation may be considered absolute; that is, for all times and all places. The principles (such as ethical and moral ones) and acts of faith and spirituality remain the same (which is what makes a religion a "tradition"); however, how these are applied and practiced changes over time (an example of this would be Thomas Jefferson's phrase that became part of the *Declaration of Independence* "all men are created equal"). A Muslim "fundamentalist" may choose to see the text in a particular way that lends itself to intolerance of other faiths even leading one to commit violence against them in the name of Islam. However, not all forms of fundamentalism would be explicitly exclusive and/or violent in their outcome. They may be "literal," "conservative," "holistic," and "absolute," or any combination of these (Lawrence 1989, 27).

Another problematic proposal in this regard is the argument that violence is considered "divinely accepted" *because of* and *due to* the extent the text is considered divine (Nelson-Pallmeyer 2005, 106–107). If this were so, how are we to explain the text's injunctions for establishing peace and justice? In fact, the same texts (the Bible, the Qur'an, the Bhagavad Gita and texts and/or teachings of other religions) also speak about a moral framework of life, our responsibility to the other, and accountability for our actions, spelled out very clearly and without ambiguity. If violence is only one part of the picture, then why would these other aspects be left unheeded if the text's influence is indeed so important in motivating human behavior *vis-à-vis* violence? With respect to Islam, this is especially problematic because injunctions for peace in the Qur'an are identified as "general" or "permanent" commands, while verses that ask a believer to "fight" are always placed within a restricted framework.

It will become evident from the discussion below that the Qur'an *permits* (not mandates) defensive violence. The question to ask is how does it regard and define this violence? What are the limits, if any, of this quranic violence? The popular "wisdom" in the world today labels violence that is committed in the name of Islam as "jihad," which is now part of the English language. There are several derivatives of this as one may have noticed in the media and other pseudo-scholarly literature. In the present, we have become accustomed to what Esposito calls, "seeing Islam through explosive headline events" (Esposito 2005, x). This is because it is easy for us to mistake the narrative advanced by the radicals as the *only* narrative due to the overwhelming exposure it generally receives in the media. When in fact there are multiple narratives today – always have been – all competing for the hearts and minds of both Muslims and non-Muslims (Said *et al.*, 2006, 3). But many of the peaceful narratives are not given the same exposure (or not given any at all) as the radical voices tend to receive.[2]

Jihad in the Qur'an

The word jihad itself comes from the Arabic root letters J H D, meaning "to strive" or "to exert" oneself, in the religious sense, in the service of God. Incidentally, this is also the meaning apparent in the Arabic Bible (1906) to refer to some of the actions of Jesus and St. Paul. In II Timothy 4:7 (RSV) it states "I have fought the good fight, I have finished the race, I have kept the faith." The Arabic translation of the Bible, *Al-Kitab al-Muqaddas* ("the Sacred Book") uses "jihad" and "*jahadto*" as equivalent to the English "fought the good fight," which is identical to the usage of jihad in the Qur'an. Another instance where jihad appears in *Al-Kitab al-Muqaddas* is in Luke 22:44, the first phrase of which states, "And being in an agony, he prayed more earnestly..." where being in agony is translated as "being in the state of jihad" (*wa is kāna fī jihadin*).[3] Once again the term jihad is used to signify "struggle" and "suffering" in the path of righteousness, which is the same as in service to God. Similarly, jihad in the Qur'an is meant to convey the "striving" that one undergoes in fighting the temptations and base desires (*jihad bin nafs*) that often lead one down the path of evil.

The term jihad appears many times in the Qur'an – according to one scholar 35 times, either as jihad or as some other derivative of the root letters J H D ("to strive"). A vast majority of these references simply imply "struggle" and some others clearly see it as a spiritual struggle. Only four of these verses that contain derivations of the term jihad "...are open ... to a 'warlike' interpretation" and even that would depend on the context in which these are received (Bonney 2004, 28). In most of the Meccan verses of the Qur'an where jihad appears, the Qur'an clearly seeks to inculcate a sense of personal effort (*jahada*). In fact, jihad appeared in verses that were revealed to Prophet Muhammad long before any fighting between Muslims and their Meccan opponents took place. The Qur'an gave Muslims permission to fight much later (in Medina), and that was primarily to defend themselves from invasion and aggression by their Meccan opponents. Similarly, in Islamic history the term jihad has been understood in a range of meanings "from political action (the jihad of the pen) to warfare (jihad of the sword) to an individual's own struggles to lead a righteous life (jihad of the soul)" (Brockopp 2004, 6A).

In the quranic usage, jihad does not appear to mean warfare, let alone "holy war" (El Fadl 2006). The word for a necessary (*not* "*holy*") war is *harb* (or *qitāl*). In the entire Arabic literature for all the centuries of Islam's presence, not a single credible reference to the term "holy war" can be found, which in Arabic would be "*harb al-muqaddasah.*" Such an expression is absent from the Qur'an as well as Muslim writings on the subject of war. In "Islamic theology war is never holy; it is either justified or not..." (El Fadl 2002, 19). Perhaps the first usage of this term "holy war" in any language may have been the one adopted by the crusaders in the middle ages. In subsequent periods a number of Muslim writers began to use it in their polemical literature against Christendom.[4] Jihad was not generally used to mean "war" in Muslim discourse, however, it was understood that when one goes to war, it constitutes a "struggle" and in that sense some wars were deemed as "jihads." Some rulers and even scholars allowed the use of jihad to refer to warfare, but that designation did not remain unchallenged. Other scholars disagreed and protested the misappropriation of this term for political purposes. Nevertheless, the political and economic weight was placed with the definition that supported the rulers' needs and whims; hence the "jihad-as-war" definition was often a preferred choice due to the religious appeal it provided to garner support for con-solidation of the empire.

Semantic bleaching of jihad

The term jihad is highly politicized today and is used in many different contexts without regard for its original spiritual denotation. One often hears words such as "jihadists" and "jihadis" to refer to either terrorists and/or separatists (and "jihad-ism" as their ideology) who claim to engage in religion-inspired activities or at least christened in such language so as to draw a sensationalist response. Seen from a purely analytical lens the political and extremist nature of these activities is apparent. However, the mainstream media outlets are not shy about appropriating the terminology used by the extremists: they often repeat terms like "jihadist" without qualification, hence they manage to create a confused state of under-standing for those who are unfamiliar with Islamic teachings. It is as though "jihad" has now become subject to a form of "semantic bleaching" where the original root meaning has undergone a "partial effacement of ... [its] semantic features, [thus] stripping away of some of its precise content so it can be used in an abstracter, grammatical-hardware-like way" (Matisoff 1991, 384). The transfor-mation of a purely spiritual concept is thus complete and its meaning broadened to such an extent that most of its "lexical content" is lost while the "grammatical content" is retained (Heine 1993, 89).

For Muslims, jihad continues to evoke religious and spiritual sensibilities. Violence associated with this term is found mostly among those who see religion – in this case, Islam – as a tool to further their ideological, political, and extremist agendas. Just as in the past some Muslim rulers abused jihad for expansionist purposes, today's political extremists seek power and influence without consideration for peace and in violation of all the basic principles of Islam. Some of these extremists cite history to argue that Muslims did use jihad to engage in defensive wars. This argument is supported by evidence from Muslims sources. Nevertheless, to base the meaning of jihad on its *abusive application in history* instead of its *import in the Qur'an* is not only misleading, it is the betrayal of the Islamic tradition itself.

If and when there comes a need for a defensive war, the rules of deciding, declaring, and the conduct in war are very clearly enunciated in the Islamic legal tradition. Only a legitimate (in today's context, popularly and fairly elected) head of government can, as a last resort, make that decision, which (again, in today's context) must meet the requirements set by the United Nations (UN). Many theologians however argue that these elaborate guidelines for what is often called the Islamic equivalent to Christian "just war" are not even relevant today since it is difficult to imagine a "just war" that can remain faithful to its own principles.[5] As a result many Muslim scholars believe the only way to resolve conflicts today is through nonviolent means (see below the discussion on Wahiduddin Khan, Jawdat Sa'id, and Rabia Harris).

The defensive war *permitted* by the Qur'an was always referred to as *harb* (warfare) *qitāl* (combat) and not by the term jihad. For example, Q. 22:39, one of the earliest verses that refers to the violence of war uses the term *qitāl* and also gives a rationale for it – that it be undertaken as a means of defense against oppression: "To those against whom war is made (*yuqaataluna* – derived from the same root letters as *qitāl*), permission is given (to fight), because they are wronged" (Ali 1992, 832). It does not sanction warfare as a means of political expansion or for hegemony over other peoples (Sachedina 1988, 106).[6] Here it is also important to note that the Qur'an offers a choice in what means one might adopt (e.g. taking up arms) to defend oneself and one's community. The Qur'an does not see it as an option *whether* one should take measures to defend oneself and stand up to injustice and aggression forced by an adversary. In other words, the Qur'an is emphatic that one must strive to eradicate injustice, but it is not suggesting in absolute terms that it must be through the use of weapons. The choice of means is left to the ingenuity and wisdom of the persons in charge of the task of defending.[7]

Jihad as struggle with the inner self

The data regarding the popular view of jihad among Muslims are quite telling. In 2002, to gauge the Muslim self-understanding of what the term jihad means to Muslims, the Gallup Poll conducted a survey of Muslims on this notion. In his report, which was based on several predominantly Muslim countries, Richard

Burkholder wrote that he found a majority of people surveyed (over 10 000) understood it to mean striving to honor one's "duty toward God" in their personal daily lives with "no explicit militaristic connotation at all" (Burkholder 2002). Despite the volatile and violent world we live in since September 11, 2001, the vast majority of Muslims regard jihad as a personal struggle. Except for a fringe minority, Muslims reject the very idea that jihad may either be translated or invoked as "holy war." Although some among the Muslims would not agree to even categorize it as either defensive or offensive, they simply prefer to see jihad as a "universal revolutionary struggle" (Peters 1979, 118 and 132–133).

According to mainstream religious thinkers it is a serious misappropriation of the *principle* of jihad when the term is employed in practice to mean something the source-principle did not intend, let alone clearly state. The principle as clearly enunciated by the Qur'an is to recognize jihad as spiritual struggle, the inner struggle of the *nafs* or self – *jihad al-akbar*, greater jihad. However, the practice as proposed by some Muslims today is in terms of war or armed struggle, *jihad al-asghar* or a lesser jihad, which is understood by the scholars to be *provisional* at best. It was identified as such by Prophet Muhammad due to the specific historical circumstances of early Muslims who were surrounded by hostile forces. Its applicability today is further complicated by the fact that there is no one unified and legitimate entity (such as the caliphate in the past) that can initiate a process by which jihad-as-war could be legally initiated. Muslim societies in the twenty-first century are part of nation-states and, in general, secular laws governing many of these societies by way of international consensus already have measures for defensive wars to be carried out through a recognized legal process. Hence the argument for a defensive "jihad of the sword" is mooted in light of the provisions already contained in the Charter of the UN. The Islamic notion of defensive war in today's terms would correspond with various articles of the UN Charter that deal with breach of peace, security, and possible actions for stopping aggression committed against a member state. These include the option to take military action as a matter of last resort.[8]

The distinction between the so-called greater and lesser jihads is also very deliberate and foundational as it is believed to be one of the important Hadiths of Prophet Muhammad. The greater jihad (understood to be as "striving in God") is evidently more difficult and is a deeply spiritual notion, while the lesser jihad ("striving for God") is understood to be a social, political, and (if necessary) military "struggle" (Ayoub 1992, 211–212). In this latter sense, jihad as armed struggle could be compared to the Christian just war tradition. It is important to note that many Muslim religious intellectuals insist that in our present circumstances, in the era of modern nation-states, emphasis must be placed on jihad's spiritual significance and that jihad should be viewed as a symbol of humility and piety (Khan 1997, 8–9; Khan 1999b). In today's world we must view jihad from a purely spiritual perspective. Political interpretations of jihad arose in a dichotomized world of the *dar al-Islam* (the Islamic state) and the *dar al-harb* (the non-Muslim state or the state hostile to Muslim state).The political (military) context is no longer viable; even if it was deemed suitable for the pre-modern era when the world was divided along religious and ethnic lines. In the spiritual sense, jihad's significance is permanent and it is in that sense that jihad must be understood and practiced today. While jihad as armed struggle may have been necessary in the early years of Islam for a strategy of defense and survival, there is very little need for it in our present-day world where violent conflicts, partly due to the nature of weapons involved, have a far greater chance of resulting in the destruction of all sides and even the annihilation of the planet itself (Khan 2003).

In the era in which the Prophet Muhammad lived, militancy was the order of the day and a primary means to secure order and pursue justice. This militant attitude, which manifested in what are known as *ghazwat* (warfare), "was a sport, a source of fame and material wealth, and a way of life" (Ayoub 1992, 206–207). It was more of an end in itself than a means to an end. But as people who have the opportunity to learn from past mistakes as well as discover newer ways of reconciliation, twenty-first-century Muslims ought to be able to move beyond medieval solutions to solve problems today. Parallel to the spiritual and political usages of jihad mentioned above, here we see two distinct understandings of the notion of jihad: (1) *textual* and (2) *historical*. It is unfortunate that what historically transpired overshadowed what was originally intended by the text of the Qur'an. The notion of jihad, from the quranic perspective, pertains entirely to an inner striving, in history, a part of which also included defending one's faith and livelihood. But the "part" came to be understood as the whole and the central feature of the notion of jihad (*jihad bin nafs*) became hostage to its historical usage.

Martyrdom or extremism? Misrepresentations of the prophetic example

Religious extremism has always been present in Islamic and other societies. Early Islamic history experienced many such groups, such as the Kharijites, who took absolutist positions with respect to judgment against others even when the Qur'an suggested that judgment belongs only to God. But never before in history had the extremists been given a free and unlimited access to what I refer to as the "loud speaker" for free publicity of their propaganda. Until very recently, they existed at the fringes of society and were tolerated but had very little impact. Today they are able to manipulate the mediums of communication while many media outlets in the world are willing to give coverage to their message of hate to be broadcast to the entire world. Muslim extremists allege that since Prophet Muhammad fought the jihad against the "infidels," they too must do so in the context of today. Taking the advantage offered through global media, extremists are able to spread their message far and wide. However, there are several problems with this view. First, the extremists mistakenly assume or falsely assert that Muhammad was involved in many violent conflicts. As a matter of historical fact, there are approximately 83 recorded incidents of conflict between Muslims and their opponents in early Islamic history. Only four of those, which happened in the life of the Prophet Muhammad, were actual armed encounters. Most of the times where conflict occurred and where violence could have erupted between Muslims and other groups, it was resolved through other means, such as treaties and negotiations. Prophet Muhammad himself spent less than 2 days in defensive fighting in his entire life of 63 years (Khan 2009, 25).

Second, during these so called "battles" Muhammad fought to defend the life and property of his followers and the right to practice their faith freely. For the first 13 years of his ministry, Muhammad and his followers experienced severe perse-cution but they did not retaliate, did not use violence and accepted the hardships for the sake of their faith. In the second phase of his ministry in Medina, Muhammad and other Muslims fought to protect the nascent Muslim community from being annihilated. A Hadith of the prophet often cited in this context says, "Do not wish confrontation with your enemy but always ask peace from God." This approach was considered radical at the time because the Arabs of Hejaz knew only one way to settle their disputes – through warfare. No difference of opinion could be resolved without violent conflict and the use of weapons. Even against such odds, Muhammad introduced peaceful means, including diplomacy and dialogue (Khan 1997). Muhammad's actions on numerous occasions provide a strong basis to argue that his policy was mainly to avoid violence and not to insist on it (Khan 2003). Thus, in the Islamic ethical framework, violence or armed struggle is only an exception to the rule and not the rule itself. In the present age, a more powerful and potent method to "fight" has gained greater currency, and that weapon is "nonviolence." Therefore it is not only prudent but also imperative that we restore the spiritual vision of jihad strongly emphasized by the Qur'an, and continue the common struggle for justice through nonviolent means. Basic famil-iarity with the Qur'an makes it plain that its message is centered on the principle of *al-sulhu khayrun* (reconciliation is best). The Qur'an, although allowing it for self-defense, sees violence as grossly displeasing to God, and repeatedly calls for resolving conflicts through peaceful negotiation. As noted earlier, jihad in the Qur'an simply means "to strive" or "to struggle"; it has no fundamental connection to the notion of *qitāl* (fighting) (Engineer 2001). In the eyes of God the struggle is meant to be spiritual, seeking inner peace, in order to achieve social peace among peoples, communities, and nations. Those who engage in such struggle would, according to the Qur'an, experience the divine reception: "*wallāhū yadū'u ilā dār as-salām*" (and God calls to the home of peace).[9]

Third, the extremists seek to dichotomize between "us" and "them" – between Muslims and non-Muslims, the so-called infidel. The Qur'an's focus is on struggle against the self, rather than against an enemy "other." It does not grant the right to anyone to call another person "infidel." The quranic usage of this term must be seen in its historical context and in light of the larger message of the Qur'an. Against the quranic imperative for a peaceful struggle in the path of self-reform, some extremist

Muslim groups today take the path of confrontation with others and portray the "West" as anti-Islamic, trying their best to vindicate, sadly, the infamous notion of the "clash of civilizations." They violate Islamic ethics on several counts. For example, they misinterpret and misuse the text of the Qur'an; they breach local laws and rules of the country where they live, which is a violation of *shari'a* law; and they cause mistrust and division between Muslim and other communities, disregarding the quranic imperative for dialogue and cooperation with other communities.

Those who through "suicide attacks" claim to seek martyrdom (*shahadah* or witness – martyr is *shahid*) stand on shaky ground; their entire philosophy – if we can call it that – contravenes Islamic ethics based on their political misunderstanding and not spiritual understanding of the term *shahid*. In Islam, martyrdom is never sought, it is given by God. If the intention of the person who stands up for justice is to get killed in the cause hoping for "martyrdom," that person may not be considered a martyr in the eyes of God. Instead, it might be regarded as suicide, which is prohibited. Intention is half of one's faith, the Prophet said, and thus one has to be quite clear in one's mind what one is seeking, personal glory or divine will. Moreover, no martyrdom can be achieved when one is knowingly willing to harm not only oneself but also others, especially noncombatants. Still, true martyrdom in Islam is that which is sought to save others and oneself from being harmed; not to cause harm at a mass scale.

Peacemaking and the Challenge of Violence

It is apparent that violence has been and is being committed by invoking the name of religion, including Islam, supposedly for reasons sanctioned by God. However, Muslim nations and Muslim violence receives far greater attention due to the nature of contemporary geo-politics and specific events since the terrorist attacks of September 11, 2001. These include the "wars" in Afghanistan and Iraq and more recently the "Arab Spring" and its aftermath. However, for our purposes in this chapter it would be important to note that despite what we witness in terms of the present state of the Muslim world, one has to distinguish between Muslim conduct and the teachings of Islam.

In this section, I will draw on select Islamic resources that highlight the importance given to the need for what are essentially peaceful and nonviolent means for social and political change rather than engaging in the violent methods that have been utilized by some Muslim groups today. Despite the odds of history, several theologians, scholars, and activists today strive (i.e. do jihad) to dig deeper into their theological resources and, using their interpretational and hermeneutical skills, they have unearthed a "theology of nonviolence" in Islam that they believe is based on both the texts as well as historical examples. It might be helpful to look at some of the terminology emanating from the Qur'an and which is employed in the service of this theology of nonviolence.

Resources from the Qur'an and the Hadith

The word Islam is derived from the verbal root 'salima', which means to be safe and secure. Salām, the noun, means safety or submission to God in peace. As-Salām is also known in the Qur'an as one of the "most beautiful names of God" (Q. 59:23). God, the source of all Peace greets His creation with Peace. The verse reads: "'Peace' a word (of salutation) from a Lord, most Merciful" (Q. 36:58).

The following four terms have been highlighted by several Muslim theologians as instrumental in arguing for a theology of nonviolence. The first and the most fundamental is al-silm (peace, reconciliation), which comes from the same root salima. Peace is defined in the sense of a relationship with others, which must remain peaceful at all costs. However, at the ultimate level, one seeks the very source of all peace, which is God. Second is al 'afw (forgiveness), which is consistently stressed in the Qur'an as the preferred option in situations even where one is entitled to compensation against injustice. The Q. 42:37 says: "true believers are those who when angered [provoked] are willing to forgive." From a justice-oriented perspective an average person has the right to demand that the violator of an injury is duly punished, and yet the Qur'an invites the victim to consider a better option: "The recompense for an injury is an injury equal thereto, but whoever forgives and makes reconciliation, his reward is due from God" (Q. 42.40). Those who are closer to God, according to the Qur'an, are inclined to forgive because "forgiveness is better." In instances of provocation and even actual physical harm the reader of the Qur'an is asked to terminate the trail of violence through forgiveness.

The third term, al-sabr (patience), is described in the Qur'an as one of the greatest virtues. It appears many times in connection with those who have faith. Some quranic verses highlighting this are as follows: Q. 39:10b: "those who patiently persevere will truly receive a reward without measure." Similarly, Q. 13:24 speaks of the greeting that will be encountered by those entering the paradise: "peace unto you for that you have persevered in patience; now how excellent is the final home." And Q. 14:23 states: "but those who believe and work righteousness will be admitted to the gardens, beneath which rivers flow, to dwell therein forever with the leave of their lord. Their greeting therein shall be 'peace!'" According to Q. 15:46, they will be welcomed and asked to: "enter here in peace and security." For the Qur'an the Garden or paradise is the place of ultimate peace (Q. 50: 32–35). And finally, la 'unf (nonviolence), which is not mentioned in the Qur'an but is always implied in various verses dealing with conflict resolution. Although it does not directly obligate one to be either nonviolent or pacifist, the Qur'an emphasizes in many instances that there is always more than one way of responding in situations of conflict and indeed better options are those that avoid violence. The verse 41:34 says: "Good and evil deeds are not equal. Repel evil with goodness; you will see that the person with whom you had enmity has become your dearest friend." For the Qur'an, nonviolence is a better and more dynamic way of persuasion. It acknowledges that nonviolence is far more effective than violence in resolving conflicts. The term *'unf* means violence, harshness, and severity and appears in a *hadith*:

> God the Blessed and the Exalted is graciously Courteous and loves 'gentle-civility' (*al-rifq*). God bestows on account of gentle conduct what God does not bestow on account of violent conduct (*al-'unf*). (Khan 1999a, 170)[10]

The practice of nonviolence can be seen as an imperative if one understands the worldview the Qur'an proposes. Through several of its verses the Qur'an obligates Muslims to engage in dialogue with people of other faiths, especially the "people of the book." The Qur'an acknowledges diversity and expects that there will always be Muslims and other religious communities. It never assumes that all human beings may one day follow the same faith tradition. Such acknowledgment and acceptance of diversity of faiths by the Qur'an necessitates that Muslims maintain good relations with other peoples who are religiously or culturally different from them. This perception of plurality is also due to the fact that Islam sees itself as part of a larger plan for humanity rather than as an exclusive ideology, which is isolated from others. It sees itself as fulfilling a role that contributes to a balanced view of the world. If there is conflict and war, it is quite difficult to keep cordial relations with others. Violence emanating from conflicts brings out the worst in all; it creates problems for all, and it almost always fails to solve the original problem that caused the conflict.

Nonviolence: A principle or a means?

The Qur'an is neutral on the issue of nonviolence even though it is not so on the question of establishing peace and justice. While it highlights the wisdom of nonviolence and forgiveness, it does so with the aim of moving towards these two goals. Justice is the basic theme in the Qur'an, violence and nonviolence are essentially means to achieve justice. As means, they can be applied according to the strategy, convention, or as a matter of principle. In history Muslims have applied it in all of these various ways in the service of fulfilling their temporal aims. Many have used it as a strategy, others have used it as a principle because of how they read the Qur'an and the life of Muhammad. In the twentieth century, we have witnessed that nonviolence is also being applied due to it becoming a convention based on the success this method has shown in resisting and overturning unjust political systems (e.g. India, Poland, and South Africa). The power of nonviolent resistance is becoming manifest at all levels of society. In fact, it threatens even the most brutal oppressors of our time. Thus where we stand today, it is a positive sign that many more Muslim theologians are becoming convinced of the power of nonviolence. They are able to see it as a viable strategy, a successfully proven conventional method, but more importantly, as a principle that is supported by the scriptural demands placed on them.

The pursuit and establishment of justice may or may not require violent methods such as war. In the context in which the Qur'an was revealed, based on the circumstances, violence was permissible within a strict framework and with specific guidelines and for specific aims that included self-defense and freedom of religion which was denied to Muslims. Any such violence was not only limited by the Qur'an, it was also strictly regulated by the *shari'a*, which is based on the Qur'an and the prophetic tradition. Thus the Qur'an approaches the issue of violence from the perspective of the victim and the oppressed. As noted earlier, this is similar to contemporary international understanding where violence as a last resort is permissible to political entities in order to defend victims of aggression by another force. The Qur'an 22:39 states, "sanction to take up arms is given to those who are attacked." This sanction was afforded to Muslims even as they were being shaped into a political entity in opposition to their persecutors in Mecca. But this permission was neither for all time nor against all people. Thus verses such as these are to be seen in their historical context, which makes it apparent that permission to defend through the use of weapons was limited by time, place and purpose. Theoretically, this may still be applicable in cases where tyrants and oppressors forcibly prevent people from "professing and practicing their religion" (Safi 2001, 12). This issue is intimately connected to the pursuit of justice. From the perspective of the Qur'an, freedom of religion is one of the most fundamental rights human beings possess and denying that right to anyone is an unjust act that must be resisted. However, even this right to fight religious persecution has been questioned by many major theologians – such as al-Ghazali (d. 1111) – on the grounds that it might create unrest and therefore disturb social peace, which is also treated by Islamic law as sacrosanct.

Both justice and peace appear to be two major concerns of the Qur'an. The Q. 2:190 says, "fight in the way of God against those who fight against you but be not the aggressors. Surely God does not love aggressors." The granting of permission to fight is qualified by the caution "do not be aggressors." In another verse the Qur'an reminds Muhammad and his followers that despite the fact that it is a defensive struggle, if the opponent side inclines toward peace, Muslims are to put down their weapons immediately. It is mandated by the Qur'an that, whenever possible, they must turn their backs on war and violence. Violence aside, in the path of justice, the Qur'an does not even absolve one's own self or one's family from being just. Here is what Q. 4:135 asks of Muslims:

> O you, who believe, stand firmly for justice, as witnesses for God, even if it means testifying against yourselves, or your own parents, or your kin, and whether it is against the rich or poor, for God prevails upon all. Follow not the lusts of your hearts, lest you swerve, and if you distort justice or decline to do justice, surely God knows what you do.

Puritanical and extremist Muslim interpretations heavily rely on verses that are read in isolation, as if the meaning of the quranic verses were obvious and "as if moral ideas and historical context were irrelevant" to how they are interpreted. The moral thrust of the Qur'an is essential in interpreting those verses that deal with inter-personal, inter-religious and even intra-religious relations and Muslim conduct over all. For example, "the Qur'an persistently commands Muslims to enjoin the good. The word used for 'the good' is *ma'ruf*, which means that which is commonly known to be good" (El Fadl 2002, 14). This same concept, when defined in a narrow ideological framework, may mean something completely different and may only include "good" works that suit the goals of an ideologically motivated extremist group. Thus we can find in the text whatever we are looking for even though the final meaning derived may be completely skewed, twisted, and even abusive. To summarize, it is pertinent to quote a prominent scholar of Islamic law, K. Abou El Fadl, concerning this misuse of the text by the Islamists and extremists:

> In regards to every ethical obligation, the Qur'anic text assumes that readers will bring a preexisting, innate moral sense to the text. Hence, the text will morally enrich the reader, but only if the reader will morally enrich the text. (2002, 15)

The Qur'an and nonviolence: The challenge ahead

The Qur'an has numerous references to peace and related terms and only a handful of verses deal with defensive war (*qital*). Based on the quranic ideas discussed above, it may be argued that the thrust of the message of the Qur'an is toward establishing peace with justice. Despite the permission given to take up arms, the quranic emphasis on the right to peace and stability seems to indicate its preference for nonviolent methods to achieve the goals of peace. The quranic text remains the same over the centuries and so are its principal aims. These aims constitute seeking justice and following a path of moderation in all things but especially in matters of faith. However, the means to pursue justice can and should be modified based on our personal and social circumstances, our collective achievements in human interpersonal relationships, engagement with newer and more reliable methods of reconciliation, our increased human and intellectual resources, and our commitment to people across various religious traditions who also struggle to achieve similar aims. Increasingly, it is recognized that the best way of pursuing justice in the present age is through nonviolence. The fact that many Muslims, like people in other faith traditions, have acknowledged these new ways of responding to violence is arguably the most positive step toward decreasing violence in the name of religion.

Muslim activism for peace currently focuses on many fronts one of which is to create local as well as sustainable mechanisms toward reforming societies. Many such efforts are not easily noticed or even considered newsworthy due to their unstructured nature. In many rural societies a local religious leader (*imam*) may act as a peace negotiator between individuals, groups, and even between villages. Such individuals may not be part of a registered organization or have physical offices out of which they work and yet they may be well known in their communities as a resource for conflict resolution and inter-faith and inter-cultural dialogue. The work of such individuals is "assumed in [their] identity" (Kadayifci-Orellana 2007, 24–25). These cultural, grassroots-based, local examples of peacemaking are abundant in the Muslim world and they often involve a re-interpretation of religious texts to challenge traditional discriminatory practices against an "other." Having a person of religious authority in that role helps provide a sustainable change over time.

However, this unstructured peacemaking style can also be problematic as it has been in some parts of the Muslim world with the rise of religious extremism and terrorism in the twentieth century. In the past few decades since the 1980s, various ideological groups (claiming religious authority) have taken it upon themselves to become vigilantes in the name of defending Islam against what they identify as Western aggression. Ironically, they have in effect violated all of the important Islamic laws and ethical principles in their attempt to supposedly defend Muslim interests. These include breaking the rule of law, violating basic human freedoms and the sanctity of life. They have engaged in uncivil and inhuman practices such as kidnappings, assassinations, destruction of towns and villages, and other forms of violence. The theological claims made by extremists for their terrorist activities are dangerous and must be countered because they tend to frame political goals in religious language and seek to confuse people into thinking these are Islamically acceptable choices.[11]

For several decades since the 1960s, a growing number of Muslim intellectuals, theologians, and religious leaders have been engaged in trying to create a theoretical foundation for civil, nonviolent possibilities, that is inclusive and pluralistic, allowing rights of others, including Muslims and non-Muslims. At the same time, numerous practical initiatives for reclaiming the spiritual heritage of the Qur'an have been launched by various scholar-activists in Muslim societies across the world.

Nonviolent Activism: Key Muslim Figures

Muslim theologians and scholars who have been at the forefront of scholarship and/or activism in advocating peace and nonviolence are generally not well known in the West and until recently were not hugely popular even in many Muslim countries. Below I will briefly note some key figures and provide a more detailed account of the views of three contemporary Muslim scholars and leaders: Mawlana Wahiduddin Khan (b. 1925, India), Shaykh Jawdat Sa'id (b. 1931, Syria), and Chaplain Rabia Terri Harris (b. 1953, United States).

Muslim Scholar-Activists and Their Contributions

One of the most prominent Muslim voices for nonviolence in the twentieth century has been that of Abdul Ghaffar "Badshah" Khan (d. 1988), who was a close friend and follower of Gandhi. One of the most absorbing biographies written in English referred to him as a "nonviolent soldier of Islam" (Easwaran 1984). Badshah Khan's achievements are noted by many as "revolutionary" simply because of the contrast between what was expected of him and what he eventually became. He was raised in a Pathan culture where defending one's independence and honor in the face of colonization and invasion came as naturally as eating and sleeping. The Pathans had a reputation for being courageous with their "violent heroics" (Easwaran 1984, 19) in the battlefield; they were feared for their strong capacity for resistance. But what terrified the British authorities in the Northwest Frontier Province – with all of the empire's mighty arsenal at their disposal – was not the Pathan with a gun, but one without one. Badshah Khan's nonviolent army of Pathans, in which there were over 100 000 soldiers, belied all the stereotypes and changed the dynamics of India's independence struggle. This was in some ways a response to Gandhi's call to engage in a "nonviolent warfare." The contrast lay in the dynamic notion of a fearless, tall and strong Pathan committed to delivering the "dove" to his oppressors. Despite savagery on the part of the British soldiers on numerous occasions, the Khudai Khidmatgars ("servants of God") of Khan's army remained nonviolent.[12]

Badshah Khan and all his companions were not acting this way as part of an anti-colonial strategy. They were inspired by the Islamic values of commitment to peace and justice and by Prophet Muhammad's methodology of using nonviolent means to struggle against oppression (recall the first 13 years in Mecca where Muhammad and his followers suffered at the hands of the pagan elite who persecuted them because of their belief in the One God). For many years, most members of the Khudai Khidmatgar organization endured severe hardships on account of their association with Badshah Khan, such as torture, imprisonment, and even death, at the hands of the British. They proved themselves to be a force greater than any with weapons; Gandhi often cited them as *actually* practicing what he (Gandhi) thought was true nonviolence – the "province of the daring and the undaunted" (Eswaran 1984, 20) and "nonviolence is not for cowards … it is for the brave" (Gandhi 2004, 140). The Islamic spiritual nature of their struggle was clear from the start as echoed by the words of Badshah Khan in a speech given to his followers:

> I am going to give you such a weapon that the police and the army will not be able to stand against it. It is the weapon of the Prophet [Muhammad], but you are not aware of it. That weapon is patience and righteousness. No power on earth can stand against it. (Easwaran 1984, 117)

Badshah Khan's ideas have found continuity today in the voices of many Muslim scholars and activists (some of whom are mentioned below) who have written

Figure 1.1   Abdul Ghaffar Khan with Gandhi and an Anglican minister. Source: © Hulton-Deutsch Collection/CORBIS

persuasively and with conviction that the Islamic tradition contains ample resources it needs for developing a nonviolent framework for action to face contemporary challenges.[13] They have argued that struggle for justice – one of the key require-ments of jihad enjoined by the Qur'an – can and must be undertaken nonviolently as is demonstrated by both the textual and historical sources of Islam. At the same time it is their contention that violence is neither the *only* nor the *best* way to "fight" for justice. Despite the fact that in Islam a defensive war is sanctioned, a strong and convincing case is being made by these thinkers for narrowing the option of using violence even further than the demands placed by the classical Islamic ethical theories. In fact it is hoped that as we learn more about human ingenuity in finding newer ways to resolve – and avoid – conflict, we would cate-gorically reject violence as a reliable means for this purpose. The list containing successful examples of nonviolent struggle in Muslim societies, past and present, continues to expand just as the resources for peace and nonviolent methodologies are becoming easily accessible and translatable from one community and country to another (several such case studies are included in Stephan 2009).

Among the notable *'ulama* (religious scholars) who have sought to further develop the views described above is Abdurrahman Wahid (d. 2009). Wahid was president of the Republic of Indonesia from 1999–2001, and for many years was president of the largest religious leaders' organization in Indonesia, the Nahdatul Ulama. He was an outspoken pro-democracy scholar-activist who advocated the idea that Muslims need to accommodate their practice to contemporary times without compromising any essential part of their faith (Wahid 2001). A formidable voice for nonviolence is that of Khalid Kishtainy, an Iraqi activist-scholar and the author of *Towards Nonviolence* (1984). He has been an outspoken proponent of nonviolence and is credited to have coined the term "civilian jihad" to give a name to the struggles of ordinary citizens, which include acts of civil disobedience and other nonviolent forms of resistance (Stephan 2009, 1). Another scholar-activist who is indispensable for anyone studying Islam and nonviolence is Chaiwat Satha-Anand, a Muslim scholar from Thailand. Satha-Anand has taken a very direct textual approach to advocate nonviolence as the most viable means for struggle. He has also been actively involved in the reconciliation efforts between conflicting groups in Southeast Asia. In his writings, Professor Satha-Anand proposed "eight theses on Muslim nonviolent actions," which offer a significant challenge to many of the violent options available (Satha-Anand 1999, 23):

1. Islam permits limited violence – it is mentioned in the Qur'an as *qital*.
2. Violence is governed by strict rules and conditions and the use of violence is understood to be the last resort.
3. These conditions include prohibition on harming noncombatants and nature.
4. Modern warfare – technology of war disallows the possibility of leaving noncombatants unharmed.
5. Therefore, under this reality of how wars are generally fought today, violence cannot be used based on religious principles.
6. Yet Islam calls for "fighting" against injustice – a call for all times to "strive" – to do jihad.
7. Therefore, the sole option for Muslims to carry out jihad for justice is through nonviolent means.
8. Quranic use of jihad as striving can be precisely followed through such nonviolent activism; it is not only sought, but demanded by the Qur'an.

Three case studies

The eight theses proposed by Satha-Anand correspond with ideas found in the thoughts of other scholar-activists promoting nonviolent struggle for peace and justice. Below I will present these ideas, highlighting the work of three individuals.

Maulana Wahiduddin Khan is a well-known Indian Islamic scholar who has been promoting his pacifist views since the early 1980s. His writings are centered on the belief that nonviolent activism and inter-religious solidarity are key to establishing peace and justice. His views are challenging in that they break the mold and ask for greater sacrifice on the part of the self and without pointing fingers at others. Khan argues that Islamic religious teachings are opposed to constructing a dichotomized view of the world where one is forced to see in terms of "them" and "us" (Omar 2008). The tendency to divide people based on cultural and religious differences is antithetical to the goals established by the Qur'an, which seeks to invite rather than alienate people by labeling them the "other." The Qur'an asks Muslims to "Invite (all) to the way of your God with wisdom and with beautiful preaching; and discuss with them in ways that are best and most gracious" (Q. 16:125). His views on violence are fairly clear; there is no justification for it in the present age, which he regards as most conducive for the intellectual jihad or jihad of reason. His philosophy revolves around a major incident in the life of Prophet Muhammad – the treaty of Hudaybiya – which Khan believes is paradigmatic for conflict resolution. The Hudaybiya principle is derived from the events surrounding this treaty.

Hudaybiya is a place 10 miles outside of Mecca where, in 628 C.E., Muslims were stopped by the Quraysh – the Meccan elites – preventing them from visiting the Ka'ba. Muslims were prepared to make the pilgrimage, and as per Arab custom, were only asking to exercise their right to access the holy shrine in Mecca. This act on the part of the Quraysh was deemed as an act of war, but Prophet Muhammad, instead of fighting for what was their right, decided to resolve the issue through negotiations with the Meccans. Despite the seemingly unfavorable terms from the Meccans and understandable resistance from some of his own companions, Muhammad went ahead with the treaty, a key feature of which was a "ten-year no-war pact" (Khan 2009, 120). As the Muslims turned back without performing the pilgrimage Muhammad received a revelation that would refer to this incident as a "clear victory" (Q. 48:10). Wahiduddin Khan sees in it much more than a peace treaty. He argues that it was a courageous step *to make peace for the sake of peace* rather than insist that peace comes only after justice has been achieved. He points out that the pact between Muslims and non-Muslims at Hudyabiya was:

> indeed a peace treaty, but the peace it ensured was not accompanied by justice, rather it was bereft of justice. Even so – the treaty tells us – it was this unilateral adjustment that led to ... peace between the two parties, [which] gave ... Muslims the opportunity to engage in activities which were more positive than just warding off enemy attacks. ... The result was truly remarkable – within a short span of two years, Islam became so powerful that Makkah was brought into its fold without any fighting. (2009, 120)

Shaykh Jawdat Sa'id is a Syrian thinker and scholar whose writings first appeared in the 1960s in Arabic and were only recently translated into English. His position on violence is similar to Wahiduddin Khan's in that he argues that, despite the hardships and persecution of Muslims in some parts of the world, the overall conditions that Muslims face do not necessitate the so-called armed jihad (Sa'id 1998a). However, the situation does require a jihad of a more fundamental nature, the one taught by the Qur'an – that is, jihad of the pen, jihad of the self (spiritual), and jihad of reaching out to others in the form of intra- and interfaith dialogue. Sa'id has been one of the earliest proponents of peace and nonviolence in the Arab world. His 1964 book, *The Doctrine of the First Son of Adam* or *The Problem of Violence in The Islamic Action* (translated from the Arabic) is one of the most thorough theological treatments of the arguments against war and violence in general. His thought has been decisively framed from the perspective of the imperative of nonviolence in Islam and has already influenced many in the Arab world. It is important to note that he did not begin writing on Islamic nonviolence in the post-9/11 world when it suddenly became fashionable in some quarters to speak of peace and nonviolence to counter the effects of the impending backlash against Islam and Muslims. Sa'id has been arguing these positions for over five decades.

Due to his emphasis on nonviolence, Sa'id often faced questions such as whether he wished to annul the notion of jihad, which is fundamentally quranic. He has responded by saying that "I am not annulling jihad; I am merely showing that the jihad [of Prophet Muhammad] is not the same as that of the '*kharijites*, the schismatics'" and in today's terms, also not that of the terrorists (Sa'id 1998b). Sa'id wants to separate jihad from the activities of the extremists and the terrorists who invoke this notion to garner support and seek false religious justification for their actions.

Sa'id believes we should be using the means of persuasion and not intimidation to resolve conflicts. Violence and weapons have no place in building a just and equitable society. But how to convince people that war and murder are not part of God's way? He argues that we must locate newer "substitute" ways to address conflict. When people only know the path of weapons and war to deal with injustice and to resolve conflicts, then they will continue to rely on it. But once they are shown an alternate and a better way, they will most likely be convinced.

> if someone were holding on to a fragile pillar as a support [while hanging above] an abyss, he would not abandon it if we were to [point out the pillar's weakness]. However, this person would certainly drop [the pillar] of support away if we were to offer him something else to save him from the danger [of the abyss]. So no sooner do we offer him a substitute, making it consciously and purposely handy to him, than he will free himself from the previous means. (Sa'id 2002, 121)

In short, Sa'id hopes that as everyone, including Muslims, realizes that there are other effective ways to resolve conflict they would be eager to let go of the weaker support mechanism (violence) to sustain their faith in the cause of peace.

Chaplain Rabia Terri Harris is an American Muslim scholar and religious leader. She is the founder of the Muslim Peace Fellowship and has been involved in the work of promoting peace and interfaith dialogue for over two decades. She is currently Scholar in Residence and Muslim chaplain at the multifaith "Community of Living Traditions" at the Stony Point Center in New York. Harris approaches the subject of jihad and violence from both a textual and spiritual perspective. She unambiguously states that the notion of jihad in the Qur'an signifies nonviolence (Harris 2010). This suggestion has substance if we acknowledge and understand two very basic meanings of nonviolence, which are: first, implicit in nonviolence is the activism for peacebuilding; and second, meaning has to with the right methodology to do it, that is, "unarmed struggle." Similarly, the notion of jihad at its core contains these two things. Thus Harris' elaboration on nonviolence below applies equally to jihad:

1. "Nonviolence is the *life decision* to live in harmony with the order of creation by giving up the domination of other people or the planet. Today, when put into community practice, this life decision is called *culture of peace* or *peacebuilding.*"
2. "Nonviolence is the *method* of pursuing necessary social change by relying upon the real long-term spiritual power of justice rather than the apparent short-term political power of injustice. Today, when put into community practice, this method is called *unarmed struggle.*" (2010)

Harris contends that many contemporary proponents of violence claim to emulate Prophet Muhammad's struggle against injustice. However in addition to misrepresenting Muhammad's actions, they fail to see his "priorities," instead focusing on

Figure 1.2   Rabia Terri Harris, Muslim chaplain, scholar and activist for peace, and founder of the Muslim Peace Fellowship. Source: reproduced by permission of Rabia Terri Harris

his "tactics" in the very few times he was on the battlefield (Harris 2007, 120). These priorities included social and communal peace, which would inevitably allow everyone to continue to seek the inner peace wherein the Qur'an's focus lies. Harris places her hopes in a struggle to revive the "alternative Islamic community tradition," which will allow Muslims to reclaim the quranic principle of "no compulsion in religion" (Q. 2:256a), "which the rest of the world calls non-violence, as our own and to share it with our global community" (Harris 2007, 123). The challenges are great but so is the reward of working for justice for all. However, Harris warns that we must guard against any form of utopianism and must learn to work with the imperfections of this world. Our "object cannot be *achieving* peace" instead it "must be the *work* of peace, for its own sake, without glory, no matter what" (Harris 2006, 69). The idea that our (interfaith) journey *is* the reward is an indispensable and wise counsel for, if the work of peace is to continue despite the immense challenges facing the global community today, we must not be disheartened if we fail to see measurable results from the work of peace.

Conclusion

Nonviolent activism assumes a posture of humility, which is also the hallmark of a pious person. Nonviolent activism for peace requires patience, restraint, and self-discipline. While violent activism is predicated on the assumption that change must begin outside of oneself, nonviolent activism involves personal commitment for self-transformation, becoming resilient, and cultivating courage, standing up for justice, not remaining silent, and, most important of all, controlling one's anger and hatred toward others. Violent activism does just the opposite; it assumes that all problems lie outside of oneself; therefore the perceived enemy is to be blamed for all ills.

From the foregoing, we can see that Muslim scholars and/or activists have been engaged at many fronts in an effort to address the challenge of violence committed in the name of Islam. Numerous resources both theoretical and practical are available and circulating even as the rise in violence continues. One of the main tasks of our time is to reclaim and reframe the notion of jihad as nonviolent struggle for justice, which may be regarded as the greatest form of jihad in Islam. As noted above, Jihad's true meaning is inner struggle; it provides a credible path for believers in the quranic message to work for justice through collaboration and in solidarity with others. It falls upon Muslims to liberate the notion of jihad from the bondage of mistranslation as well as misappropriation by terrorists and Islamophobes alike. Against the collective memory of misuse of the notion of jihad in history, we must seek to re-employ this notion once again in the service of unarmed struggle for justice.

The Qur'an could not be any clearer on violence and why it is problematic. Under certain conditions Muslims are/were permitted to take up arms (Q. 22:39). In other instances, the same Qur'an seeks to promote values of tolerance, patience, and peace. Justice remains the key objective, but the ultimate goal of the quranic sanction for war (*qital*) and jihad (all forms of struggle) is to achieve peace (*al-Salam*). To consider violent conflict as a means to pursue peace and justice has become increasingly problematic and even self-contradictory because of the nature of warfare today. Similarly it can be said that violence always generates more violence. The path to eradicate terrorism does not begin with more senseless violence but with wisdom and compassion, with dialogue and moral persuasion.

In the years after Prophet Muhammad's death and especially after 680 C.E., the increasing use of the word jihad to mean "jihad of the sword" made it difficult to distinguish between the quranic jihad and armed struggle. The lines became blurry at some point in history when the Muslim elite, preoccupied with empire building, failed to see the quranic emphasis on human liberation rooted in the notion of justice. In the present, the process of reclaiming the spiritual meaning of jihad has once again galvanized many secular and religious intellectuals. It is imperative to realize that the vision of pursuing peace (within ourselves and between people) is the *overriding message* of the Qur'an. It is on this basis that Muslims seek to establish a fundamental relationship between the quranic message of compassion, forgiveness, patience, and nonviolence – the most effective weapon for achieving peace. Following the successful examples of many nonviolent movements witnessed in the last century, the option of war today is viewed by many as neither necessary nor just. Activists and scholars in all religious traditions are joining forces with many other supporters of nonviolence and pacifism to oppose war as a solution. Muslim thinkers and concerned citizens from both religious and secular perspectives have called for a rethinking of the notion of jihad in light of the demands of our contemporary age. Working across religious, cultural, and

Figure 1.3 An example of Chinese-style Arabic calligraphy found in the worship hall of the tenth century "Niujie Mosque" in Beijing. The text reads "Surely, God loves those who are God conscious, mindful." (Qur'an 3:76b). Source: Irfan A. Omar

ethnic lines provides the optimism that nonviolence as a religious imperative can be established. Such interfaith collaboration may be our best hope to curtail the spread of the culture of violence that surrounds us today.

Questions for Discussion

1. Discuss the meanings of the words "Islam" and "Muslim." What do they say about the identifiable goals of the religion of Islam?
2. What does the Qur'an say about using violence against another? How might it be read and interpreted?
3. If in history some Muslim rulers justified and used violence against other groups (Muslim and non-Muslim) does it mean that Islam is a violent religion? What are some ways to differentiate between collective teachings (as opposed to disparate, stand-alone quotes from the text) and the actions of those who claim to practice the teachings?
4. What quranic notions can be drawn upon to promote peacemaking and the nonviolent struggle for justice for all?
5. Jihad is a much-abused term today with many negative derivatives in circulation such as "jihadism" and "jihadists" – should Muslims abandon the use of this term and replace it with some other to refer to inner spiritual struggle? Why or why not?
6. This chapter introduces several Muslim activists for peace and nonviolence. Which of these would you be interested in exploring further and why? Are there specific ideas with which you agree or disagree?
7. What are some of the most pressing issues facing Muslim communities and groups today?
8. Reflect on the vast majority of Muslims who often feel the brunt of violence as a result of terrorism and "counter-terrorism" operations sponsored by state actors (such as the United States military involvement in Afghanistan and Iraq during most of the first decade of the twenty-first century). It may be argued that in such circumstances an average person's perseverance and struggle to survive and make ends meet, despite all odds, represents a form of nonviolent resistance? Do you agree? Why or why not?

Notes

1 There are numerous works available in English on the life of Muhammad. Two recent and accessible studies are Armstrong and Ramadan. For details, see "Further Reading."
2 To find news and reports of positive interfaith and intercultural interactions and activities about/by/among Muslims, one has to go off the "mainstream" media grid. One web source that seeks to report on and collect positive stories of peacemaking and

community building is www.TheAmericanMuslim.Org. See "Good News Stories About/By/For North American Muslims in 2013" compiled by Sheila Musaji, http://theamericanmuslim.org/tam.php/features/articles/good-news-2013/0019814, accessed November 28, 2014.

3　The Greek "agōn" in its general meaning does seem to support the Quranic meaning of "struggle" and "fight" in metaphorical sense. See *A Greek-English Lexicon of the New Testament* (1954), s. v. "agōn".

4　For this information, I am indebted to Professor Mahmoud Ayoub for allowing me to rely on his encyclopedic knowledge of Arabic religious literature.

5　For in depth discussion of an "Islamic Just War" see Kelsay 2007.

6　Some quranic references to the term jihad or its derivatives are found in the following verses, all of them meaning "to strive": 9:19, 9:24, 22:78, 25:52, 29:6, 49:15, and 60:1. The term *qitāl* (defensive war) appears in 2:190, 4:75, 9:12–13, 9:29, and 22:39.

7　Of the over 6600 verses in the Qur'an there are about 40 that deal with defensive war. That amounts to less than 1% of the quranic content (Khan 2003, 119). Most numerous are those verses that speak of peace, patience, and the eternal life after death.

8　See chapter VII, http://www.un.org/en/documents/charter/index.shtml, accessed November 28, 2014.

9　A reference to Q. 10:25. See also Q. 89:30 where the "soul at peace" (a righteous person) is invited by God to "enter the Garden" affirming that God's paradise is the core of all peace and conversely, being at peace is like being in paradise.

10　A fuller version of this Hadith is found in *Sunan Abu Da'ud*.

11　At present, the so-called "Islamic State in Iraq and Syria" or ISIS – with its violent and destructive actions against civilians – represents one such pseudo-Islamic organization that seeks to use religion to pursue purely political aims.

12　For a fuller discussion on the irenic ideas and activism of Badshah Khan (India/Pakistan), see Gandhi 2004.

13　Within the West, there are several scholars and activists whose voices have become influential and have impacted both the activism and the discourse. In the United States, scholars such as Abdulaziz Sachedina, Mahmoud Ayoub, Amina Wadud, Azizah Al-Hibri, Abdul Aziz Said, Riffat Hassan, Muhammad Abu Nimer, Meena Sharify-Funk, A. Rashied Omar, Farid Munir, Eboo Patel, Ayse Kadayifci-Orellana, Najeeba Syeed-Miller, and Amir Hussain are part of a growing body of scholars and leaders who are engaged in dialogue and outreach to make a difference for peace.

References

The Arabic Bible. 1906. *Al-Kitab al-Muqaddas*. Cambridge: Cambridge University Press.

Ali, Abdullah Yusuf, trans. 1992. *The Meaning of the Holy Qur'an*. Brentwood, MD: Amana Publications.

Ayoub, Mahmoud M. 1984. *The Qur'an and Its Interpreters*, vol. 1. New York: State University of New York Press.

Ayoub, Mahmoud. 1992. "Jihad: A Source of Power and Framework of Authority in Islam." *Bulletin of the Institute of Middle Eastern Studies*, volume 6.

Bonney, Richard. 2004. *Jihād: From Qur'ān to bin Laden*. New York: Palgrave Macmillan.

Brockopp, Jonathan. 2004. "Understanding Islamic Ethics." *Centre Daily Times* (State College, PA). November 1, 2004.

Burkholder, Richard. 2002. "Jihad – 'Holy War', or Internal Spiritual Struggle?" Accessed November 28, 2014. http://www.gallup.com/poll/7333/Jihad-Holy-War-Internal-Spiritual-Struggle.aspx.

Easwaran, Eknath. 1984. *Nonviolent Soldier of Islam: Badshah Khan, A Man to Match his Mountains*. Petaluma, CA: Nilgiri Press.

El Fadl, Khalid Abou. 2002. *The Place of Tolerance in Islam*. Boston, MA: Beacon Press.

El Fadl, Khaled Abou. 2006. "Islam and Violence: Our Forgotten Legacy." In *Islam in Transition: Muslim Perspectives*. Edited by John Donohue and John Esposito. Oxford and New York: Oxford University Press, pp. 460–464.

Engineer, Asghar Ali. 2001. "Islam and Doctrines of Peace and Non-violence." *Islam and the Modern Age*, 32, 1 (February).

Esposito, John L. 2002. *"Foreword" in Muslims in the West: From Sojourners to Citizens.* Edited by Yvonne Yazbeck Haddad. New York: Oxford University Press.

Esposito, John L. 2005. *Islam: The Straight Path*, third edition. New York: Oxford University Press.

Gandhi, Rajmohan. 2004. *Ghaffar Khan: Nonviolent Badshah of the Pakhtuns*. New Delhi: Viking Penguin.

A Greek-English Lexicon of the New Testament. 1957. *Chicago*, IL: The University of Chicago Press.

Harris, Rabia Terri. 2006. "Bismi Llah Ir-Rahman ir-Rahim." In *Shalom, Salaam, Peace: Peace Services in the Abrahamic Traditions*. Edited by Mary Evelyn Jegen, SND. Alkmaar: IFOR.

Harris, Rabia Terri. 2007. "Nonviolence in Islam: The Alternative Community Tradition." In *Subverting Hatred: The Challenge of Nonviolence in Religious Traditions*. Edited by Daniel L. Smith-Christopher. Maryknoll, NY: Orbis Books, pp. 107–127.

Harris, Rabia Terri. 2010. "On Islamic Nonviolence." *Fellowship* (Spring 2010). Accessed November 28, 2014. http://forusa.org/fellowship/2010/spring/islamic-nonviolence/11639.

Hasan, Ahmed, trans. (1984). *Sunan Abu Dawud*. Lahore: Sh. M. Ashraf.

Heine, Bernd. 1993. *Auxiliaries: Cognitive Forces and Grammaticalization*. Oxford: Oxford University Press.

Hinze, Bradford E. and Irfan A. Omar (eds). 2005. *Heirs of Abraham: The Future of Muslim, Jewish, and Christian Relations*. Maryknoll, NY: Orbis Books.

Kadayifci-Orellana and S. Ayse. 2007. "Living Walls: Among Muslims Peace Takes on its Own Distinct Forms." *Harvard Divinity Bulletin* 35, 4 (Autumn): 24–29.

Kaltner, John. 2003. *Islam: What Non-Muslims Should Know?* Philadelphia, PA: Fortress Press.

Khan, Wahiduddin. 1997. "The Concept of Jihad," *Al-Risāla* (English), July–August.

Khan, Wahiduddin. 1999a. *Islam and Peace*. New Delhi: Goodword Books.

Khan, Wahiduddin. 1999b. "On Islam and Jihad," *Al-Risāla* (English), July–August.

Khan, Wahiduddin. 2003. *The Ideology of Peace: Towards a Culture of Peace*. New Delhi: Goodword Books.

Khan, Wahiduddin. 2009. *The Prophet of Peace*. New Delhi: Penguin.

Kelsay, John. 2007. *Arguing the Just War in Islam*. Cambridge, MA and London: Harvard University Press.

Kishtainy, Khalid. n.d. "Nonviolence and 'Civilian Jihad." Accessed November 28, 2014. http://www.commongroundnews.org/article.php?id=21078&lan=en&sp=1.

Kishtainy, Khalid. 1984. *Towards Nonviolence* (in Arabic). Amman: Dar al-Karmal.

Lawrence, Bruce. 1989. *Defenders of God: The Fundamentalist Revolt against the Modern Age*. San Francisco, CA: Harper & Row.

Matisoff, J. 1991. "Areal and Universal Dimensions of Grammaticalization in Lahu." In *Approaches to Grammaticalization vol. II*. Edited by E.C. Traugott and B. Heine. Amsterdam: Benjamins, pp. 383–454.

Nelson-Pallmeyer, Jack. 2005. *Is Religion Killing Us? Violence in the Bible and the Qur'an*. New York and London: Continuum.

Omar, Irfan A. 2008. "Towards an Islamic Theology of Nonviolence: A Critical Appraisal of Maulana Wahiduddin Khan's View of Jihad." *Vidyajyoti Journal of Theological Reflection* (India), 72, 9: 671–680, and 72, 10: 751–758.

Peters, Rudolph. 1979. *Islam and Colonialism: The Doctrine of Jihad in Modern History*. The Hague: Mouton.

Sachedina, Abdulaziz. 1988. *The Just Ruler* (al-sultān al-'ādil) *in Shi'ite Islam*. New York: Oxford University Press.

Safi, Louay M. 2001. *Peace and the Limits of War*. Herndon, VA: International Institute of Islamic Thought.

Sa'id, Jawdat. 1964. *The Doctrine of the First Son of Adam* or *The Problem of Violence*. Accessed November 28, 2014. http://www.jawdatsaid.net.

Sa'id, Jawdat. 1998a. "Paths of Social Order," an unpublished paper presented at the Symposium on "Islam and Peace," Washington DC.

Sa'id, Jawdat. 1998b. "Jawdat Sa'eed Answers Twelve Questions Posed by the Journal 'Current Islamic Issues.'" Accessed November 28, 2014. http://www.jawdatsaid.net/en/index.php?title=Main_Page.

Sa'id, Jawdat. 2002. *Nonviolence: the Basis for Settling Disputes in Islam*. Damascus and Beirut: Dar al-Fikr.

Said, Abdul Aziz, Mohammed Abu-Nimer and Meena Sharify-Funk (eds). 2006. *Contemporary Islam: Dynamic not Static*. London and New York: Routledge.

Satha-Anand, Chaiwat. 1999. "The Nonviolent Crescent: Eight Theses on Muslim Nonviolent Action." In *Islam and Non-violence*. Edited by Glenn D. Paige, Chaiwat Satha-Anand, and Sarah Gilliatt. Hawaii: Center for Global Nonviolence.

Stephan, Maria J. 2009. *Civilan Jihad: Nonviolent Struggle, Democratization, and Governance in the Middle East*. New York: Palgrave Macmillan.

Wahid, Abdurrahman. 2001. "Islam, Nonviolence, and National Transformation." In *Islam and Nonviolence*. Edited by Glenn D. Paige, Chaiwat Satha-Anand, and Sarah Gilliatt. Hawaii: Center for Global Nonviolence.

Further Reading

Abu Nimer, Muhammad. 2003. *Nonviolence and Peace Building in Islam: Theory and Practice*. Gainesville, FL: University Press of Florida. This is one of the most comprehensive accounts of the subject in English. It provides a good survey of quranic teachings on peace and nonviolence and includes numerous case studies on religious and cultural dimensions of peacebuilding in the Muslim world.

Armstrong, Karen. 1993. *Muhammad: A Biography of the Prophet*. San Francisco, CA: Harper San Francisco. Armstrong writes from a world religions perspective. She is a keen observer and meticulous scholar who has studied and written about several major religious figures. Here she unpacks Muhammad for a twenty-first-century reader

Faith-Based Peace-building: Mapping and Analysis of Christian, Muslim and Multi-faith Actors. Accessed November 28, 2014. http://www.clingendael.nl/publications/2005/20051100_cru_paper_faith-based%20peace-building.pdf. An in-depth analysis of Christian, Muslim, and other faith organizations documenting their innovative methods of peacebuilding often in collaboration with other religious and secular groups and individuals.

Nusseibeh, Lucy. "Palestinian Women and Nonviolence." Accessed November 28, 2014. http://www.commongroundnews.org/article.php?id=21088&lan=en&sp=1. This article by a Palestinian scholar describes the journey of women's nonviolent struggle against the violence inflicted due to Israeli occupation of the Palestinian territories.

Ramadan, Tariq. 2007. *In the Footsteps of the Prophet: Lessons from the Life of Muhammad.* Oxford and New York: Oxford University Press. This is an accessible work written by one of the most prolific European Muslim scholars.

Smock, David and Qamar-ul Huda. 2009. "Islamic Peacemaking Since 9/11." United States Institute of Peace (USIP) Special Report. Accessed November 28, 2014. http://www.usip.org/publications/islamic-peacemaking-911. This report documents the efforts by Muslim leadership in peacebuilding activities and advocacy around the world. It also provides key sources for further study and reflection.

Muslim Peacemaking and Civil Rights Organizations/Resources

The American Muslim (TAM) www.TheAmericanMuslim.Org (accessed November 28, 2014).

Center for Peace and Spirituality www.cpsglobal.org (accessed November 28, 2014).

Council on American-Islamic Relations (CAIR) www.cair.com (accessed November 28, 2014).

Daughters of Abraham Book Group. http://daughtersofabraham.com (accessed November 28, 2014).

The Imam and the Pastor – a documentary film set in Nigeria.

Inner-City Muslim Network (IMAN) www.imancentral.org (accessed November 28, 2014).

Inside Islam: Dialogues and Debates, University of Wisconsin-Madison and Wisconsin Public Radio. http://insideislam.wisc.edu (accessed November 28, 2014).

Karamah: Muslim Women Lawyers for Human Rights. http://karamah.org (accessed November 28, 2014).

Muslim Peace Coalition. http://muslimpeacecoalition.org (accessed November 28, 2014).

Muslim Peace Fellowship. http://mpf21.wordpress.com/about-2 (accessed November 28, 2014).

Newground: Muslim-Jewish Partnership. http://www.muslimjewishnewground.org/index.html (accessed November 28, 2014).

Salam Institute for Peace and Justice. http://salaminstitute.org/new (accessed November 28, 2014).

Scholar of the House, a web site dedicated to promote peace through the works of Dr Khaled Abou El Fadl. http://scholarofthehouse.org/index.html (accessed November 28, 2014).

Glossary

dar al-Islam: the Muslim polity where social and legal spheres may be informed by Islamic teachings.

dar al-harb: the political entity hostile to Muslims.

Islamism: in Islamic studies discourse, an equivalent term for fundamentalism. It seeks to separate between Islam as faith, and an ideology or ideologies that appropriate Islamic form and terminology to express their political and/or extremist objectives.

Islamophobe: a person harboring irrational fear of and/or prejudice against Islam or Muslims.

Jihad bin nafs or Jihad al-akbar: struggle against the self, or the greater jihad.

Jihad al-asghar: the lesser jihad, sometimes also used to refer to the "struggle" in the battlefield.

Kharijites: a group of Muslims in early Islam who took the extreme position of declaring someone "unbeliever" based on apparent action deemed to be against God.

The Prophetic tradition: the beliefs, practices, and decisions that emerged on the basis of the Muhammad's teachings based on the Qur'an.

qital: defensive war.

Quraysh: the Meccan leaders opposed to Muhammad and his message of monotheism. They persecuted him and many of his followers until they were defeated by Muslims in a nonviolent conquest of Mecca in 631 C.E.

shahadah: the first pillar of faith, the creedal statement, also means "witness" and is a term commonly associated with "martyrdom."

Schools of Law: Hanafi, Maliki, Hanbali, Shafi'i (Sunni), and Ja'fari (Shi'a). There are five major schools of law; each recognizes all the others as valid ways of practice. The differences are often cosmetic but in some instances they have led to major shifts in theological thinking. Separation among these first arose mainly due to the differing interpretations of the source materials, the Qur'an and the Hadith.

Shi'a: smaller of the two sects in Islam, Shi'a have a special reverence for Ali, Muhammad's son-in-law and his family.

Sunni: the larger of the two sects in Islam.

1.1

A Confucian Response

Sin Yee Chan

In his chapter, Irfan Omar has given a nuanced and meticulous scholarly analysis of the much-contested term "jihad" and tried to detach the term from its associations with violence and terrorism. According to Omar, jihad's primary meaning in the Qur'an is "to strive" or "to exert" oneself, in the religious sense, in the service of God. In brief, it means "personal spiritual struggle." It is deemed problematic to use the term for a violent endeavor. The concept of jihad as defensive warfare emerged during the early Muslims' battles against the Sassanid Empire and other political powers, and many political authorities have since then invoked jihad as part of armed campaigns for their ideological and political undertakings, especially during the era of the crusades. Consensus among scholars of Islam, however, is that in the Qur'an defensive, last resort war is not referred to as jihad, but as "*qital*" (fighting). Jihad in the Qur'an therefore is distinguished from "*harb*" (war), "*futuhat*" (conquest), and "*qital*" (fighting). Omar conceives of this effort to "reclaim" jihad as a contribution to counter extremism and violence by depriving the extremists of their ideological resources. Omar emphasizes that the Qur'an's general and permanent stance is for peace and nonviolence; violence is only permissible in a very limited context. This can be seen from the cherished Islamic virtues such as *al-silm* (peace, reconciliation), *al 'afw* (forgiveness), *al-sabr* (patience), and *la 'unf* (nonviolence).

Omar carefully demonstrates a case in which an ideological element has been misappropriated by some political authorities and contemporary extremists. Misappropriation is a common fate of most, and perhaps all, major ideologies, religions, and traditions in the world. Confucianism is not immune from this misfortune. For example, while philosophical Confucianism emphasizes hierarchy, it also stresses the importance of reciprocal duties between the parties in a hierarchical relationship, as well as the importance of remonstrance from the party in an inferior position to ensure that the superiors follow the right path. However, when the political authorities enforced Confucian ideology in the past, it was the

Peacemaking and the Challenge of Violence in World Religions, First Edition.
Edited by Irfan A. Omar and Michael K. Duffey.
© 2015 John Wiley & Sons, Ltd. Published 2015 by John Wiley & Sons, Ltd.

hierarchical and not the reciprocal elements that were emphasized. The result then is the association of Confucianism with authoritarianism and blind obedience. This feature is still central to the image many have of Confucianism today.

Reflections on the case of Confucianism bring out some questions about Omar's analysis. Though the idea of hierarchism in Confucianism suffers from misappropriation, there is no denial that hierarchism is indeed a central element in Confucianism and that there is an intrinsic tension between it and the element of reciprocity. The misappropriation removes the tension by making hierarchism one-sided. In contrast, in Omar's analysis, it is not clear whether jihad is a central element in Islam and whether there is any intrinsic tension between spiritual struggle and violence inherent in the concept of jihad. Otherwise, the chapter only shows that the extremists have used a concept wrongly, but not that the extremists are purported to embrace something central to Islam. It may be that jihad in the Qur'an does not mean war or fighting, but is the term jihad still somehow related to the concept of violence? What does jihad as striving or struggle mean? Does it imply or is it associated with vehement use of force, if not exactly violence? One would suspect that the association of jihad with war or fighting is not a matter of mere coincidence or total arbitrariness; there must be some elements in the concept that enable the misappropriation to happen.

Moreover, while it is important to reclaim the concept, it is also important to acknowledge the historical understanding of the concept and its impact on the culture. Otherwise we may not be able to fully understand the basis that anchors the concept in people's psychology – its associations, connotations, and connections with other elements in the history and tradition.

Furthermore, it does seem that jihad as armed struggle is a well-established concept in Islamic history and traditional culture. If so, whether jihad as armed struggle is still called for or not requires a political and not a mere religious or scholarly judgment. Omar explains that jihad as armed struggle in the current time is unjustified because the nature of the weapons involved makes war an extremely destructive endeavor and that the extreme ethnic and religious repressions which happened in the past are no longer true in the same way today. We have greater freedom of speech and freedom to practice religion and many more methods of political reconciliation and mediation. Many extremists, on the other hand, contend that the political, religious, and ethnic repressions are just as severe as before, though perhaps not as blatant. Moreover, on top of all these traditional repressions, they claim, there are also the more debilitating economic and cultural repressions by the capitalist, imperial powers. To fully divest the ideological resources of the extremists, it seems that theoretical and political analysis are also needed to address the issues of economic imperialism and ethnic and religious segregations in the various parts of the world.

Another point of comparison with the Confucian tradition concerns the Confucian notion of a just war – punitive expedition. One major reason for launching a punitive expedition is to remove tyrants who have caused immense suffering to the people and destroyed the social order. Omar emphasizes the peaceful and nonviolent elements of Islam and points out that war is justified only for the defense of one's state or one's religious freedom. Does this rule out the kind of humanitarian intervention and regime change implied by the Confucian notion of punitive expedition? Would Islam really prohibit military humanitarian intervention? Wouldn't emphasizing nonviolence and forgiveness in the face of horrendous atrocities practically mean bolstering the oppressors? Moreover, the Confucian punitive expedition is also about retribution, which the Confucians believe is a part of the moral order. What does Islam say about retribution and war? Is it permissible to launch a war to punish a tyrant?

Regarding the nonviolent nature of Islam, it would be helpful for Omar to explain the issue of martyrdom a bit further. He claims that the extremists cannot achieve martyrdom because to achieve martyrdom:(1) martyrdom has to be given by God and cannot be sought by oneself; (2) the intention can never be about personal glory; and (3) one can never knowingly be willing to harm any noncombatant. But can the extremists still claim that they meet all the above conditions because (1) they receive God's calling; (2) the intention is to achieve moral revolution, not personal glory; and (3) they do not aim to harm, but rather the will is to achieve moral revolution, the harm is a byproduct. And harm must be permissible as a byproduct, they will claim, otherwise, any military confrontation would be deemed impermissible. Or alternatively, the extremists can claim that they are not achieving martyrdom, they are mere soldiers of God and God will reward them in heaven. (It might help therefore to also explain briefly the myth of the heavenly rewards that the extremists often claim that they will receive after their sacrifice.)

The major aim of Omar's chapter is to defend Islam as a religion preaching peace and nonviolence. One question then is why Islam, more than any other religion in the world, is often associated with extremism and violence. Does it have a more vivid appeal to the underclass and the oppressed because of some of its doctrinal ideas? Or is it because of certain nondoctrinal related historical and sociological factors such as the association between Islam and the Third World? I do not know if answering these questions is beyond the scope of Omar's chapter, but they are worth raising.

1.2

A Jewish Response

Joshua Ezra Burns

In today's world, the object of peace in Islamic thought can seem like a rare commodity. Irfan Omar is justified in lamenting that those few Muslims who perpetrate violence in the name of a radical fundamentalist Islam tend to get more press than the vast majority who reject that interpretation of the concept of jihad as a betrayal of their core ethical principles. The resulting imbalance in the public discourse on Islam has been to the detriment of those both within and without the Muslim community advocating the less authentic interpretation urging the individual to seek social change through introspective means. I commend Omar for his intellectual honesty in considering both approaches and thank him for providing a constructive counterpoint to the prejudicial portrayal of Islam.

Speaking from my own admittedly idiosyncratic Jewish perspective, I find much with which to identify in Omar's comments on the scriptural foundations of Islam's teachings on violence and peacemaking. He appropriately acknowledges that the Qur'an and the Hadith contain statements supporting both alternatives. Urging, however, the critical reader of these texts to consider their pronouncements in their literary and historical contexts, Omar shows that they prescribe no uniform doctrine to be asserted as the only way for the devout Muslim to conduct his or her behavior. I reach an identical conclusion with respect to the Hebrew Scriptures in my study of peace and peacemaking in the Jewish tradition. In both Judaism and Islam, it is therefore the prerogative of the individual to decide how best to interpret the revealed word of God. And while both religions recognize the contributions of past interpreters, neither compels the individual to imagine the present in past terms simply for the sake of tradition.

Of course, religion is only one of the factors which determine the practice of Judaism and Islam. In the case of Islam, the political interests of the Islamic state have always conditioned the enforcement of certain religious customs in the interest of public mores. As Omar points out, many contemporary movements involving radical Islamists are predicated on political ideologies of a bygone era

Peacemaking and the Challenge of Violence in World Religions, First Edition.
Edited by Irfan A. Omar and Michael K. Duffey.
© 2015 John Wiley & Sons, Ltd. Published 2015 by John Wiley & Sons, Ltd.

when theologians knew of only two states comprising the "us" of the Islamic caliphate and the "them" of the world beyond its borders. The desire of those fundamentalists to press Islamic law upon unwilling subjects both Muslim and non-Muslim is a residual effect of a break between past and present owing to geopolitical and sociocultural developments well beyond their purview. What they desire is nothing less than a reversal of history. That many have resorted to violence to achieve that impossible goal is no wonder. There simply are no rational means whereby to achieve their goal.

As I discuss in my chapter, the Jews too have had occasion to reflect on the loss of political power. Yet where the developments of the past 100 years served to debase Islam's ancient political constitutions, the same developments galvanized Judaism's. I refer here to the birth of the modern State of Israel. The creation of a dedicated Jewish nation-state in May of 1947 was facilitated by the decline of the Ottoman Empire and the consequent emergence of local Arab nationalist movements throughout the Middle East. What was once an impossible dream for the Jews became a reality in part due to the dissolution of Islam's political hegemony over Palestine, a place where Jews and Muslims had lived in relative harmony for nearly 1400 years. Of course, Jews in Palestine and elsewhere in the Islamic world during those centuries had no need for political theologies of their own. Lacking the social apparatus to exercise their political will, they relied entirely on the allowances of their Muslim protectors. The only sovereign Jewish state of which they dared to conceive was the eschatological kingdom of the Messiah, a state to be ruled directly by God through His earthly regent.

Though decades in the making, the declaration of the State of Israel suddenly forced Jews around the world to digest a clash of traditional values no less upsetting than that incurred by the dissolution of the Ottoman caliphate. Many liberal Jews, including the most vocal proponents of the Zionist movement, envisioned their new state as a secular political entity bound by Jewish national interests rather than the long disused political dictates of the Jewish religion. Even those religious Jews who supported the Zionist movement largely disassociated its aims from the Messianic beliefs of their theological tradition. But Jews from both camps were quick to realize the difficulty of serving the political needs of their state without trampling on on the venerable ethical principles of their faith. Judaism was not well equipped to wield power over non-Jews, even if its proponents were to imagine that power as civil rather than religious.

Just as some Muslims have struggled to come to terms with their inability to restore the religious order of ages past, some Jews of a similar fundamentalist bent have resisted letting go of the idyllic eschatological kingdom of which their ancestors dreamt. These Jews assert their rights and the rights of all Jews to settle the entirety of the biblical Land of Israel, an area encompassing the politically contested Palestinian territories and the Golan Heights. The pull of tradition has proven strong, influencing the domestic policies of the Israeli government and the organizational agendas of right-leaning Jewish advocacy groups throughout the world. The resulting conflict of interests between Jewish and Muslim claimants to these disputed areas thus remains a point of controversy in the broader conflict between the Israelis and the Palestinians and, to the minds of many on both sides, a major obstacle to peace.

I will conclude by commending Omar and other scholars of his noble tempera- ment for continually striving to remind us all of Islam's ethical conscience in these trying times. While I am sure that these efforts are appreciated by likeminded Muslim audiences, they stand to teach just as much to those of us less well acquainted with the venerable ideas behind the Islamist slogans menacingly touted on the evening news. Countering prejudice with authentic knowledge of Islam might be a radical idea in its own right. But it is an idea with which all morally driven people should be able to relate.

2

Christianity
From Peacemaking to Violence and Home Again

Michael K. Duffey

At that moment one of those with Jesus reached for his sword and drew it, and he struck the High Priest's servant and cut off his ear. But Jesus said to him, "Put up your sword. All who take up the sword die by the sword. Do you suppose that I cannot appeal to my Father, who could at once send to my aid more than twelve legions of angels?"

Matt. 26.52; an incident at Jesus' arrest; this saying of Jesus
is repeated in The Book of Revelation, 13.10

Christian Religious Texts

The New Testament comprises four gospels (an old English word meaning "good news") written between 70 C.E. and the end of the first century. The Gospels of Matthew, Mark, and Luke include some of the same material (Jesus' teachings and stories about him) each edited to emphasize certain aspects about him. For example, Mark's Gospel has been called the story of the crucified messiah; Matthew emphasized Jesus as the messiah, the son of David; Luke focuses on Jesus as the fulfillment of Jewish hope; and John stresses the preexistence of Jesus.

Pauline Letters are 21 letters written to early Christian communities or individuals; seven definitely by St Paul and another eight possibly written by him or by his disciples. The letters address the fulfillment of God's plan through Jesus, his teachings, and the behavior of the Christian community.

The Acts of the Apostles tells the story of the early Christian community in Jerusalem, including the decision that St Paul will carry the revelation of Jesus to the gentiles.

Peacemaking and the Challenge of Violence in World Religions, First Edition.
Edited by Irfan A. Omar and Michael K. Duffey.
© 2015 John Wiley & Sons, Ltd. Published 2015 by John Wiley & Sons, Ltd.

The Book of Revelation offers encouragement in the time of persecution, foretelling the overcoming of the "beast," the leaders of Rome who have rejected Christ.

Early Church Fathers' writing from the second to the eighth centuries C.E.

Church Councils (to date the Catholic Church has had 21 ecumenical councils): The first two were in Nicea in 325 and Constantinople in 381. Most churches recognize the pronouncements of the first seven councils as authoritative.

The Nicene–Constantinople Creed

I believe in one God, the Father Almighty, Maker of heaven and earth, and of all things visible and invisible. And in one Lord Jesus Christ, the only-begotten Son of God, begotten of the Father before all worlds; God of God, Light of Light, very God of very God; begotten, not made, being of one substance with the Father, by whom all things were made. Who, for us men and for our salvation, came down from heaven, and was incarnate by the Holy Spirit of the virgin Mary, and was made man; and was crucified also for us under Pontius Pilate; He suffered, died, and was buried; and the third day He rose again, according to the Scriptures; and ascended into heaven, and sits on the right hand of the Father; and He shall come again, with glory, to judge the living and the dead; whose kingdom shall have no end.

And I believe in the Holy Spirit, the Lord and Giver of Life; who proceeds from the Father and the Son; who with the Father and the Son together is worshipped and glorified; who spoke by the prophets.

And I believe in one holy catholic and apostolic Church. I acknowledge one baptism for the remission of sins; and I look for the resurrection of the dead, and the life of the world to come. Amen.

This chapter describes the peacemaking and nonviolence within Christianity, as well its violence. The first section is a very brief description of the Jewish origins of Christianity and the identity of Jesus. It includes the texts that record the actions and teachings of Jesus: testimonies about him offered to early Christian communities, rules for Christian life, and the pronouncements of early church councils. The following section highlights Jesus' teachings on peacemaking. Next, I offer a very brief examination of Christian history from the point of view of nonviolence and peacemaking. For much of history Christian churches used violence to achieve their ends. Finally, there is a hopeful account of contemporary Christian communities striving to rekindle a peacemaking vision of Jesus. This presentation is in the main descriptive, although as the chapter makes clear it is also prescriptive.

Who was Jesus?

Jesus was a Jew, as were his disciples and the crowds who were drawn to him. He was born around the year six of the Common Era near Jerusalem in the town of Bethlehem. Jesus was conceived by the power of the Holy Spirit and born of a virgin, Mary. His early life is obscure. At around the age of 30 he began his public ministry of miraculous healing and of preaching what he called the coming of the "kingdom of God." He was a faithful Jew, teaching that the Jewish laws should be observed and that they could be summarized in the commandments to love God and to love thy neighbor. But he criticized certain Jewish religious leaders for their hypocrisy.

Three years later, Jesus' charges of hypocrisy led Jewish leaders to conspire to get rid of him. The Roman governor of Palestine complied. He was arrested and executed by crucifixion. Three days later he rose from the dead. After ascending into heaven he sent his Spirit to assist and guide the community in its continuation of his ministry. News of his resurrection attracted many followers, first Jews and then Gentiles (non-Jews). He was worshipped as Jesus the Christ (*Christos:* messiah). Christianity spread rapidly beyond the borders of Palestine into the gentile worlds of Rome and Greece as Christianity's familial relationship with the Jewish faith gradually diminished.

As Jesus was a Jew, his message of God's compassion and forgiveness and his call for justice for the poor and scorn for the greedy were rooted in the Jewish tradition. However, the deeper question about him was his identity. His disciples hoped that he would be the one to redeem Israel from the oppression of the Roman occupation. Many people debated that question. Jesus' identity is tied to two dimensions of Jewish religious faith: the promise of the covenant and of a messiah. The way followers of Jesus interpreted the covenant and the messianic hope defines Christian faith and also offers clues to its notion of peace.

God made a covenant with the Israelites through Moses. They were promised divine protection and prosperity if they kept God's commandments. The history of Israel was one of both fidelity and infidelity. The "golden age" of Israel was the reign of King David and the construction by his son Solomon of the temple in Jerusalem. But the infidelity of the Israelites resulted in the conquering of Israel by the Babylonians in 587 B.C.E. and the exile of Jewish leaders. During the exile the prophet Jeremiah delivered God's promise of a new covenant:

> I will make a new covenant with Israel and Judah ... I will set my law within them and write it on their hearts; a will become their God and they shall become my people ... I will forgive their wrongdoings and remember their sins no more. (Jeremiah 31:31–32, 34)

Likewise, the prophet Isaiah spoke God's reassuring words: "my love will be immovable and never fail and my covenant of peace shall not be shaken. So says the Lord who takes pity on you" (Isaiah 54:10). The new covenant is identified with Jesus' pronouncement at the outset of his public preaching. He went into the synagogue of his hometown and read from the scroll of Isaiah: "The Kingdom of God is upon you. Repent and believe the good news" (Matt. 4:17). Luke's gospel elaborates:

> The Spirit of the Lord is upon me because he has anointed me; he has sent me to announce good news to the poor, to proclaim release for prisoners and recovery of sight for the blind; to let the broken victims go free, to proclaim the year of the Lord's favor. (Luke 4:18–19)

Immediately following the announcement of the Kingdom is Jesus' Sermon on the Mount in which he commends a particular way of life – peacemaking, forgiveness of enemies, and suffering for justice's sake.

As I have noted, Israel yearned for the coming of a messiah who would redeem the nation and save it from its enemies, who in the time of Jesus were the Roman occupiers. The disciples of Jesus shared the messianic hope for an "anointed one" who would restore the throne of King David. They saw Jesus as the one who had the power to do this. However, their understanding of Jesus had to change in the aftermath of his crucifixion and resurrection. Jesus would become identified with the "suffering servant" of God whom Isaiah described, and not as a royal figure:

> He had no beauty, no majesty to draw our eyes ... he was despised, he shrank from the sight of men, tormented and humbled by suffering; we despised him, we held him of no account, a thing from which men turn away their eyes. Yet on himself he bore our sufferings. He was afflicted, he submitted to be struck down and did not open his mouth. (Isaiah 53:3–4, 7[1])

The image of the messiah was now seen through the lens of the cross. Jesus linked God's making of a new covenant to his own death. On the night before his death he gathered his disciples to share the Passover supper. There he blessed bread and wine and identified consuming them with his death, calling the wine the "the blood of the covenant shed for many for the forgiveness of sins" (Matt. 26:28).

Jesus, Nonviolence, and Peacemaking

Jesus is revealed as a new kind of messiah, one committed to the Kingdom of God, marked by forgiving, loving of enemies, accepting suffering for the sake of love, and being compassionate to the poor and suffering. Most unexpected was the means through which he would save Israel and all the nations. He would allow himself to be subjected to suffering and death.

The Hebrew word for peace, *shalom*, has several meanings. One sense is of inner peace, suggested in the quotation from the gospel of John: "Peace is my parting gift to you, my peace, such as the world cannot give. Set your troubled hearts at rest, and banish your fears" (John 14:27). Jesus offered comfort and encouragement to his disciples as he was about to depart from them after his resurrection. *Shalom* also refers to the collective wellbeing of the Jewish people and of universal wellbeing and concord between individuals and groups. Elsewhere in this volume Professor Joshua Burns described the vision of shalom as national wholeness with which the Israelite Prophets characterized the reigns of King David and King Solomon. The prophets envision a universal peace in which the Messiah would

> instate a new world order bringing harmony not only to the nation of Israel but to all the nations of the world who would defer to the authority of God's chosen earthly sovereign

[and]

> a universal peace to be achieved when God would set a new king of David's line on the throne of Jerusalem.

At the birth of Jesus an angel proclaimed "Glory to God in the highest heaven and peace to all men who enjoy his favor" (Luke 2:14). Pope Benedict XVI referred to Jesus revealing a "new kind of power, unlike that of Emperor Caesar Augustus, who held the title 'bringer of world peace'" (Pope Benedict XVI 2007, 84). At the beginning of his public ministry Jesus retreats to the desert. There, the devil tempts him with worldly power, which Jesus rejects. Jesus preached the Sermon on the Mount in which he described eight characteristics of holiness ("beatitudes"): humility, solidarity with those who are "sorrowing," hungering and thirsting for righteousness, mercy, gentleness of spirit, and purity of heart (Matt. 5:4–7). The final two marks of holiness he described were: "Blessed are the peacemakers, for they will be called children of God" and "Blessed are those who are persecuted for righteousness' sake, for theirs is the kingdom of heaven" (Matt. 5:10).

Jesus called his followers to forbearance: do not kill or harbor hatred; instead "love your enemies and pray for those who persecute you" (Matt. 5:21–22; 44–45). Overcome evil with good and suffer evil rather than defend yourselves through violence. Make peace with those with whom you have grievances (Matt. 5:23). Forgo retaliation: "You have heard it said, an eye for eye, tooth for tooth. But what I tell you is do not set yourself against the man who wrongs you" (Matt. 5:38–39). Enemies were to be loved and persecutors prayed for (Matt. 5:44–45).

Jesus' peacemaking was not passivity. He offered three scenarios to suggest how powerless people could affirm their dignity without resorting to violent against their oppressors. Addressing the master–slave relationship – an instance of class oppression – he advised a slave struck by his master to turn the other cheek. By turning his cheek it was not possible for the master to repeat a backhanded slap but he would need to use his forehand, used only with a social equal. By being "cheeky" the slave was defying his master and emphasizing his own humanity (Wink 1998). In a second example, a poor man was taken to court because he could not repay a debt to a rich man. So he was forced to surrender his cloak – a form of economic oppression. Jesus advised the debtor to give the rest of his clothing as well, departing the court naked, which in that culture was the shaming of the rich man. In a third example, a peasant is forced by a Roman centurion to carry his pack for a mile – an instance of political oppression. By carrying it a second mile the peasant complicated the life of the centurion, who was restricted by military regulations from forcing a peasant to carry his pack further than a mile. While these examples have been interpreted to mean that Jesus was urging passive submission, the teaching bears another interpretation: Jesus was prescribing a nonviolent strategy in which the oppressed could challenge oppression and assert their dignity. By responding in an unexpected way that asserts human dignity those who are seemingly powerless can alter the behavior of the oppressor[2] (Matt. 5:39–42).

Jesus was prepared to die for his message of justice for the poor and end oppressive use of power. As noted, he was crucified for his activism and suffered his fate without raising a hand to defend himself. Furthermore, he forgave his executioners: "Father, forgive them; for they know not what they do" (Luke 23:34). Other teachings of Jesus include: "If you have a grievance against anyone, forgive him, so that your Father in heaven may forgive you the wrongs you have done" (Mark 11:25); "Pass no judgment and you will not be judged" (Matt. 7:1). The only formal prayer he taught his disciples, the "Our Father," includes the call to forgive as God has forgiven us. All of these are the marks of the Kingdom that Jesus proclaims: doing justice nonviolently, loving enemies, and forgiving (Mark 1:15).

Jesus' most dramatic act of nonviolence was crucifixion. The night before, he explained its meaning at a supper celebrating Passover, which marked the Israelites' liberation from slavery in Egypt.

> Jesus took bread, and having said the blessing he broke it and gave it to his disciples with the words: "Take this and eat; this is my body." Then he took a cup, and having offered thanks to God he gave it to them with the words: "Drink from it, all of you. For this is my blood of the covenant, shed for many for the forgiveness of sins." (Matt. 26:27–29)

In Christian traditions this meal is known as the Last Supper or Lord's Supper, and in some churches is called the Sacrament of the Eucharist, the Greek word for thanksgiving. Participation in the meal marks the unity – based on just relationships – of the community, which now makes the community part of the mystical body of Christ.

Figure 2.1 Crucifixion in the Church of the Gesu, Milwaukee, Wisconsin, USA. Source: Michael K. Duffey

St Paul's letters to the early Christian communities – the earliest Christian writings – echo Jesus' message:

> Never repay evil with evil. Do not seek revenge, but leave a place for divine retribution. … If your enemy is hungry, feed him; if he is thirsty, give him a drink; by doing this you will heap live coals on his head. Do not let evil conquer you, but use good to defeat evil. (Romans 12:19–21)

Paul also uses a description of a soldier arrayed for battle:

> When things are at their worst stand firm. … Fasten on the belt of truth, for the coat of mail put on integrity, let the shoes on your feet be the gospel of peace, take up the great shield of faith…take salvation for your helmet, for sword take up that which the spirit gives you. (Ephesians 6:14–17; cf. Romans:13:12)

What can be concluded from these passages is that the community must do these things to be true followers of Jesus. A contemporary New Testament scholar concludes his examination of these texts: "the community of Jesus' disciples is to be meek, merciful, pure, devoted to peacemaking, and willing to suffer persecution – and blessed precisely in its faithfulness to this paradoxical vision" (Hays 1996, 322).

Jesus the nonviolent compassion of God

There is a critical issue on which violence and nonviolence turns for Christians, an issue that goes to the heart of Christian belief about the character of God. It ultimately may determine whether we can forgive and be reconciled with one another. The Nicene Creed professes that Jesus "for our sake was crucified, died and was buried and on the third day rose again." How, in fact, did Jesus' death on the cross save us?

Throughout the centuries Christian theologians have argued various theories of how Jesus' death functioned to satisfy the affront to God's majesty by sinful humanity. In some of these explanations Jesus' death was the requirement of divine justice, which had been offended by human sinfulness. A popular but mistaken understanding of what it means is "to be saved" actually encourages Christians to respond violently against "evildoers."[3] When Jesus is the sacrifice, which commutes the human death sentence, we are left with the image of God as a harsh and unforgiving judge. Christianity goes astray when God is understood primarily as a judge who exacts a brutal judgment. So God's wrath is to be feared. Christians may also come to believe that they are instruments of God's judgment. They may harbor a new crusade mentality, whether it be against communists, Muslims, or anyone else who seems to threaten the faith. A fundamentalist preacher writes that Christians "cannot ignore the battle [against Communists] ... nowhere in Scripture, nowhere, does the Lord God tell us to love His enemies or to make covenant with them in any way" (Walton 1987).

Such a view dismisses the Jesus of the New Testament, where Jesus' forgiveness and mercy made him "the one in whom the fullness of God was pleased to dwell" (Col 1:19). But Jesus' life and teaching revealed nonviolent compassion in word and deed. In this he revealed the heart of God. In terms of history, Jesus was put to death because he challenged Jewish religious authorities and the political status quo by taking the side of the poor and oppressed. His was a politically and religiously motivated death. He went to his death without resorting to violence or resisting the violence done to him. Contemporary theologians reject "divinely sanctioned violence" as a perversion of the Gospel. An adequate soteriology affirms that God is not violent but with Jesus suffers human violence and yet shows forgiveness and mercy. Richard Rohr writes:

> Jesus came to change the mind of humanity about God. This grounds Christianity in
> love and freedom from the very beginning. ... A nonviolent atonement theory says

that God is not someone we need to fear or mistrust. Healing and forgiveness have not been at the forefront of Christian history, even though it is almost the only thing that Jesus does. (Rohr 2007, 209–210)

When Christians profess that God is not a god of vengeance but is all loving, all forgiving, and all suffering in solidarity with the oppressed as they struggle for life, then the Christian way of life is very different. From what are we saved? Not from hell but from violence that is a living hell.

Contemporary theologian Anthony Bartlett writes about the peacemaking necessity of Christians:

The world and the church in it are at a moment of unparalleled crisis. It is a crisis brought about by the Gospel itself when God introduces God's truth to the world and does so in the most intimate depth of our humanity. It is a kind of radiation therapy, pinpointing the most secret cancer of our being. The cancer is the deep violence within human history and the pinpointing of God is not to destroy by reciprocal violence, but to bring to light and at once to offer the healing of love. (Bartlett 2007, 406)

It can only be concluded that God loves everyone by giving his son to die for them.

A Brief History of Christian Nonviolence and Violence

The early church

Neither Jesus nor the writers of the New Testament addressed serving in the Roman military. But a century later Christian writers took up the issue. The context was the charge leveled against Christians that they posed a threat to the virtues and welfare of the Empire. Christian writers denied the charge of disloyalty but nevertheless affirmed that Christians could not bear arms in defense of the Empire. We consider four eminent voices, Justin Martyr, Terullian, Origen, and Cyprian:

- St Justin Martyr (103–165 C.E.) spoke of his conversion: "we who delighted in war, in the slaughter of one another, and in every other kind of iniquity have in every part of the world converted our weapons into implements of peace – our swords into plowshares – and we cultivate, piety, justice, brotherly charity, faith and hope, which we derive from the Father through the crucified Savior" (Falls 1949, 318).
- Tertullian (160–220 C.E.) defended the virtues of Christians and asserted that Christians prayed for the Empire's wellbeing. But he insisted that they gave Jesus and his Father their ultimate loyalty and could not bow to Roman deities. Tertullian asked rhetorically: "How will a Christian man go to war? ... the Lord, in subsequently disarming Peter disarmed every soldier" (Cairns 1929, 170–171).

- Origen (c. 185–25), as had Tertullian, denied the charge that Christians cared little about the welfare of the Empire, saying that they prayed for its security and for "those who are fighting for a righteous cause" (Crombie 1922, 156). He allowed that Roman soldiers could use force, but not Christians. Followers of Jesus by their prayers and exemplary lives defeat the interior devils and demons "who stir up wars" (Crombie 1922, 303). In this way Christians could help to preserve civil order. That the entire Christian community should react to war in this way was a revolutionary ideal. Origen embraced pacifism, denying that Christians could participate in war because of their conviction that killing is prohibited. He proclaimed: "No longer do we take the sword against any nations nor do we learn war anymore since we have become sons of peace through Jesus who is our author instead of following the traditional customs by which we were strangers to the covenant." Origen called Christians "sons of peace" who do not "learn war anymore." (Roberts and Donaldson 1923, 303) He wrote:

Christians have been taught not to defend themselves against their enemies; and because they have kept the laws which command gentleness and love to man, on this account they have received from God that which they would not have succeeded in doing if they have been given the right to make war, even though they had been quite able to do so. (Roberts and Donaldson 1923, 303)

- Cyprian of Carthage (c. 200–258 C.E.) was martyred during the era of Roman persecution. He testified that Christians "do not even fight against those who are attacking since it is not granted to the innocent to kill even the aggressor" (Clark 1986, 90).
- The church praised those who resigned their military commissions, such as St Martin of Tours (born c. 316 C.E.) son of a Roman soldier, who refused military service and lived as a hermit until called to become a bishop.

For these Christians, nonviolence was required of those who would imitate Jesus, who accepted death rather than defend themselves and therefore were glorified by God. Like Jesus, his disciples might also be called to forfeit their lives, but by imitating him they would share in his resurrection.

Christians and Empire

Mohandas Gandhi was once asked about his impression of Christianity. He replied that the example of Jesus and the Sermon on the Mount "went right to my heart." "Jesus," he said, "possessed a great force, the love force, but Christianity became disfigured when it went to the West. It became the religion of kings" (Gandhi 1947). He did not mean that Christians sometimes succumbed to the temptation of violence, but that Christianity justified violent defense of its beliefs. History gave Gandhi reason to conclude that Western Christian leaders often supported Empire. As we have seen, in the first three centuries the church preached and practiced pacifism. But beginning in the fourth century the church's relationship to the Empire changed fundamentally.

The Emperor Constantine

In the early fourth century, the Christian church's status in the Roman Empire changed fundamentally. In 312 C.E. the Roman emperor Constantine issued the Edict of Toleration, removing the ban on the practice of Christianity. Within a century Christianity had a privileged status as the official religion of Rome, enjoying the patronage of the state. This is often referred to as the "establishment" of Christianity. The Emperor had reason to keep the Christian communities united. When religious disagreement threatened to divide the church during Constantine's reign, the emperor convened a church council to settle the dispute in order to maintain the unity of the church. The Council of Nicea (325 C.E.) hammered out the orthodox Christian belief about the full divinity and humanity of Jesus. The confession of Christian beliefs is succinctly stated in the Nicene Creed, approved at a church council in the city of Constantinople in 381 C.E.

Distinguishing between orthodox beliefs and heretical formulations was intended to preserve Christian unity. But it also contained the seeds of the suppression of heresies. Exile, torture, execution of heretics – especially during the Spanish Inquisitions – are sad facts of Christian history. It was a reflection of the power of the churches to define orthodoxy and to enlist the secular authorities to enforce it Punishing heretics – often very cruelly – was a form of institutional violence that is part of Christian- history.

St Augustine's Just War

The *Pax Romana* ensured the security of the Empire and of the church. St Augustine (354–430) taught that the use of limited warfare was a legitimate means of defending the Empire. Augustine taught that Christians were obligated to defend the Empire by military means if necessary. He adopted criteria developed by older Roman moralists for justifiable war making: war must be waged for defensive purposes, by legitimate authority, with honorable intentions, and with minimal harm.[4]

Augustine argued that Christian soldiers served God by protecting the peace of Rome from barbarians and the purity of the church from heresy (some of those barbarians were the very sources of heresies) by force if necessary. The soldiers' vocation was the protection of innocents, and as such an act of love. But soldiers needed to conduct themselves virtuously, never succumbing to the temptation of plundering and pillaging. "Be peaceful ... in warring," he wrote to Boniface, the Christian governor of North Africa, "so that you may vanquish those whom you war against, and bring them to the prosperity of peace" (Brown 1969, 366). Augustine reasoned that defeating invading armies was an act of love for enemies, for the purpose of war was to bring them to Christianity. He went so far as to require that soldiers act as virtuously as monks. Such was Augustine's naiveté about the nature of war. He did recognize a minority of Christians, monks who maintained a nonviolent witness in imitation of Jesus, living the unarmed life. Their witness also extended beyond the monastery walls to lay people, as we shall see below.

The purpose of war for Augustine was to preserve "good order." It was the long-lasting influence of St Augustine's teaching on war and violence that shaped mainstream Christianity for 1500 years. Augustine fathered the mainstream Christian view that violence was a just means for just political purposes. Some historians have argued that Augustine represented a "pronounced change from the beliefs of the early Christian Church" and a "milestone in the process of relativizing and accommodating Christ's teaching ... to the views of right and wrong that were generally accepted in the world into which Jesus came" (Deane 1963, 156). Indeed, Augustine's perspective was not based on the New Testament. A damaging result of Constantine and Augustine was a distinction that grew up between the behavior required of monks and the behavior of "worldly" Christians.[5] The view that Deane holds reflects the view of many others. However, as the note below indicates, others do not agree that Constantine and establishment amounted to a dangerous compromise for Christianity. I leave it to readers to ponder this disagreement.

In later centuries a full blown just war theory emerged in Christianity – justifiable war included requirements that there be a declaration of war, a calculus that more good than evil would result, that war be a last resort, that direct harm to civilian be avoided, and that the enemy be defeated with the least amount of damage.[6]

The Western world of the "Dark Ages" was indeed violent: Muslim political forces' penetration into the erstwhile Western territories, Christian incorporation of violent tribes, and Viking raids are a few of the features that made it so. The feudal period was also marked by frequent war-making between feudal lords. Churchmen condemned their incessant warring. In the eleventh century a church council condemned war, and imposed regulations to limit it. The "Peace of God" prohibited attacks on clergy, religious pilgrims, townspeople, peasants, and property. The "Truce of God," banned warfare on Sundays, Fridays, Lent and Easter, Advent and Christmas. The Church also imposed severe penances on soldiers for killing and injuring, asserting that "shedding the blood of human being was shedding the blood of Christ" (Musto 1986, 65).

Christian crusaders

In 1094 Pope Urban II rallied Christian princes to organize armies to drive Muslims from the Holy Land:

O what a disgrace if such a despised and base race, which worships demons, should conquer a people which has the faith of omnipotent God and is made glorious with the name of Christ! (Thatcher and McNeal 1905)

Ironically, Urban imposed the "Truce of God" on the princes in order to unite them for the Crusades. Eventually as many as 10 brutal Crusades over 300 years attempted to capture Jerusalem (and other lands considered holy by Christians), wipe out Muslims, and regain territory from the Turks in the eastern part of the Roman Empire. In addition, en route to Jerusalem crusaders also attacked Jewish communities and even some fellow Christians.

There were notable exceptions to this violent march. St Francis of Assisi (1182–1226) preached and exemplified the nonviolent message of the Gospel. He became one of the most revered Christian saints for his peacemaking and reconciliation efforts among his fellow Christians and with Muslims. Francis's life may be summarized in this portion of the peace prayer attributed to him: "Lord, make me an instrument of your peace, where there is hatred let me sow love." Intent on the conversion of Muslims, Francis travelled to Egypt and went unarmed into the camp of the sultan. While Francis did not succeed in converting him, he won the sultan's admiration. Francis founded a religious order, the Franciscans, as well as a lay order, the "Third Order Franciscans," whose rule forbade "taking up lethal weapons, or bearing them about, against anybody."

Despite all the violence in this period, the majority of Christians were not active participants and were more often its victims (Musto 1986). The impact of St Francis extended well beyond the orders he founded. A large movement known as the "Great Alleluia" began in Northern Italy around the time of his death. It involved massive numbers of people from peasants to merchants and nobles renouncing violence, making peace with neighbors, and reconciling with neighbors. As alternatives to the Crusades, this movement, called the Great Alleluia brought tens of thousands of people into the streets of major cities to embrace peace. The Great Alleluia continued throughout the fourteenth century (Musto 1986, 85–86).

Christian invaders

In the fifteenth century, Europeans invaded and conquered indigenous people in the Americas. To the Mayas of Guatemala Pedro Alvarado proclaimed:

Let it be known ... our coming is beneficial. We bring tidings of the true God and Christian religion so that you may become Christians peacefully. ... But should you refuse the peace we offer, then the death and destruction that will follow will be entirely of your own account. (Lovell 2005)

His troops killed them and destroyed their city. Only a handful of missionaries that followed respected and sought to protect the Indians. One of them, Bartolome de las Casas (1484–1566) influenced the Spanish monarchy to outlaw some of most abusive colonial practices and to declare indigenous peoples Spanish subjects protected by the monarch. In 1543 Pope Paul III affirmed that Indians possessed souls and prohibited their enslavement, forced conversion, and theft of their land.

Christians often converted non-Christians by force. For centuries the religious practices of conquered peoples were deemed superstitions or devil worship. Christian conquests in the Americas and in Africa were fueled by racism: people of color were considered inferior, needing to be saved and civilized by European Christians.

The Protestant reformers

Developments from the sixteenth to the nineteenth centuries helped to shape the modern world. In the sixteenth century the Protestant Reformation continued the Catholic tradition justifying violence to protect social order and the church. The Protestant Reformation began when Martin Luther (1483–1546), an Augustinian monk, nailed his "Ninety-Five Theses" to the church door in Wittenberg as a protest against the abuse of power of the Roman Catholic Church. His protest would mark the end of the uncontested spiritual and political authority of the Roman Church.

The fresh air of religious and political freedom that he brought to the German principalities had unforeseen consequences: peasants demanded greater religious autonomy from the princes and an end to economic exploitation. Luther supported their causes, counseling them to press their demands by calling on God and enduring patiently (Luther 1974a). But peasants were to obey those in authority. When instead they revolted, Luther called on authorities to "swiftly take to the sword" (Luther 1974b). God would punish corrupt civil authorities even though they were also God's instrument for enforcing worldly order.[7] Wars between Protestants and Catholics were fueled by contention over who would have political and religious authority, as much as by doctrinal differences. But some Christians rejected war altogether. Desiderius Erasmus (1466–1536) was a Catholic contemporary of Luther who tried to reconcile Protestant and Catholic leaders – earning the gratitude of neither. He urged princes, kings, and popes to stop warring and dismissed arguments for justifiable war, condemning Christians for killing one another "with all the weapons of hell" (Dolan 1964). St Ignatius of Loyola (1491–1556), a soldier in his early life, eschewed violence against Protestants and promoted a spirituality that focused on the passion, death, and resurrection of Christ.

The Radical Reformation

Some sixteenth-century Protestant reformers established "Peace Churches" rejecting the justification of violence that emerged after Constantine. Another branch of the Protestant reformation called the Radical Reformation emerged shortly after Luther. Cells of German and Swiss Anabaptists arose, renounced the use of the sword, and expressed their intention to live according to the scriptures as the early church had. While acknowledging that political authorities might use the sword to keep order and punish evildoers, they claimed that those who followed Christ were forbidden from taking up the sword. Worldly authorities were "armed with steel and iron," while Christians were "armed with the armor of God, with truth, righteousness, peace, salvation and the Word of God."[8] Anabaptists refused the use of violence to defend the public order and hence would not participate in the coercive work of the political order. This led to the charge by other Protestants and Catholics that the Anabaptists ignored their Christian responsibilities to maintain civic order. For this they were persecuted. Michael Sattler (1490–1527) was the leader of the Swiss and southern German Anabaptist movement. Shortly after publishing the "Schleitheim Confession" (1527), Sattler was arrested by Roman Catholic authorities, put on trial along with a number of other Anabaptists, found guilty, and executed.

The Mennonite Church, descending from the Anabaptists (named for Menno Simons, 1496–1561) maintained that true Christians follow the Prince of Peace, renounce war, and "do not know vengeance" (Holmes 2005). With the Church of the Brethren, the Quakers, and several other smaller churches, they comprise what are called "peace churches." Until recently the peace churches were labeled "sectarians" with unrealistic and irresponsible political views. Despite their persecution, the peace churches maintained their nonviolent witness. By the twentieth century their successes in resolving conflicts nonviolently at the communal and social levels around the world won them the respect of other Christian churches.

Nationalism and Christianity

The rise of the European nation-state system in the seventeenth century encouraged the violence of the state to expand its control over other states, usually with the support of churches, both Catholic and Protestant, except for the peace church Protestants. Nation-states raised levies to create large war chests and conscripted large numbers of citizen-soldiers rather than make war with small mercenary armies. By the end of the nineteenth century, nations had at their disposal weapons producing destructiveness on a scale never before seen. The tide of violence rose quickly. Nationalism pervaded European and American Christianity: Anglicans supported their country's militarism, as did French Catholics, German Lutherans, Italian Catholics, and American Christians, and most supported violent defense of their country's colonies.

The twentieth century: War of slaughter

The twentieth century was cursed with ferocious wars. World War I was fought to defeat German aggression, but was fueled by wider national self-interest among the Allies. In 1914 Pope Benedict XV condemned "the strongest and wealthiest nations" armed with "the latest weapons devised by military science" (Pope Benedict XV 1914). He lamented that:

> while the mighty hosts are contending in the fury of combat, cities, families, and individuals are being oppressed by those evils and miseries which follow at the heels of war; day by day the numbers increase of widows and orphans.

Whatever war produced was only the "peace of the dead." Pope Pius XI condemned "the state of armed peace which is scarcely better than war itself" (Pope Pius XI 1932). The peace churches were committed to providing humanitarian aid to war victims, healing the wounds of war, and working for its abolition.[9] After the war, Quakers established the International Fellowship of Reconciliation.

A secular pacifism arose after World War I, though all but disappearing with the rearmament of Germany in the 1930s. In the United States, Dorothy Day and Peter

Figure 2.2 Dorothy Day. Source: Milwaukee Journal photo, courtesy of the Department of Special Collections and University Archives, Marquette University Libraries

Maurin founded the Catholic Worker Movement in 1933, which championed the rights of workers, served the poor, and represented a very small minority of Catholic pacifists in the United States. Day wrote:

> The increasing horror and immorality of modern war which because of the means used necessitates the slaying of the innocent should serve to recall the latent pacifist tradition so that the Sermon on the Mount will be seen to confirm and sanction nonviolent procedure[s]. (Day 1952)

At the outbreak of World War II and throughout the war Pope Pius XII made numerous appeals for disarmament and international legal mechanisms to end the war. World War II defeated totalitarian and fascism, but at the cost of 60 million lives, the majority civilians. The anti-Semitism that lay dormant led to the Holocaust in "Christian Europe." After the defeat of Germany an international Catholic peace organization called *Pax Christi* was founded to foster reconciliation between France and Germany. It now has over 60 national chapters.

Christian Conscience

Very few Catholics refused to serve in World War II. One who did was Franz Jaegerstaetter a 22-year-old Austrian peasant who declared that Hitler's war was unjust. He refused induction into the German Army and was later executed. His last communication from prison was a reminder of the beatitude "blessed are the persecuted." Later the Catholic Church pronounced Jaegerstaetter an exemplary Christian for refusing to conform to the immense pressure put on him to obey unjust political authority. His conscientious objection contributed to the Catholic Second Vatican Council (1963–1965) teaching on conscience.[10] The Bishops called for

> laws making humane provisions for the case of those who for reasons of conscience refuse to bear arms, provided, however, that they accept some other form of service to the human community. (Vatican Council II 1965, 79)

They also expressed "praise for those who renounce the use of violence in the vindication of their rights and who resort to methods of defense which are otherwise available to weaker parties" (Vatican Council II 1965, para 78):

The Council also declared that targeting cities with nuclear weapons "merited unequivocal condemnation as a crime against God and humanity," and condemned modern weapons that can lead to "an almost total and altogether reciprocal slaughter of each side by the other." They urged "an evaluation of war with an entirely new attitude" (Vatican Council II 1965, 80).

Gandhi, King, and Chavez

Amidst the violence of the twentieth century arose an alternative, nonviolent resistance. Mohandas Gandhi was its great initiator in South Africa and India. Gandhi was influenced by eastern religions, especially Hinduism, Jainism, and Buddhism, and also by his familiarity with Jesus and the Sermon on the Mount. Gandhi pioneered skills such as boycotts, civil disobedience, strikes, and fasts to overcome injustice through nonviolent means.

Martin Luther King, Jr wrote that Gandhi lifted "the love ethic of Jesus above mere interaction between individuals to a powerful and effective social force on a large scale." For Gandhi and King, love was a potent instrument for social and collective transformation (King, Jr 1958).When accused of disturbing the peace, King responded that there was only a negative peace whereas Jesus came to "bring a positive peace which is the presence of justice, love, yea, even the Kingdom of God" (King, Jr 1958).

In the 1950s and 1960s King used Gandhian methods of nonviolent resistance as potent means for achieving desegregation. King was co-founder of the Southern Christian Leadership Conference, a large group of black ministers whose nonviolent activism was crucial for gains in racial equality in the United States.[11] As a result of their nonviolent campaigns against segregation, two landmark federal pieces of legislation were passed, the Civil Right Act of 1964 and the Voting Rights Act of 1965.

Another nonviolent advocate arose in those years, Cesar Chavez, who led the struggle of US migrant farmworkers for dignified working conditions and just wages. Chavez criticized the lack of church support but never wavered in his nonviolent struggle. He wrote:

> I think that once people understand the strength of nonviolence – the force that it generates, the love it creates, the response it brings from the whole community – they will not be willing to abandon it easily. (Chavez 1969)

Issues of war and peace have continued to dominate the United States, especially the American war in Vietnam.[12] In 1967 King condemned the war in Vietnam (1963–1975) as racist, a war against Asians fought by poor people of color conscripted in disproportionate numbers. He condemned the racism, militarism, and poverty of the United States as the source of the moral decay of the nation. Though antiwar sentiments and nonviolent protests had grown throughout the war, it was not until 1972 that the US Catholic bishops declared that the war in Vietnam was morally unjustifiable because of widespread attacks on civilians and disproportionate destructiveness. They also advocated the legal recognition of selective conscientious objectors who refused to serve in particular wars that they believed violated just war criteria. This led to important moves for nonviolence in the coming decade.

Peace through Nonviolence

In the 1980s Catholic bishop conferences around the world strongly supported nonviolent national defense. In *The Challenge of Peace* the US Catholic bishops promoted nonviolent "defense instituted by government [using] peaceable non-compliance and non-cooperation ... [for] blunting the aggression of an adversary and winning the other over."[13] The bishops of Holland, Germany, and Japan also echoed the American bishops, endorsing nonviolence defense as in keeping with the Gospel. The German bishops advocated "discovering nonviolent solutions to overcome conflicts." The Japanese bishops said that it is self-evident that endeavors for peace should be nonviolent (*The Challenge of Peace* 1983). The same emphasis can be seen in the advocacy of other Christian denominations, such as that of the United Methodists Bishops, *In Defense of Creation: The Nuclear Crisis and Justice and Peace*. Their emphasis moved from praising individuals for adopting a nonviolent stance to urging oppressed groups to work for nonviolent social change. They also urged nations to "defend against unjust aggression without using violence."[14]

The most significant antiwar development in the Roman Catholic Church has been its virtual rejection of the just war tradition. Following the 1991 US invasion of Iraq, an editorial in *La Civilita Cattolica*, a Roman Catholic journal wrote that "we can only conclude that modern war is always immoral."[15] The 1500-year-old just war tradition no longer lay at the center of Catholic teaching on war. However, the reality is that "just war" is still the measure of the morality of war; that is, unless the crusade mentality still motivates the resort to war. Yet in the wake of 9/11, Pope John Paul II linked justice with forgiveness, writing "there is no peace without justice; no justice without forgiveness."[16] The last word in the Pope's call is forgiveness as the essence of justice.

Liberation theologians of various churches urged Christians to make a "preferential option for the poor" through nonviolent methods of overcoming injustices and affirming human dignity. Churches have urged their members to actualize social principles by working for the common good, distributive and social justice, solidarity, defending the right of people to determine their own future by organizing, and protecting the environment. "The new name for peace is development," wrote Pope Paul VI in 1967. He also asserted that "if you want peace, work for justice" (Pope Paul VI 1967, 21, 20).

Many have worked nonviolently for justice across the Americas. Clergy and lay Christians in the Third World have advocated on behalf of the powerless. Bishops in El Salvador, Guatemala, Chile, and Chiapas, among other places have stood with the poor.[17] Lay movements have included hundreds of organizations protesting – at the risk of death – government repression, torture, and the "disappearance" of hundreds of thousands of loved ones by the military. Bishop Cornelius Korir of Kenya mediated a truce between political factions when civil war was imminent. The Bishop invoked the Eucharist as "a symbol that we are united in Christ's body, no matter our tribe, nation, or color."[18]

Activists around the world learned lessons from Gandhi and King on how to use nonviolent methods to defeat repression states.

- Mairead Corrigan, a Catholic and Betty Williams, a Protestant organized large demonstrations and marches in Northern Ireland to protest the sectarian violence. Their movement, called the Peace People, won them the Nobel Peace Prize in 1976.
- In the 1980s the Catholic Church of Poland encouraged nonviolence as the "Solidarity" worker movement struggled with the Communist government for freedom. Throughout the Gadansk shipyard strike led by Lech Walesa the Church urged both the striking workers and the communist government not to use violence.
- In East Germany the Lutheran Church did the same. The Bishop broadcast over loud speakers to opponents of the regime to remain calm and not resort to violence.
- The Catholic bishops of the Philippines orchestrated the nonviolent ousting of the Marcos dictatorship in the 1980s. The main player in the popular movement was the Cardinal of Manila, Cardinal Sin, who rallied thousands of people to block the streets of Manila so that Marcos's troops could not proceed. None of the people in this mass activity behaved violently.
- In Chile and Guatemala the Catholic Church established truth commissions to uncover the truth of the violence perpetrated by governments and to work for national reconciliation.
- The World Council of Churches led the way in condemning apartheid in South Africa and by 1986 a coalition of South African organizations that included every Christian denomination was putting effective pressure on the government to end apartheid. Bishop Desmond Tutu counseled nonviolent activism to defeat apartheid and later chaired the country's Truth and Reconciliation Commission promoting truth telling and forgiveness.
- In 1997 the Serbian Orthodox Patriarch joined a demonstration of 100 000 in Belgrade demanding that Slobodan Milosevic step down. This was an extraordinary event, given the Orthodox Church's long identification with Serbian nationalism. In 1999, in the wake of revelations of atrocities committed by Serbian forces in Kosovo, the Serbian bishops expressed the Church's commitment to nonviolent means of ousting Milosevic:

> The Orthodox Church must always use evangelical means. We cannot say to the people rise up and throw off your Government. We cannot use evil means to overcome evil. We can say obey the statutes of the law. That's it. (Harden and Gill 1999)

Clearly, Gandhi's movement has made a strong impression on the churches, as have the nuclear threat, the recognition of "structural injustices" in the Third World, ethnic animosities, and militarism.

Peace churches

Many Christian denominations have declared their intent to become "peace churches" and have developed organizations to pursue peace.

Among them are the Baptist Peace Fellowship, Catholic Peace Fellowship, Episcopal Peace Fellowship, Fellowship of Reconciliation (Quakers), Lutheran Peace Fellowship, Methodist Peace Fellowship, Mennonite Central Committee, Orthodox Peace Fellowship, and the Presbyterian Peace Fellowship. So has the World Council of Churches, an affiliation of 350 churches. Their missions include resisting militarism, nuclear weapons, torture, the death penalty, and gun control, as well as reform of trade policies that do systemic violence to poor countries. Their methods range from education of their congregations, to advocacy and family peace camps. An affirmation by the Episcopal Peace Fellowship (formerly the Anglican Peace Fellowship) puts it succinctly: "War ... is incompatible with the teachings and principles of our Savior Jesus Christ."[19] These peace fellowships represent small percentages of congregations but nonetheless are organizations that would not have existed 50 years ago.

Notable international peacemaking groups include *Pace e Bene* (named for St Francis's traditional greeting: "peace and good") based in Italy, which has trained 25 000 people to apply peacemaking skills in conflict situations. *Sant' Edidgio* works in more than 70 countries and has trained over 50 000 peacemakers and mediators who have worked in Africa and the Balkans. Christian Peacemaking Teams were initiated by Mennonites, Quakers, and the Church of the Brethren and are now ecumenical. They work in conflict zones with local peacemakers through nonviolent direct action. Christian relief and development agencies teach conflict resolution skills to foster peace in the war zones where they work.

Institutions of higher education are making peace studies programs part of their mission. Inter-religious dialogues especially with Muslims have begun.

Addressing Christianity's institutional violence

I have described the peacemaking of Christians in the last decades of the twentieth century, but cannot ignore the violence and injustices in its institutional structures. The church has often strayed far from the teaching and witness of Jesus. If it is to build a community in his name, it must make amends for three instances of its institutional violence: a history of violent conversion, racial and ethnic violence, and violence against women. Christians are peacemaking disciples of Jesus when they overcome these instances of structural violence.

Institutionally, Christianity must confess its history of disrespect for other faiths and forcible conversion. Recall Gandhi's criticism of Christianity as having long ago become a religion of kings. Making a preferential option for the poor is now recognized as the essential Christian work in the world.

Jesus praised non-Jews, be they Samaritans or gentiles, on various occasions. In the parable of the Good Samaritan, it was the latter who came to the aid of a Jew when other Jews passed by. At the foot of the Cross it was a Roman centurion who professed Jesus' divinity. The Gospel was preached to the gentile as well as the Jew. But when Christians encountered the indigenous peoples of the Americas, Africa, and elsewhere they regarded them as inferior. Gustavo Gutierrez, a Latin American theologian, notes that while St Paul approached the Greco-Roman world "attentive to the religious values to be found outside Christianity," Spanish missionaries regarded the peoples of the Americas as belonging to a "socially and culturally inferior world" (Gutierrez 1993). Color was often at the root of the disrespect.

The fruit of 500 years of European conquest of the Americas has been massive injustices and violence, now called "structural violence" in the forms of massive poverty, malnutrition, ill health, and lack of education. Churches in Latin America have addressed the wholesale violations of human rights by dictators. In 1968 the Catholic bishops of Latin America declared that the church was obligated to work for justice for and with the poor. In 1970 the World Synod of Catholic Bishops declared that proclaiming the Gospel required working for justice (Synod of Bishops 1970). The 500th anniversary of the Conquest was an occasion for the Catholic Church to acknowledge the truth of the past. The Guatemalan bishops invited the Mayas to tell their own story. The latter spoke of "the violation, abduction, prostitution, and robbing of our mother earth" that violated "the life of God and of his children."[20] In their response, the bishops pledged to enter into cultural dialogue that recognizes "the sense of God and power of the Spirit" already present in the culture and "beating in heart of the Mayas." The church, they continued must be "promoter of their cultural values, and defender of their rights." This must be the determination of all Christians.

Jesus had much contact with women: some sought his healing and others were his disciples. Women were the last to remain at his crucifixion and the first to be told by the angel of his resurrection. Among them was Mary of Magdala who carried the news to his apostles and would later to be known as the "apostle to the apostles." Jesus revealed the good news of salvation to a Samaritan town through a Samaritan woman he encountered at a well. On one occasion Jesus defended a woman accused of adultery, telling the men about to stone her "let the one who is without sin cast the first stone." From the beginning women played an important role in the evangelical work of the church. St Paul mentions several women in authority in the earliest Christian communities. In his letter to the Church of Rome he mentions seven women who lead Christian communities, including Phoebe, "a fellow Christian who holds office in the congregation at Canchreae."[21]

Rather than being a radical challenge to societal attitudes toward women, Christianity has reflected strong gender bias. Women have been barred from leadership positions. While Mary the mother of Jesus is exalted, other women are praised for their subservience. If they are to practice nonviolence, Christians must overcome its view of male superiority and repent of the sexism that pervades its institutions. Christian peacemaking cannot do without women peacemakers.

Conclusion

The teachings found in the New Testament and in many of the writings of the early church fathers are emphatically opposed to the use of violence. While Jesus never addressed the vocation of soldiers, the church fathers explained to Romans why Christians could not defend the Empire by the use of force.

Christian history proved to be a temptation to secure and defend earthly power by war. The Christian church became a political and spiritual power after Constantine. From the teachings of Augustine, Christianity until very recently justified war by appealing to the just war doctrine. The wars of the twentieth century were only opposed by the peace churches. Even the use of the atomic bomb against Japan drew little protest from Christians.[22] It was in response to the Vietnam War and the nuclear threat that Christians began to question war and to recommend nonviolent means of conflict resolution, inspired by the work of Gandhi, King, St Francis, Mennonites, and Quakers. Hopefully, it will not be only monks, minorities, and Mennonites (and other peace churches) who urge, teach, and practice nonviolent peacemaking.

Thomas Merton (1914–1968) was a monk whose writings on spirituality, war, the nuclear threat, race, violence continue to be widely read and have been translated into many languages. His most trenchant criticisms of war were of the war in Vietnam and the possibility of nuclear war. Merton spoke eloquently about the power of nonviolence, declaring that the beatitudes of the Sermon on the Mount,

> convey a profound existential understanding of the dynamic of the Kingdom of God – a dynamic made clear in the parables of the mustard seed and of the yeast. This is a dynamism of patient and secret growth, a belief that out of the smallest, weakest, and most insignificant seed the greatest tree will come. (Merton 1968)

The peace that Jesus preached and exemplified is the fruit of living nonviolently and compassionately. Living a life of healing and forgiveness, Jesus struggled to bring the Kingdom of justice and love nonviolently. His disciples are called to repent for their violent history as they profess their belief that the reign of God is manifested in their nonviolent peacemaking. The Christian communities:

> will become the sphere where the future of God's righteousness intersects – and challenges – the present tense of human existence. The meaning of the New Testament's teachings on violence will become evident only in communities of Jesus' followers who embody the costly way of peace. (Hays 1996)

This chapter is in memory of Dr Martin Luther King, Jr for his nonviolent struggle for racial justice and his effort to end the American war in Vietnam.

Questions for Discussion

1. What is significant about Jesus being a Jew?
2. What attribute of Jesus' messiahship did his followers at first find very troubling?
3. In the New Testament Jesus is described as having exhorted nonviolence strongly. Why do you think that many Christians do not interpret his teachings that way?
4. Why was Gandhi critical of Christianity?
5. Why have the Mennonites historically been maligned?
6. What impact has Franz Jaegerstaetter, the Austrian farmer had on contemporary Catholicism?
7. Why has the just war tradition today all but been discredited?
8. How much progress do you think Christians have made in overcoming the institutional kinds of violence described in this chapter?

Notes

1   The suffering servant remains an enigmatic figure within Judaism. The most common interpretation is that the servant is the Jewish community itself.
2   It would hardly have made sense that Jesus, announcing a new way of life, would have counseled suffering humiliation, which is the naturally fearful response of the oppressed to oppressors.
3   I am indebted to Terrence Rynne for his formulation of this idea. See the references for the details of his monograph, which explains this Christian soteriology.
4   Augustine taught that Christians should never use violence in their personal defense, but only in the defense of innocents.
5   Some historians do not see the establishment of Christianity under Constantine as a corruption of the Christian way of life but as an organic evolution of the church into an institution with greater civic responsibility. It is my view that while such was a theoretical possibility, in fact the church too often abused its power and compromised its principles.
6   It must be noted that in the Middle Ages wars to expand religion were not justified. James Johnson writes that "as to just cause, defense of religion was allowed, as was restoration of the right of religious practice ... but force could not be used to propagate religion." There was no "holy war" doctrine. James Turner Johnson "Just War and Jihad of the Sword," in *The Blackwell Companion to Religion and Violence*, Andrew R. Murphy, ed. (Oxford, 2011), 274.
7   See Luther's treatise "Whether Soldiers Too Can be Saved" (1526). All of Luther's political essays bear the theme of protecting the social order.

8   Schleitheim Confession, Article 6. The author was later hanged.

9   In most Western nations peace churches won the right of conscientious objection for their members.

10 Jaegerstaetter was actually a "selective" conscientious objector, because he only declared that Hitler's war, rather than all wars, was unjust.

11 No other organized group of church leaders in the United States have ever used nonviolence so effectively.

12 Thich Nhat Hahn, a Vietnamese Buddhist monk, toured the United States during the war appealing for peace. He made a telling comment about the United States that would seem to apply equally to many Christians: "If only the United States had had a vision of non-duality concerning Vietnam, we would not have had so much destruction in both countries. The war continues to hurt both Americans and Vietnamese." *Peace is Every Step: Paths of Mindfulness in Everyday Life* (New York: Bantam Books, 1991), 101–102. Christians have much to learn in terms of discovering deeper realities through disciplines of discernment.

13 *The Challenge of Peace* (1983), para 223, 225. Similar statements were issued by the Catholic bishops of France, Belgium, Japan, and others.

14 *The Challenge of Peace*, para 77. Now aggression refers to aggression against nations.

15 July, 1991. The editorial positions of this journal are reviewed by the Vatican.

16 John Paul II's Message for World Day of Peace, January 1, 2002. It may seem odd to call for justice and at the same time for forgiveness but readers should consider the logic of justice, peace, and forgiveness.

17 Some have paid with their lives. Bishops Oscar Romero (El Salvador) and Juan Gerardi (Guatemala) were among them.

18 Bishop Korir describes his step-by-step method of creating a peace resolution in *Amani Mashinani*. http://www.crsprogramquality.org/storage/pubs/peacebuilding/AMANI%20peace-grassroots.pdf, accessed December 3, 2014.

19 Episcopal Peace Fellowship, http://epfnational.org. In 1982 England waged a short war against Argentina over the Falkland Islands. In the wake of their success the government of Margaret Thatcher requested that the Anglican dean of St Paul's Cathedral in London preside over a religious service of thanksgiving. With the support of Rowan William, the Archbishop of Canterbury and head of the Church of England, the dean refused. The government was most unhappy, even appealing to the Queen to change their minds. The dean explained his reason for refusing to hold such a religious service, saying that war and destruction were not a cause for rejoicing but for penitence and mourning. His only regret, he said, was not having the Lord's Prayer recited in Spanish, as he had planned to do. An overwhelming majority of public respondents agreed with him.

20 "500 anos sembrando el Evangelio" reprinted in *Christus* (August 15, 1993), 10.1–2. Never before had the church heard directly from the ingenious.

21 See Romans 16:1–15.

22 A notable exception was the Catholic chaplain to the pilots who dropped the atomic bomb over Hiroshima and Nagasaki. Fr. George Zabelka wrote "I was … heir to a tradition that had for seventeen hundred years engaged in revenge, murder, torture, the pursuit of power and prerogative violence, all in the name of our Lord." He continued that "the just war theory is something that Christ never taught or even hinted at." "I Was Told It Was Necessary" [interview]. *Sojourners* 9/8: 1980, 14.

References

Bartlett, Anthony. 2007. "Atonement: Birth of a New Humanity." In *Stricken by God: Nonviolent Identification and the Victory of Christ*. Edited by Brad Jersak and Michael Hardin, 406. Grand Rapids, MI: Eerdmans.

Brown, Peter. 1969. *Augustine of Hippo*. Berkeley, CA: University of California Press.

Cairns, W.H. 1929. *Ante-Nicene Christian Library: The Writings of Tertullian*. Edinburgh: T and T Clark.

Clark, G.W., trans. 1986. *Ancient Christian Writers: Letter to Cornelius*. New York: Newman Press.

Chavez, Cesar. 1969. "Creative Nonviolence." *The Catholic Worker*, June.

Day, Dorothy. 1952. *The Long Loneliness*. New York: Harper and Row.

Deane, Herbert A. 1963.*The Political and Social Ideas of St. Augustine*, 156. New York: Colombia University Press.

Dolan, John P. 1964. *The Essential Erasmus*. New York: Mentor-Omega.

Falls, Thomas B. trans. 1949.*St. Justin Martyr*. New York: Christian Heritage.

Gandhi, Mohandas K. 1947. "Speech before the Inter-Asian Relations Conference." New Delhi.

Gutierrez, Gustavo. 1993. *Las Casa: In Search of the Poor of Christ*. Maryknoll, NY: Orbis Books.

Harden, Blaine and Carlotta Gill. 1999. "Crisis in the Balkans: The Serbian Orthodox Church of Milosevic's Rise Now Sends Mixed Message." *New York Times*, July 4.

Hays, Richard. 1996. *The Moral Vision of the New Testament*. New York: Harper One.

Holmes, Arthur. 2005. *War and Christian Ethics*. Grand Rapids, MI: Baker Academic.

King, Jr, Martin Luther. 1958. *Stride toward Freedom*. New York: Harper and Row.

Lovell, W. George. 2005. *Conquest and Survival in Colonial Guatemala: A Historical Geography of the Cuchumatán Highlands, 1500–1821*. Montreal: McGill-Queen's University Press.

Luther, Martin. 1974a. "Admonition to Peace" (1525). In *Selected Political Writings*. Edited by J.M. Porter. Philadelphia: Fortress Press.

Luther, Martin. 1974b. "Against the Robbing and Murdering Hordes of Peasants" (1525). In *Selected Political Writings*. Edited by J.M. Porter. Philadelphia: Fortress Press.

Merton, Thomas. 1968. "Blessed Are the Meek: The Christian Roots of Nonviolence." In *Thomas Merton Peace*. Edited by Gordon Zahn, 201. New York: The McCall Publishing Company.

Musto, Ronald G. 1986. *The Catholic Peace Tradition*. New York: Orbis Press.

Pope Benedict XV. 1914. *Ad Beatissimum*. Vatican City.

Pope Benedict XVI. 2007. *Jesus of Nazareth: From the Baptism in the Jordan to the Transfiguration*. Translated by Adrian J. Walker. New York: Doubleday.

Pope Paul VI. 1967. *Evangelii Nuntiandi*. Vatican City.

Pope Pius XI. 1992. *Ubi Arcano Dei Consilio*. Vatican City.

Roberts, Alexander and James Donaldson (eds); Robert Ernest Wallis, trans. 1923. *Ante-Nicene Christian Library: The Writings of Tertullian*. Edinburgh: T and T Clark.

Rohr, Richard. 2007. "The Franciscan Opinion." In *Stricken by God: Nonviolent Identification and the Victory of Christ*. Edited by Brad Jersak and Michael Hardin, 209–210. Grand Rapids, MI: Eerdmans.

Synod of Bishops.1970. *Justice in the World*. Vatican City.
Thatcher, Oliver J. and Edgar Holmes McNeal. 1905. *A Sourcebook for Medieval History*. New York: Scribners.
Vatican Council II 1965. *The Church in the Modern World*. Vatican City.
Walton, Russ. 1987. *One Nation under God*. Nashville, TN: Thomas Nelson, Inc
Wink, Walter. 1998. *The Powers that Be*. New York: Doubleday.

Further Reading

Bainton, Roland. 1960. *Christian Attitudes toward War and Peace: A Historical Survey and Critical Re-evaluation*. New York: Abingdon Press. This is an excellent description of the development of just war and pacifism within Christianity.
Haring, Bernard. 1987. *The Healing Power of Peace and Nonviolence*. Mahwah, NJ: Paulist Press. Haring was the most prolific Catholic moral theologian of the twentieth century, teaching in a Catholic seminary in Rome for 40 years.This book was his last and he considered it the most important, especially as the world lived under the nuclear threat. The passion of the book reflects his experience as a medic in World War I and his reading of the New Testament.
Hays, Richard. 1996. *The Moral Vision of the New Testament: Community, Cross, New Creation: A Contemporary Introduction to New Testament Ethics*. New York: HarperCollins. Hays, a prominent New Testament scholar, explores the meaning of the teachings of St Paul and of the Gospels. He then applies those teachings to the question of "defense in the cause of justice." His conclusion, based on the texts, is that Christian violence cannot be biblically defended.
King, Jr, Martin Luther. 1963. *Strength to Love*. Minneapolis, MN: Fortress Press. This is a collection of Dr King's sermons in which he articulates the New Testament basis of nonviolent action for justice.
King, Jr, Martin Luther. 1958. *Stride toward Freedom: The Montgomery Story*. New York: HarperCollins. In this work, King tells the story of the churches' nonviolent activism to overcome segregation in Montgomery, Alabama, which was a watershed event that paved the way for ending legal segregation in the United States.
Musto, Ronald. 1986. *The Catholic Peace Tradition*. Maryknoll, NY: Orbis Press. Musto's book is one of the most comprehensive writings on the history of Christian nonviolence.
Rynne, Terrence. 2008. *Gandhi and Jesus: The Saving Power of Nonviolence*, Maryknoll, NY: Orbis Books. Rynne provides an excellent account of Gandhi's values in conversation with four contemporary Christian theologians. He argues that Jesus' death reveals the call to nonviolence.
United States Conference of Catholic Bishops. 1983. *The Challenge of Peace: God's Promise and Our Response*. Washington, DC: United States Catholic Conference. The Bishops assess the morality of the US nuclear policy, conscience, and nonviolence national strategies.
Wink, Walter. 1998. *The Powers that Be*. New York: Doubleday. Wink translates the meaning of New Testament texts, set in a first-century worldview, into a contemporary view to stress the relevance of the texts for today's Christians.

Yoder, John Howard. 1972. *The Politics of Jesus*. Grand Rapids, MI: Eedrmans. Yoder, a Mennonite theologian, demonstrates the nonviolent revolutionary intent of Old Testament and New Testament texts.

Yoder, John Howard. 2009. *Christian Attitudes to War, Peace, and Revolution*. Grand Rapids, MI: Brazos Press. This is a collection of Yoder's essays and class notes on the ethics of war.

Zahn, Gordon. 1964. *In Solitary Witness: The Life and Death of Franz Jaegerstaetter*. Collegeville, MN: The Liturgical Press. Zahn tells the little known story of the man who refused to fight in Hitler's army.

2.1

A Buddhist Response

Eleanor Rosch

The Christian religion is primarily about a transformation of consciousness...
Keating 2008, xii
The Christian of the future will be a mystic or he will not be anything at all.
Rahner 1981, 149

Buddhism is a contemplative religion.[1] In the Buddhist view, the royal road to a peace that is lasting and fulfilling is contemplative practice. Only thus, it is believed, can minds and hearts be transformed and an enlightened society made possible. One of the most important effects of the introduction of Eastern religions, such as Hinduism and Buddhism, into the West may be the way they have inspired Christianity and Judaism to find and reestablish aspects of their own contemplative traditions and to purvey those more generally to the laity. The growing practice of Buddhist meditation among Westerners, even in secular contexts, demonstrates how hungry people are for what such practices can provide. However meditation and contemplation are far from mainstream yet in Christianity. For example, Catholic and Episcopal churches might have a few parishioners who meet to practice centering prayer, but where would you find such a practice as a regular part of the church service?

Michael Duffey's clear and heartfelt account of the history of Christian peace-making and nonviolence (and their opposites) illustrates this state of affairs. Although there is mention of peace churches, such as the Society of Friends (Quakers), which have a base in contemplative prayer and although he cites modern Christian contemplatives, such as Thomas Merton and Richard Rohr, the issue of contemplative practice as such in Christianity is not brought to the fore. In the following discussion, I would like (1) to show how Buddhism and Christianity (and by extension other religions) might find a more fruitful meeting ground in the realm of meditation and contemplation than in discussion of doctrines; and

Peacemaking and the Challenge of Violence in World Religions, First Edition.
Edited by Irfan A. Omar and Michael K. Duffey.
© 2015 John Wiley & Sons, Ltd. Published 2015 by John Wiley & Sons, Ltd.

(2) to indicate ways in which that understanding could affect both personal and social peacemaking and nonviolence.

If you look at the doctrines of different religions they may appear hopelessly different[2] and in conflict with one another. However, if you look from the point of view of contemplative practice you might discover that many of the same issues arise for the practitioners of different religions (and can have doctrinal import) even though they may be dealt with differently.[3] Buddhism and Christianity would certainly appear polar opposites at first glance. But let's look at the Buddhist contemplative path and note possible Christian equivalents.

The Buddhist path begins with the mindfulness meditation of early Buddhism in which the practitioner learns to be present with him/herself and the world around. That might seem an alien notion to Christianity, however Father Thomas Keating points out that we are given two sources of revelation; one is scripture and the other the creation itself. Thus in Christian terms, the mindfulness meditator is learning to attend to the creation, surely not a bad idea. What that attention reveals in Buddhism is that the ordinary life lived from the perspective of a false sense of oneself and of what is real can lead only to endless cycles of dissatisfaction and suffering. This (ideally) brings earnest renunciation and a turning of the mind toward a deeper life of simplicity and meditation. The aim is to empty oneself of grasping, clinging, greed, fear, anger, aggression, jealousy, ignorance, and all the karmic seeds that keep one bound to these patterns. Renunciation, purification, and self-emptying (kenosis) are also basic aspects of the Christian contemplative path, with resonances in Judaism and Islam as well.

As Buddhism evolves, Mahayana adds emptiness and compassion as major aspects of the path. Emptiness can be off-putting to people of any persuasion as it suggests nihilism, a claim long refuted in Buddhist polemic. Interestingly, at least one mainstream Buddhist interpretation of emptiness as inherent purity finds resonance in the teachings of Thomas Merton; "At the center of our being is a point of nothingness which is untouched by sin and illusion, a point of pure truth, a point or spark which belongs entirely to God" (Merton 1989). The Vajrayana Buddhist might put it that since God (the basic ground of existence) is empty of sin and illusion (samsara), when seen with the pure vision of the illuminated wisdom mind, so also is the whole of the creation (the phenomenal world). Compassion, of course, is a near universal religious teaching, but the Buddhist and Christian, as well as those with a religious perspective in general, might add that unless the compassionate impulse is allied with something deeper than our fickle psychology, it can easily slide into the manipulative self-interest of the false or surface self.

The teachings of Vajrayana Buddhism, particularly the paths of Dzogchen and Mahamudra, point to a basic goodness (complete perfection) beyond emptiness that is primordial—far deeper than our mind's conception of good versus bad. Beyond our conceptual mind altogether, it is an aspect of the basic ground of existence and thus of the unobstructed radiance of that ground (see Rosch chapter, this volume). The enlightened person lives with the fullness of such presence moment by moment in a way resonant with Christian statements such as, "The fullness of joy is to behold God in everything" (Julian of Norwich 2008, 171). The enlightened person acts from that, not from ego. Because the ground has no causes and conditions for being, one cannot get to it from anything that one does—the type of issue that Christianity deals with through the concept of grace.

Vajrayana could be of special interest to Western religions in that it is separated from theism only by the hair's breadth of its staunch repudiation of anthropomorphic language to describe the basic ground. People who call themselves spiritual but not religious are sometimes drawn to Vajrayana because it offers a devotional path that does not require them to believe in human-like supernatural beings. Contemplative paths in Western religions may also reach stages beyond anthropomorphic language as they progress, giving further credence to the argument that the contemplative aspects of religions provide an especially fertile ground for dialogue.

How does all of this apply to peacemaking and nonviolence? It applies first to the state of being of individuals. One's false and ego-oriented sense of self thrives on drama and conflict. Were a person immersed in such a sense of self to arrive at a peaceful heaven, he might well reject it as insufficiently entertaining. A peacemaker must be strong, stable, and grounded in her own relationship to peace in order to withstand the temptations and challenges arising from the manipulative aggression inherent in present societies. Belief in a doctrine is unlikely to provide all that is needed to do this. Beliefs are made of words; they are cognitive events in the mind. Beliefs shift and twist. One can have many contradictory beliefs. When beliefs get entangled with the emotional system they can become rigid and dogmatic or automatic and powerless. People struggle to have conceptual faith in their religious beliefs, but wherever there is conceptual faith alone, there will be doubt; faith and doubt are two sides of the same coin.

The power of contemplative practice is to go deeper than words, thoughts, beliefs, and emotions. While this is the aim of all such practice, two examples specifically directed at beliefs and faith may be illustrative. In Chinese Chan, Yuanmiao taught a system where both great faith and great doubt were aroused together again and again, eventually intensified with such ferocity that they would explode the struggling mind, allowing the practitioner to settle back into his primordial and ever-present enlightened nature (Buswell 2013). A second technique, taught by the Korean Zen teacher Chinul, is called, "tracing back the radiance." Instead of focusing on the words, concepts, or even meaning of a particular teaching, the practitioner arouses an intense questioning of the state of mind of the teacher who gave that teaching. By this means, in stages, the practitioner (ideally) is able to trace the teaching all the way back to its enlightened source (Buswell 1992). Duffey used a closely related form of questioning in his rich exploration of what Christ might have been communicating in allowing himself to be crucified. Such techniques can apply to working with concepts, beliefs, faith, and doubt in relation to whatever source one's religion (or secular belief system) takes as most primal and meaningful.

Other skills needed by a peace worker are also blocked by the mind of concepts, beliefs, and self-referential motivations. Such a mind judges constantly and takes sides between disputants. Its idea of justice is an eye for an eye and a life for a life. It cannot admit not knowing. The contemplative mind in both Christianity and Buddhism is humble enough to let go beyond knowing. It can leave guilt and judgment to God or karma, and work for the best outcome that is realistically possible in this world of apparent imperfections. The contemplative mind is (ideally) observant enough to catch its own wavering, at least some of the time, and it is at least capable of inclusiveness and nonjudgmental empathy with others regardless of their social status or what harm they may have done. One of Richard Rohr's recurring examples of the nondualistic contemplative mind at work (Rohr 2009) is people's struggles with the shocking and difficult idea that God loves everyone equally: the idiot, the wealthy snob, and the sociopath as much as oneself who is trying so hard to be good.

In the political sphere, the contemplative mind is not per se rebellious, but neither is it subservient. That may be why the Christian church, through most of history, has suppressed large-scale contemplative practice. Christianity and Buddhism show a striking parallel history in that both were primarily pacifist in their early days, but when they became state religions – Christianity under Constantine and Buddhism under King Ashoka – they were faced with new challenges and became more subtle and slippery about condoning violence. Part of this may be realpolitik, but much of it may be the truth that many, perhaps most, members of established religions do not work very hard at embodying that religion. Imagine what the history of Christianity and Buddhism (in fact of the world) might have been like had the members of those religions, including those highly placed, steadfastly adhered throughout the vicissitudes of history to nonviolent intentions and to the guidance and power that comes from beyond the mind.

A final point has to do with how suffering can be transformed into a path in both Christianity and Buddhism. Christianity is masterful at this; identification with Christ on the cross has opened hearts and granted succor to untold masses of people throughout the ages. The first word of teaching that the Buddha is said to have uttered after his enlightenment was *dukkha*, meaning suffering or unsatisfactoriness. The truth of suffering is the First Noble Truth in Buddhism and is considered the beginning of the path. Experiencing suffering is the great crossroads; it can make a person angry, bitter, and small (and a nation paranoid and violent) or can open one's heart to the world. That is where peace may hang in the balance. As the Venerable Maha Ghosananda, the great contemporary peacemaker of Cambodia (who lost his entire extended family in the killing fields of the Khmer Rouge) has put it:

> The suffering of Cambodia has been deep.
> From this suffering comes Great Compassion.
> Great Compassion makes a Peaceful Heart.
> A Peaceful Heart makes a Peaceful Person.

A Peaceful Person makes a Peaceful Family.
A Peaceful Family makes a Peaceful Nation.
And a Peaceful Nation makes a Peaceful World.
May all beings live in Happiness and Peace. (Ghosananda 1992)

Notes

1   This is how Buddhist teachers tend to present their tradition in the contemporary world, however there is scholarly dispute about the extent to which it was true historically. See for examples, McMahan (2008) and Sharf (1995).
2   The one exception is the almost universal acknowledgment of the virtue of compassion as is demonstrated by the growing number of religions, organizations, and individuals who are signing Karen Armstrong's Charter for Compassion.
3   A related point was made in the perennialism movement that focused on the mystical elements in religions. See, for example, Huxley (1945).

References

Buswell, Robert E. (ed. and trans.) 1992. *Tracing Back the Radiance: Chinul's Korean Way of Zen*. Honolulu, HI: University of Hawaii Press.

Buswell, Robert E. 2013. "The Transformation of Doubt in Zen 'Questioning Meditation.'" Paper given at a conference at the Mangalam Research Center, Berkeley, CA. April 6, 2013.

Ghosananda, Maha. 1992. *Step by Step: Meditation on Wisdom and Compassion*. Berkeley, CA: Parallax Press.

Huxley, Aldous. 1945. *The Perennial Philosophy*. New York: Harper & Brothers Publishers.

Keating, Thomas et al. 2008. *Spirituality, Contemplation and Transformation: Writings on Centering Prayer*. New York: Lantern Books.

McMahan, David L. 2008. *The Making of Buddhist Modernism*. Oxford and New York: Oxford University Press.

Merton, Thomas. 1989. *A Merton Reader*. Edited by Thomas P. McDonnell. New York: Image Books.

Rahner, Karl. 1981. *Concern for the Church*. New York: Crossroad.

Rohr, Richard. 2009. *The Naked Now: Learning to See as the Mystics See*. New York: The Crossroads Publishing Company.

Sharf, Robert H. 1995. "Buddhist Modernism and the Rhetoric of Meditation Experience." *Numen* 42: 228–283.

2.2

A Muslim Response

Irfan A. Omar

Christianity and Islam have a lot in "common"; some of us may be shocked by that statement but it is true – of course – depending on how and what we choose to see in these two religions. At the exoteric level they may have very different historical and structural elements, but, as we look deeper, the esoteric dimension of these two religions is remarkably quite comparable. They both have a rich tradition of saints and mystical practices. They are both universalistic in their claims with a strong focus on the interrelation between the divine and creation.

Over the centuries, scholars and practitioners alike have reflected on many shared aspects such as the sincere reverence for Mary, high regard for Jesus, and the quranic view of those "who are pious and humble" – a reference to Christian monks (and nuns). As a child, I grew up listening to stories about Jesus (and other world teachers, Prophet Muhammad, the Buddha, Mirabai, Kabir, etc.). These became and still remain part of me. Muslim cultures around the world have a deep reverence for what one Islamic scholar calls the "Muslim Jesus" (Khalidi 2001). The stories that I heard were adaptations from the biblical and quranic sources and they left no doubt in my mind that the message of Jesus was one of peace. This was confirmed for me in this chapter as Michael Duffey systematically lays out the evidence and shows the development of peacemaking traditions among Christians.

One particular point of divergence for me as a Muslim was to read about the suffering of God and the particular way it was described in this chapter, which is an integral part of the Christian thinking, although it is moving to see the narrative about Jesus as revealing a suffering God who is suffering *with* people and is doing so for the sake of their (humanity's) salvation. In Muslim theology such descriptions of God are non-existent. Theologians often do not entertain the how, what, and who types of questions about God except to discuss things that the Qur'an itself says about God (e.g. God's attributes – such as Most Merciful, Most Compassionate, Most Just, Source of All Peace, The Friend, The Protector, and so on).

Peacemaking and the Challenge of Violence in World Religions, First Edition.
Edited by Irfan A. Omar and Michael K. Duffey.
© 2015 John Wiley & Sons, Ltd. Published 2015 by John Wiley & Sons, Ltd.

A point of convergence for me was when Duffey mentioned the "just war" tradition. It seems there was a great deal of give and take between Islam and Christianity in the early Middle Ages as Islamic theology was being developed. The chapter is very explicit about the permissible warfare: citing St Augustine, Duffey argues that "war must be waged for defensive purposes, by legitimate authority, and with honorable intentions." Similar ideas are found in the writings of early Muslim leaders who faced the challenge of conflict and war after the death of Muhammad. As a result of Muslims' historical experience, there developed a strong Islamic just war theory that contained some of the same elements as its Christian counterpart. Also similar to the Christian historical reality, many Muslim rulers violated the teachings of their own scriptures and those of Prophet Muhammad. Many wars were fought for less than noble objectives – for expansion and for power. If we need proof of this, just think of the sobering fact that most Christians in history were harmed/killed by their fellow Christians and the same is true for Muslims.

There were also instances of hope and peace in this chapter. Duffey mentioned the name of one of the rare examples from among the spiritual teachers of the past – St Francis of Assisi. Although it was only as a passing reference, Duffey noted the journey made by St Francis to Egypt where he would meet the ruler of that region, Sultan Malik al-Kamil. For many proponents of interfaith dialogue, this meeting was paradigmatic in Christian–Muslim relations. The Sultan, as the ruler of Egypt, was also the leader of the Muslim forces facing the crusaders coming from the West. In most Western accounts, the meeting between St Francis and the sultan was cast in polemical terms until only a few years ago when Franciscan scholars began to re-examine the available documents. They soon discovered that it contains a rich story of dialogue and mutual respect and even recognition. This narrative is in fact quite contrary to the larger narrative about that (late medieval) period, which is about the Crusades. As a result of this re-examination, there are now series of works on this historic and factual meeting centered round the possibilities and promises of interfaith encounter (see Hoeberichts 1997; Warren 2003; Cosato 2008; Moses 2009; Dardess and Krier Mich 2011). The findings of numerous scholars today reveal that each of the two parties in that encounter came away with greater knowledge and appreciation of the other. Each of them did things slightly differently after the encounter, which advanced the cause of peace and opened new pathways for dialogue.

References

Cusato, Michael F. 2008. "From Damietta to laVerna: The impact on Francis on his Experiences in Egypt." *Spirit and Life: A Journal of Contemporary Franciscanism* 12: 81–112.

Dardess, George and Marvin L. Krier Mich. 2011. *In the Spirit of St. Francis and the Sultan: Catholics and Muslims Working Together for the Common Good.* Maryknoll, NY: Orbis Books.

Hoeberichts, Jan. 1997. *Francis and Islam*. Quincy, IL: Franciscan Press.
Khalidi, Tarif, ed. and trans. 2001. *The Muslim Jesus: Sayings and Stories in Islamic Literature*. Cambridge, MA: Harvard University Press.
Moses, Paul. 2009. *The Saint and the Sultan: The Crusades, Islam, and Francis of Assisi's Mission of Peace*. New York: Doubleday.
Warren, Kathleen A. 2003. *Daring to Cross the Threshold: Francis of Assisi Encounters Sultan Malek al-Kamil*. Rochester, MN: Sisters of St. Francis.

3

Jewish Ideologies of Peace and Peacemaking

Joshua Ezra Burns

Come, my children, listen to me; I shall teach you fear of the Lord. Who is the man who desires life, who cherishes the days to see goodness? Keep your tongue from evil, your lips from deceitful speech. Flee from evil and do good, seek peace and pursue it.

Psalm 34:12–15

Judaism's Sacred Texts

The **Torah** encompasses the first five books of the Hebrew Scriptures, that is, Genesis, Exodus, Leviticus, Numbers, and Deuteronomy. These books contain narrative accounts of the birth of the nation of Israel along with divine laws relating to ethical conduct and the worship of Yahweh, the God of Israel. To varying degrees of applicability and interpretation, these laws are considered authoritative in all contemporary Jewish denominations.

The **Hebrew Scriptures** are a collection of sacred books roughly equivalent to the Christian Old Testament. These texts narrate in reverent terms the early history of Israel and their gradual evolution into the Jewish people. Also included are books of prophecies, songs, poems, proverbs, folktales, and other cultural effects of Judaism's most primitive era.

The **Mishnah** is the earliest work of Judaism's rabbinic movement. It is a compilation of scholarly opinions relating to the interpretation of the laws of the Torah culled from the so-called rabbis or Jewish teachers of the first and second centuries of the Common Era.

The **Talmud** is either of two compendious rabbinic commentaries on the Mishnah compiled in Palestine during the fourth century and in Babylonia

Peacemaking and the Challenge of Violence in World Religions, First Edition.
Edited by Irfan A. Omar and Michael K. Duffey.
© 2015 John Wiley & Sons, Ltd. Published 2015 by John Wiley & Sons, Ltd.

(modern Iraq) between the fifth and sixth centuries. The Babylonian Talmud is generally considered an authoritative source of religious law among contemporary Orthodox and Conservative Jews.

The **Mishneh Torah** is a synopsis of the Mishnah, the two Talmuds, and other classical rabbinic texts written by the twelfth-century Jewish philosopher Maimonides. It is meant to offer practical moral guidance drawn from lessons within those voluminous treatises. Although not considered an authoritative code of law in its own right, the Mishneh Torah is widely regarded as a touchstone of the classical Jewish legal tradition.

The **Kabbalah** is a genre of Jewish mystical literature originating in medieval Europe. Though seldom read for devotional purposes, its mythical poetry and esoteric retellings of scriptural narratives have influenced expressions of Jewish spirituality for generations.

"Seek peace and pursue it." The term in the Psalm translated as "peace" is the well-known Hebrew word *shalom*. Traditionally offered as a blessing of greeting, this concise formula functions as "hello" when joining another's company, "goodbye" when parting ways, and a gesture of goodwill in general conversation. But although Jews often will express their desire for peace as a common courtesy, the ideology of *shalom* is easily misunderstood. For amidst the diverse elements of practice and belief that define Judaism, the language of peace bears several meanings. In certain contexts, *shalom* connotes the welfare of the individual, whether Jewish or non-Jewish. In other contexts, it connotes the collective wellbeing of the Jewish people. In yet others, *shalom* connotes a more universal peace touching all peoples and even the earth itself. Depending, therefore, on how one chooses to imagine peace, the active pursuit urged by the author of the Psalm might be taken to imply any of a number of initiatives nominally to be defined as peacemaking. In the essay to follow, I shall describe some notable efforts by Jewish thinkers of the past and the present to capitalize on the Psalm's promise of divine fulfillment on behalf of their selves, their fellow Jews, and the world at large.

What is Judaism?

Before we proceed, a few words on the term Judaism are in order. Today, Judaism is typically regarded as a religion rooted in the theology of ancient Israel and developed by its Jewish practitioners over the centuries. The origins of the Jewish religion are described in the Hebrew Scriptures, the collection of ancient books constituting the Jewish Bible and the Christian Old Testament (Carr 2010). The narrative portions of those books recount the history of a nation called Israel said to have entered a series of covenants or agreements with Yahweh in return for

His eternal commitment to their descendants. Abraham, the forefather of Israel, is said to have been chosen by God to depart from his father's household to found a new nation in the land now comprising the State of Israel and the Palestinian territories. As his family grows, a famine in the land sends his descendants to Egypt, where they are ultimately enslaved by a heartless Pharaoh. Amidst their despair, a hero arises in Moses, an Israelite foundling raised as an Egyptian prince who uses his position to confront the king and demand the liberation of his downtrodden people. Aided by God, Moses brings chaos to Egypt, upsetting nature through a series of miracles until the Pharaoh finally relents to his demands. But even when Israel wins their freedom, an arduous trek through the wilderness stands between them and their ancestral homeland. To see them through their journey, God issues Moses a set of commandments known as the Torah or "the instruction," a guide for worship and upright living to be observed by Israel in the present and in perpetuity. Henceforth, loyalty to God would mean fidelity to His Torah, and with it, the promise of God's reciprocal loyalty to Israel.

The synthesis of narrative and law comprising the five books of the Torah is traditionally taken as the charter document of the Jewish religion. All of Judaism's central ethical and ritual tenets originate in these texts. But the dramatic experiences of the first generations of Israelites are only part of the story informing the mythic imagination of the Jewish people. For upon their return, Moses's descendants are said to have spent centuries staking their claim to Abraham's inheritance, first establishing their territorial right, then establishing a kingdom, and enduring the division of that kingdom into the rival states of Israel and Judah. All the while, their leaders must defend their towns from the incursions of neighboring kingdoms and mighty foreign empires seeking to claim their lands as their own. Preserved in the biblical books of Joshua, Judges, Samuel, and Kings, the stories of these challenging times follow a consistent pattern of ebb and flow. When Israel and her leaders follow His commandments, God rewards His people with peace and prosperity. When they lapse in their observance, God punishes them with war and misfortune. The whole of the narrative thus elaborately demonstrates both the benefits of Israel's ancestral covenants and the risks incurred by failing to meet its terms.

As the kings of Israel and Judah struggled to maintain peace in their lands, certain of their subjects were presumed to maintain peace with God. These were the prophets, dynamic individuals who professed to speak on God's behalf. Although the Hebrew Scriptures ascribe many and varied motivations to these men, those whose words proved the most enduring were those who championed the Torah, promising good fortune in return for responsible leadership and faithful worship at the Temple of Jerusalem. The prophetic refrain was simple but effective: obey the commandments of God and things will get better. This call would prove ever more attractive as things actually got worse. In 722 B.C.E., the northern Kingdom of Israel fell to the Assyrians. Its people, representing the greater part of the Israelite nation, were dispersed among the nations of the Middle East. Only the southern

Kingdom of Judah remained to sustain God's ancient promise to Abraham. After years of fending off further attacks, Jerusalem fell to the Babylonians in 597 B.C.E. Over the next 10 years, some survivors of Judah fled for safety. Others were deported to Mesopotamia. Others still remained in their impoverished land for lack of resources to go elsewhere.

The Babylonian Exile would prove to be the catalyst for the formation of Judaism. As the once stern warnings of the prophets turned to words of hope and consolation, the displaced survivors of Judah looked inward for cause to survive. Many continued to follow God's commandments to the best of their abilities in the hope that their patron deity might forgive their past trespasses and restore them to their ancestral homeland. Resisting assimilation to the cultural norms of their foreign environments, they maintained a separate Jewish estate in exile. Their optimism was unexpectedly vindicated in 539 B.C.E., only 49 years after the final liquidation of Jerusalem, when the Babylonians were conquered by the Persians under the command of the benevolent King Cyrus II. As accounted in the biblical book of Ezra, Cyrus permitted those of his Jewish subjects who wished to return to Jerusalem to do so, even providing funds and manpower for the reconstruction of its ruined temple. To those Jews who had remained true to God, it now seemed that their divine guardian had returned to their corner.

Though now lacking political sovereignty, the leaders of the Persian province of Judea were wiser for their people's experiences of exile and restoration. They therefore took pains to ensure that their harrowing history would not be repeated. They rebuilt Jerusalem and its temple, restoring its sacrificial services and supporting its priesthood. They disseminated the word of God through public readings of the Torah. They compiled records of their national history emphasizing the vitality of their covenant, writing the very books since preserved as the Hebrew Scriptures. New Jewish prophets arose preaching cooperation and understanding with the other nations of the world. Amidst these efforts, a new cultic ideology emerged casting the God of Israel as the God of the entire world, a God faithful to those faithful to Him regardless of where they happen to live. It was in this ideology that Judaism was born.

Yet despite its ingrained theological tradition, one must acknowledge that the Jewish people did not begin to think of Judaism as a religion until fairly recently. To be clear, the contemporary religious category popularly known as Judaism can be traced back to an ancient Jewish culture traditionally entailing certain fixed ideas about God. That culture also involved unique rites and behaviors related to the worship of God later to be construed as key elements of the Jewish faith. But these cultural effects did not constitute a religion in the formal sense of the word (Nongbri 2013, 46–50). They entailed no compulsory system of belief or regulatory ritual program by which to measure one's Jewish identity. To be a Jew was primarily a matter of national or ethnic identification, a function of being born into a family of Jewish descent or choosing to disavow one's own ancestral culture to become a Jew. By and large, it was not a matter of confession or creed (Satlow 2006, 1–14).

It was not until the nineteenth century that Jewish thinkers began to conceive of their ancestral culture in systematized religious terms. Seeking entry into a European civil society dominated by Christian values, many Jews touched by the liberal values of the European Enlightenment undertook to interpret their Judaism in terms analogous to Christianity. Only as a result of those efforts did the prospect of theological normativity enter the realm of Jewish popular thought. Yet the realization of Judaism as a religion yielded disparate results across the wide spectrum of Jewish society. Some Jews opted to loosen the bonds of tradition, while others preferred to maintain continuity with their people's past. Others still positioned themselves between these poles, preferring to balance the old and the new. The modern Judaism to which they all contributed was therefore marked by diversity in its theology and its practice, encompassing a range of religious ideologies commonly indebted to the Hebrew Scriptures yet open to their continual reinterpretation (Batnitzky 2011, 13–28; cf. Shavit and Eran 2007).

Prior to the modern era, therefore, the Jewish people operated with no prevailing standard by which to measure any given belief or cultural value as normative. Consequently, one cannot presume to discern a uniform theology of peace or agenda for peacemaking at any given time or in any given location of Jewish activity in the past, much less in the present. For to describe a fundamental doctrine of peace or peacemaking "in Judaism" would be to read the varied record of Jewish engagement with these ideologies through a tendentious interpretive lens. I do not mean, of course, to disparage the admirable efforts of scholars who have sought to discern theological justifications for contemporary peacemaking on the basis of classical Jewish texts. I mean merely to state that the critical reader must acknowledge that such efforts are driven by modern religious sensibilities. By way of contrast, my purpose here is historiographical. I aim merely to provide examples of ideologies of peace and peacemaking in pre-modern Jewish thought. I will leave it to the discriminating reader to decide how best to make use of those examples in his or her own efforts to pursue peace within the Jewish community or in dialogue with activists seeking moral guidance from within the Jewish tradition.

Jewish Terms for Peace and Peacemaking

Let us begin by returning to *shalom*. The standard Hebrew expression for peace has a long history. The word *shalom* appears throughout the Hebrew Scriptures. But not every instance of *shalom* in the Bible signifies what modern readers would objectify as peace. The word derives from the verbal root *šlm*, which means "to complete." On its basic semantic level, therefore, the nominal form *shalom* might best be rendered as "completeness" or "wholeness," indicating, in other words, a state of personal perfection. For one to achieve *shalom* would seem to necessitate a prior state of imperfection or disarray which the individual would have to overcome in order to improve his or her condition.

It was as an effect of this figurative quest for perfection that the classical Israelite ideology of *shalom* evolved (Talmon 1997). Thus, throughout the Hebrew Scriptures, *shalom* typically refers to the welfare of an individual at ease and free of peril. The implied wholeness of one who possesses *shalom* suggests a contrast with the individual who is wracked with disease or anxiety, one lacking peace of body or peace of mind (e.g. Genesis 43:27; Exodus 4:18; Numbers 9:26; Judges 6:22–23; Psalm 119:165). This seems to be the idea behind the Psalm's encouragement to pursue peace by choosing righteous conduct over evil. Elsewhere, the logic of personal *shalom* is extended to indicate concord between two parties; that is, between two individuals or two groups of people (e.g. 1 Samuel 16:4–5; 1 Kings 5:12; 2 Kings 5:1–22; Psalm 120:6–7). In these instances, therefore, the object of *shalom* represents not a state of personal perfection but the opposite of mutual hostility, a concept arguably anticipating our contemporary understanding of peace as the absence of violence or ill will between persons of disparate interests.

These, then, were the primary objects of peace in classical Israelite culture. Only in subsequent Jewish traditions did the ordinary language of personal and inter-personal *shalom* acquire a distinctly idyllic quality. Following the fall of the Kingdom of Judah, peace seemed impossible for many of its survivors. Those Jews who sustained their ethnic identities through the Babylonian Exile to return to Judea wished to capitalize on their newfound freedom by establishing a provincial commonwealth free of conflict. The leaders of the Jews therefore remained loyal to their Persian governors and refrained from wars of conquest. They sought to maintain good relations with God by worshipping at His newly restored temple in Jerusalem. The once elusive promise of *shalom* for all of Israel finally seemed tenable (e.g. Isaiah 45:7; Jeremiah 39:4; Ezra 9:12).

But throughout their trials of devastation and reconstruction, some Jews dreamt of an even more ambitious peace. Prophetic authors trained on the tales of David and Solomon preserved in their sacred books imagined that those legendary Israelites kings had ruled their subjects in perfect *shalom*. It was that state of national wholeness that inspired their visions of the Jewish future. In their hands, therefore, *shalom* became an eschatological objective, a universal peace to be achieved when God would set a new king of David's line on the throne of Jerusalem. This anointed one, or Messiah, would instate a new world order bringing harmony not only to the nation of Israel but to all the nations of the world, who would defer to the authority of God's chosen earthly sovereign (e.g. Micah 5:4–5; Isaiah 9:5–6; Haggai 2:7–9).

The Messianic dream of universal *shalom* did not supplant the earlier, arguably more tenable notion that one can achieve personal peace simply by serving the will of God. Yet if the object of *shalom* is to be understood in part as the restoration of global perfection, one might well question the relationship between the piety of the individual and the fate of the world at large. In this philosophical dilemma lies the meaning of another Jewish term key to our discussion. The Hebrew phrase *tikkun olam* literally translates to "restoration of the world." Today, it is generally used to signify the core Jewish value of social justice, a rubric including, although not restricted to, peacemaking. Like *shalom*, the idea of *tikkun olam* is firmly rooted in classical Jewish traditions encouraging active agency in bringing about positive social change. But also like *shalom*, the contemporary ideation of *tikkun olam* must be understood in view of its evolution in pre-modern Jewish thought (Rosenthal 2005).

The language of *tikkun olam* originated in the works of the rabbinic sages, specifically the Mishnah and the Talmud. In these ancient compendiums of post-biblical Jewish legal traditions, the figurative "world" subject to restoration was the rather restricted world of the sages and their disciples, in antiquity a rather small subset of the general Jewish population. Rabbinic legislators applied the term *tikkun olam* to decisions meant to improve social relations between Jewish hus-bands and wives as well as other litigants at odds over civil disputes prone to regulation by the Torah or the Law of Moses. For those sages to have enacted rulings ostensibly helping to "restore the world" was, in fact, merely to reconcile one Jew with another (e.g. Mishnah *Gittin* 4:2-3; Babylonian Talmud *Pesaḥim* 88b). This, then, was the rather quaint concept of *tikkun olam* first impressed on the Jewish popular imagination. Overtures to repairing the world outside the Jewish community are not to be found in Judaism's classical source texts.

The move toward externalizing the restoration effort came with the Kabbalists, Jewish mystics of later medieval Europe and Palestine. These Jewish mystics adapted the language of *tikkun olam* to a novel cosmology whereby God, in creating the physical world, was thought to have destroyed a more perfectly ordered metaphysical world affording no quarter to evil and sin. According, therefore, to the Kabbalah, one of the prime operatives of human existence is to restore the physical world to its primordial state of perfection. The Jewish people in particular were supposed to achieve this *tikkun olam* by living lives of constant holiness, following the laws of the Torah in order to overcome the immorality of the world around them. Only fidelity to God's commandments would bring about the advent of the Messiah and his reign of peace. It was among the Kabbalists, therefore, the ideology of *tikkun olam* was retrofitted to complement the classical Jewish ideology of *shalom*, promising a restoration of the world to the state of wholeness in which they imagined its existence before the creation of the earth.

Although this mystical theology of Torah no longer guides the religious disci-plines of the Jewish majority, its ideology of *tikkun olam* has persisted. Revived by the influential twentieth-century Jewish thinkers Martin Buber and Abraham Joshua Heschel as a call for moral action, the mission to "restore the world" by improving the living conditions of all its inhabitants has become a slogan even among Jews disabused of the Messianic motivations of the Kabbalists (Buber 1948, 185-187; Heschel 1955, 379-380). The task of *tikkun olam* has thus been taken up not only by the ultra-orthodox Hasidic Jews, who still maintain elements of its mystical theology, but by socially conscious Jews of every denominational variety, including the Reform, the Conservative, the Reconstructionist, and the Modern

Orthodox. Among these diverse Jewish populations, many continue to see fidelity to the Torah as their foremost religious responsibility and, moreover, as a necessary prerequisite for restoring the world to its mythical state of primordial perfection. But most would agree that the righteous Jew must also do right on behalf of others, supporting social justice as a fundamental and fundamentally Jewish ethical commitment.

To this end, a major component of the contemporary Jewish agenda for social justice is peacemaking, fostering healthy relations between the Jewish people and their neighbors in the global community. As we shall see, the popular call for *tikkun olam* thus functions as a vital religious directive in the pursuit of *shalom*. But before discussing this effort, we should consider its relationship with past ideologies of peace and nonviolence rooted not in Judaism's theological imagination but in the harsher realities of human conflict and warfare.

War and Peace in the Hebrew Scriptures

As noted, the Hebrew Scriptures represent the founding charters of the Jewish people and their religion. All of Judaism's moral teachings originate in these ancient texts, whether directly or indirectly. Naturally, therefore, one would expect to find in the pages of the Jewish Bible notices of God's desire for peace. In fact, the books of the Israelite prophets furnish ample evidence to this effect. Isaiah, for instance, famously envisioned a Messianic age when "the wolf shall live with the lamb and the leopard shall lie down with the kid," when natural enemies, in other words, would become friends and violence a thing of the past (Isaiah 11:6). The visionary Micah similarly foretold a day when human beings would beat their weapons into agricultural tools and "nation shall not take up sword against nation," never again to know war (Micah 4:3). These expressions speak to an idyllic conception of peace as the ultimate goal of humanity and of all God's creation.

And yet, these placid images appear amidst a literary record of ancient Israel replete with evidence of its violent reality. The Israelites were constantly at war. The authors, moreover, of the narrative books of the Hebrew Scriptures generally believed that God sanctioned their people's military triumphs, if only when their leaders deserved His protection by virtue of their fidelity to God's commandments. At times, therefore, they depict God as having ordered Israel to vanquish entire nations standing the way of their national sovereignty (Niditch 1993; Firestone 2012, 17–25). So, for instance, is God said in the book of Deuteronomy to have bid His chosen people, "Clear away many nations before you. ... You must utterly destroy them. Make no covenant with them and show them no mercy. ... Break down their altars, smash their pillars, hew down their sacred poles, and burn their idols with fire" (Deuteronomy 7:1–6). These verses and countless others depict God not as hostile toward other non-Israelite nations in general but specifically toward those of Israel's neighbors who stood to corrupt His followers with foreign modes of worship. But their violent rhetoric is unavoidable. While the Hebrew Scriptures, therefore, certainly do not promote war as an ideal, they seem to offer ample justification for its pursuit, if only in a distant frame of historical reference whereby its outcome might be construed as advantageous to God (Collins 2003). This fact naturally complicates any effort to read the Jewish Bible as an unequivocal commission for peace.

The paradoxical nature of the Hebrew Scriptures' take on war and peace is perfectly exemplified in the following ethical directive recorded elsewhere in Deuteronomy:

> When you approach a city to attack it, you shall offer it peace (*shalom*). Should it accept peace and let you in, all the people found therein shall be put to forced labor and serve you. Should it refuse to make peace with you but offer you war, you shall besiege it. And when the Lord your God delivers it into your hand, you shall put all its men to the sword. (Deuteronomy 20:10–13)

The book of Deuteronomy likely dates to the reign of the Jewish king Josiah, circa 640–609 B.C.E. This was a time of relative calm in the Kingdom of Judah, well past the age when Israel had the need or political wherewithal to launch attacks on neighboring cities for the sake of territorial gain. But the speaker is Moses, the ancient lawgiver reputed to have delivered God's word to the Israelites before they possessed a land or kingdom of their own. The author's likely purpose in ascribing these words to Israel's first prophet was to revise an existing scriptural record wherein God was said to have sanctioned Israel's territorial conquests without ethical compunction. Though affixed in their cultural memory, that amoral way of thinking had become a cause for concern for the Jews following the fall of the northern Kingdom of Israel. The Deuteronomic author seems to acknowledge that God will go only so far to protect his chosen people in battle. He therefore depicts God as advocating negotiated peace as a preferable alternative to war. Even so, however, the author does not see peace as a necessary alternative to war. His ethical objective remains not with the will of God but with the needs of the nation of Israel.

How should the modern reader account for this moral equivocation? Why would God sanction war while telling His prophets to espouse peace? From a critical standpoint, one might explain the inconsistency of the scriptural record as a function of its diverse composition. The Hebrew Scriptures were written neither by one author nor in reference to a single set of historical circumstances. They were written by many authors, first Israelite and later Jewish, over several generations. Each of these authors was of his own mind and each responded to the unique theological and social challenges of his day.

Among the greatest challenges for these authors was the constant stream of foreign nations into the land of Israel and, in turn, into the cultural sphere of her people. To their minds, the Egyptians, the Canaanites, the Assyrians, the

Babylonians, and other nations ever threatened to break Israel's national constitution by undermining their covenants with God (Goldenberg 1998, 9–27). As a result, virtually every surviving literary artifact of ancient Israel shows concern for either the prospect or the actuality of international conflict. Only those Israelite authors daring enough to imagine a world without war were prone to promote peace as more true to the design of God's creation. Their sense of theological dissonance accounts for the tranquil, if patently unrealistic, visions of Isaiah, Micah, and the other Israelite prophets who yearned for a divine resolution to their people's seemingly unending hostilities with their neighboring nations.

The ultimate failure of the Israelites to withstand their Assyrian and, later, Babylonian foes did not dash their survivors' hope for peace. As noted earlier, the revival of the Kingdom of Judah as the Persian province of Judea saw a renewal of Jewish interest in the pacifistic prophecies of old. In time, however, the disparity between the real and the ideal grew so stark that the new prophets of Israel could not help but to conclude that their people would not find peace before sustaining a final, devastating war with the nations at large. This motif most famously finds expression in the book of Daniel, its latest stage of composition dating between 167 and 164 B.C.E. during a tragic struggle between the Jews and their imperial masters in Hellenistic Syria. In chapters 7–12, an anonymous prophetic author speaking in Daniel's voice offers a series of apocalyptic visions of a war to end all wars pitting the Greeks against the Persians in simultaneous battles on heaven and earth. Only, in his estimation, when God would intervene and send His Messiah to earth would Israel and all the other nations aligned with his chosen people enjoy true and enduring peace.

On the whole, therefore, it seems fair to conclude that the Hebrew Scriptures offer little aid to the modern reader seeking coherent Jewish rationales for peace or peacemaking. To be certain, these books record numerous examples of righteous behavior in wartime, offering the contemporary reader potential models of reconciliation and nonparticipation (Niditch 1993, 134–149). But these rare examples do not obscure the dominant message proclaiming that that the prerogative of peace belongs to God alone. We must therefore look elsewhere to discern when and under what conditions influential Jewish thinkers of later times began to conceptualize peace not merely as an eschatological goal but as a temporal goal as well.

Pacifism in the Rabbinic Tradition

The Jewish victory over the Syrian Greeks would be their last military success for quite a while. Losing their political independence to Rome in 63 B.C.E., the people of Judea would later undertake two disastrous rebellions, the first from 66 to 70 C.E. and the second from 132 to 135 C.E. Each resulted in heavy losses and mass destruction. The failure of the first revolt incurred the devastation of the Jewish Temple in Jerusalem, until then the focal point of worship for Jewish communities throughout the world. The failure of the second revolt, led by the would-be Messiah Simon bar Kosiba, saw his people symbolically stripped of their national identity when the Romans renamed their province from the traditional Judea to the archaic Greek ethnic designation Palestine. These disasters suggested to the most faithful Jews that God had not approved of their people's militaristic actions. Though ostensibly fighting for much the same reasons as the Israelites once had, their own Jewish contemporaries seemed not to have merited the same measure of divine protection as their ancient forebears.

The breaking of Israel's national will had many negative effects on the formative Jewish tradition, but one positive consequence was an important social movement initiated by the rabbinic sages (Cohen 2014, 211–229). Between the first and second wars, a small cadre of rabbis, which is Hebrew for teachers, set about to create a new paradigm for Jewish culture to be focused on piety and the betterment of the self in the service of God. With Jerusalem in ruins and no temple to frequent, the rabbinic movement took root in small discipleship circles in the Galilee region of northern Palestine. There, over the course of the next several centuries, the rabbis and their disciples studied the Torah fastidiously. They produced traditions of learned commentary to be encoded in the Mishnah and Talmud. And in their gradual rise to popular influence among the Jewish people in Palestine and abroad, the rabbinic sages saved their nation from the precipitous decline in morale that followed their ill-fated campaigns against Rome. Ever since, observant Jews of every philosophical disposition have held the writings of the rabbis in high esteem, second in sacred significance only to the Torah and the other books of the Hebrew Scriptures.

Given the circumstances of its origin, it is no surprise that one of the rabbinic movement's most prominent innovations was the preference of its proponents for peace. In general, the rabbinic sages focused on matters of ritual law to be practiced by the individual Jew and between Jewish parties. They devoted none of their many and voluminous treatises to matters of warfare (although cf. Kiel 2012). Chastened by their people's failures to banish the Romans from their land, the rabbis exhibited a distinct distaste for international conflict aptly expressed in the Talmudic maxim, "God does not rejoice in the downfall of the wicked" (cf. Exodus 14:26–28). Alluding to the fall of the Pharaoh's army at the Sea of Reeds, an event recounted in the biblical book of Exodus as a great triumph for Israel, this saying tempers the jubilation of Moses and his cohort with a sobering reminder that the Egyptians, too, were God's children. The sages preferred to imagine that God prefers to give the wicked their due in the world to come than to punish them on earth. This cautious attitude marks a major shift from that of a past when their ancestors deemed war on behalf of God as a legitimate option for pursuing the greater good of Israel (Goldenberg 1998, 81–98). Recent history had shown otherwise; the rabbis adjusted their beliefs accordingly.

So deeply ingrained was the principle of pacifism in the rabbinic imagination that subsequent generations of sages actually wrote it into the founding of their discipline. A well-known legend originating in third- or fourth-century Palestine describes how one of the rabbinic movement's founders, Rabbi Yoḥanan ben Zakkai, found himself trapped within the walls of Jerusalem during its besiegement by the Romans during the first Jewish revolt. Offered terms of peace by the Roman general Vespasian, Rabbi Yoḥanan pleaded with the Jewish rebels to surrender, thereby sparing the temple and the city. But the rebels refused. The intrepid rabbi thus devised a plan to escape the siege and personally appeal to the mercy of Vespasian. However, upon reaching the Roman camp, the rabbi asked the general only that he and his disciples be afforded a place to pray, to study the Torah, and to abide by God's commandments. Vespasian agreed to this request, issuing an official charter for the emerging rabbinic movement even as Jerusalem burned under Roman fire (*Avot de-Rabbi Natan* [A] 4; see Goldin 1955, 35–37, and cf. *Avot de-Rabbi Natan* [B] 6, Babylonian Talmud *Gittin* 56a–b, Lamentations Rabbah 1.31, and Midrash Proverbs 15).

The historicity of this story is subject to question. One must wonder, for instance, whether a Roman general would have entertained such a trivial request during the heat of battle, much less whether Rabbi Yoḥanan might better have pled on behalf of Jerusalem and her stubborn civic leadership. But these issues need not concern us here. This is a tale scripted long after the events it purports to relate. Its rhetoric belongs to an age when the Jews of Palestine, including the sages and their disciples, were thoroughly beholden to their Roman masters and far removed from the experience of war (Schofer 2005, 34–36). The author's portrait of Yoḥanan ben Zakkai serves to inscribe an ideology of pacifism upon the early history of the rabbinic movement, suggesting that the great sage, unlike other of his Jewish contemporaries, wished nothing more than to serve God in peaceful repose. God, the author suggests, had abandoned His holy city and His holy people, if only for the time being. Better, therefore, for Yoḥanan to have retreated from Jerusalem so as to preserve the Jewish tradition for future generations rather than to allow the senselessness of war to destroy his people entirely.

The Roman seizure of their last grasp of political independence would relieve the Jews of their militaristic ambitions for a long time to follow. For although many Jews continued eagerly to wait for Daniel's apocalyptic conflagration, the seemingly endless delay of its onset likewise hindered its Messianic promise of peace for the nation of Israel (Schiffman 2006). Subsequent transfers of Palestine to the Byzantines, the Persians, the Arabs, the Franks, and the Turks served to push the dream of a Jewish kingdom further into the reaches of fantasy. Throughout the Middle Ages, faithful Jews the world over monitored the international scene for signs of prophetic fulfillment, ever hopeful that the latest outbreak of hostilities among their Christian and Muslim neighbors would herald the advent of their divinely appointed sovereign (Idel 2003). In the meantime, they had recourse only to invoke the lessons of their ancient masters asserting that war was to be waged no longer by the Jewish people but by God alone.

Lacking the political clout to do otherwise, medieval Jews typically had no choice but to retreat to the rabbinic position when caught in the net of warfare.

A tragic example is the response of the Jewish communities of the German Rhineland when put to the sword by the Frankish crusaders in 1096. Rather than resist the marauding Christian armies, many Jews willingly gave up their lives in the manner of the ancient sages thought likewise to have submitted to the tortures of the Romans. Their survivors construed these acts of martyrdom as sanctification of the name of God, realizing an ideology of nonviolent resistance later to serve the Jewish people in countless other bouts of persecution targeting their communities (Chazan 1987, 85–136). Meanwhile, however, those Jews in Palestine who witnessed the crusaders rout their local Arab lords wondered whether the violent clashes unfolding before their eyes would serve to ready the city of Jerusalem for the arrival of their long-awaited Messiah (Prawer 1988, 6–7, 110, 222–223, 258–259). Clearly, the pursuit of peace signaled different approaches to Jewish constituencies experiencing war in different ways. Yet both their responses speak to a mentality locating the object of peace in the hand of God and, unfortunately, beyond the reach of the Jewish people.

Even in times of relative calm, medieval Jews were mindful of their powerlessness. The renowned twelfth-century Iberian philosopher Moses Maimonides was perhaps the most notable of his age to warn his fellow Jews against taking up arms against their gentile neighbors (Firestone 2012, 99–126). Considering the scriptural statutes urging violence against the enemies of Israel, Maimonides sought to dispel any notion that God's decrees extended to gentile nations of his own day. He emphasized, for instance, in his widely read commentaries on Jewish law that gentiles who subscribe to monotheistic ethical principles also held by Jews were not to be deemed idol worshippers according to the logic of the Torah. Consequently, he argued, Jews minded to carry out the Deuteronomic order to root out foreign cultic influences had no cause to cast any contemporary national or religious collective as potential corruptors of Israel. Maimonides thereby sought to disarm those overzealous Jews apt to begrudge their Christian and Muslim masters in the name of their own opposing theological viewpoints (*Mishneh Torah* 14.6.1, 4; see Hershman 1949, 220–221).

But despite his conciliatory impulses, it would be a mistake to characterize Maimonides' position as a coherent ideology of peace or peacemaking. He merely devised a scientific rationale for the tradition of reflexive pacifism that he had received from earlier rabbinic generations (Wilkes 2012). War, he aimed to show, was not God's will, at least not for the nation of Israel and not for the foreseeable future. This, in short, was the lot of the disempowered Jewish believer in Maimonides' day just as it had been for centuries past and just as it would remain for centuries to follow.

The State of Israel

In the year 1947, the international community sanctioned the formation of an independent Jewish state, the first in over 2000 years. Following the tragic losses incurred during the Holocaust, the humanitarian need for a Jewish homeland became clear enough to persuade the majority of voting members of the United Nations to adopt a resolution partitioning Palestine into two self-governing states, one Jewish and the other Arab. The ensuing declaration of the State of Israel initiated a series of armed confrontations between its Zionist founders and their regional neighbors over its geographical parameters and, to the minds of some, the very existence of a Jewish republic in a land home to a sizable Palestinian Arab population. These issues have remained matters of controversy to this day, eliciting intermittent violence between partisans in the Israeli and Palestinian camps as well as philosophical debates between their supporters and their detractors in the Middle East and throughout the world.

This is not the occasion to explore the many political and ideological disputes dividing the Israelis and the Palestinians, the latter of whom are still struggling to come to terms amongst themselves and with the international community over their own long-delayed bid for statehood. My objective, rather, is to discuss how the ongoing conflict has affected Jewish ideologies of peace and Jewish efforts at peacemaking. I shall therefore begin by briefly describing what each party to the conflict believes it justifiably needs in order to achieve peace in view of the contentious past circumstances that led to the current state of affairs (cf. Tessler 2009; Adwan *et al.* 2012).

The Palestinians, above all, need political independence. Their manipulation by other Arab states during the war of 1948 dashed the prospect of creating a state of their own to operate alongside and in cooperation with the State of Israel in their shared ancestral homeland. Another major offensive in the summer of 1967 resulted in the surrender by the Jordanians and the Egyptians of territories populated predominantly by Palestinian Arabs, namely the West Bank and the Gaza Strip. Following a final failed offensive in 1973, Jordan and Egypt resolved no longer to engage in combat against the Jewish state, ultimately agreeing to peace treaties with Israel in 1979 and 1994, respectively. Meanwhile, the Palestinian people who endured these battles were left in the disadvantaged position of political nonentities lacking a formal governmental apparatus whereby to negotiate their peace.

As a result of the Arab–Israeli wars, the Israelis came to occupy the Palestinian territories, which, though now relinquished by their former claimants, have not been assigned to Israel by international consensus. Though today governed by elected Palestinian officials, the Arab inhabitants of these areas would prefer that the Israelis vacate the territories entirely, thereby paving the way for their genuine political autonomy. The global Palestinian population also encompasses persons living outside of the territories whose ancestors were displaced from their homes during the wars. Many of these self-described refugees seek repatriation not only in the disputed territories but within the internationally recognized borders of the Jewish state. To the minds, therefore, of the Palestinians and their sympathizers, Israel's apparent refusal to address the aforesaid needs stand in the way of peace in the Middle East as well as peaceable relations between Jews and Arabs across the globe.

The Israelis tend to see the situation differently. Having won their independence in the war of 1948, Israel's Zionist leadership, they assert, earned the right to establish a Jewish state in their people's ancestral homeland. Successful efforts to protect their borders in 1967 and 1973 solidified their prerogative to hold their ground both strategically and ideologically. That their defensive maneuvers pushed some unwilling Arab populations out of the Jewish state while drawing others within its borders is certainly regrettable from a humanitarian perspective. Even so, they argue, Arab residents of the State of Israel are eligible for Israeli citizenship and, therefore, free to live as ethnic minorities with rights equal to the Jewish majority in a democratic state supporting their religious, cultural, and economic freedoms.

As for the situation in the Palestinian territories, it is an ethical quandary that many in Israel would rather not have to face. To be fair, some radical Jewish ideologues have passionately maintained their people's sovereign right to the entirety of the historic "Land of Israel" said in the Hebrew Scriptures to been promised by God (Firestone 2012, 221–318). But the current military positions in and around the lands gained in 1967 speak more to the commitment of Israel's government to protect its citizens, both Jewish and Arab, from the radical religious ideologies still tragically troubling the discontented Arab populations of the territories. For even as some Palestinian factions have rejected terrorism in favor of diplomatic relations with Israel, others have refused such overtures. Consequently, to the minds of Israel's domestic policymakers and their international allies, restricting the nationalistic ambitions of the Palestinians is the only way to maintain Israel's security, if only ideally for the time being. To their minds, successful negotiations for the future of the Palestinian people must proceed on preconditions of peaceful coexistence mutually agreeable to all who stand to benefit from these efforts.

Figure 3.1 The Western Wall and the Dome of the Rock in Jerusalem. Source: © stellalevi / iStockphoto

Since my primary concern in this essay is to discuss Jewish ideologies of peace, I shall now explain how those I've already described have been brought to bear upon the current political impasse. As we have seen, Jewish statehood was not a tenable reality during Judaism's formative age. It was, at best, a goal for a far off future when God would intervene in human affairs. But that Messianic ideal was not among the chief driving forces of the Zionist cause prior to 1947. To the minds of its leading proponents, the advantage of statehood was to afford those Jews persecuted in other countries a national homeland tied to the Jewish past and a corresponding political apparatus with which to defend their nation when necessary.

The Zionists, in other words, operated not in the realm of theology but in that of *realpolitik* (Firestone 2012, 141–142; Batnitzky 2011, 147–162). That their proposed state would be a constitutional democracy rather than the divinely ordained kingdom of their people's Messianic imagination was immaterial to their agenda. A national home promised better conditions in which to live and worship irrespective of whether or how their plans stood to impact God's plans for a hypothetical apocalyptic future (Firestone 2012, 163–178). Once, therefore, the foundations of the modern State of Israel were in place, Jews there and abroad had to confront the task of reconciling the ends of political Judaism with its means. On the one hand, they assumed that the Jewish state should be governed by traditional principles of Jewish ethics. On the other, they realized that those principles were conceived without due regard for the needs of non-Jewish parties within their state and its regional compass.

But as we have seen, the rabbinic sages and their medieval successors whose teachings inform contemporary Jewish thought had counseled peace from positions of utter powerlessness. As for the Hebrew Scriptures, the ethnic prejudices of Israel's most ancient age seemed entirely out of step with the modern reality of as state accountable not to God but to the international community. Their classical sources thus offered scant precedent on which to plot a new moral course for a global Jewish population beholden by their treasured bonds of nationhood to the political movements of the State of Israel.

Pursuing Peace

To the conscientious Jewish activist, the objective of peacemaking must account both for theology and political reality. To privilege peace for Israel over peace for Palestine is to betray a basic tenet of the scriptural ideal of *shalom*, namely its promise of peace for all Jews. To privilege peace for Palestine over peace for Israel is to betray another, its promise of peace for all nations and all of God's creation. One must therefore consider the perspectives of Israeli and Palestinian, Jew and Arab, Christian and Muslim. One must acknowledge, in other words, the rights and needs of everyone who stands to benefit from harmonious intergroup relations within the transnational and multicultural society whose diverse constituencies are invested in the territorial disputes in Israel and Palestine (Gopin 2003).

But how can one solve a seemingly intractable conflict of interests? To many Jews, asking God for assistance remains a feasible option. Songs of praise invoking the ancient prophetic calls for *shalom* are to be found throughout the traditional Hebrew liturgies recited by members of all contemporary Jewish denominations. These classical prayers affirm the traditional Jewish belief in divine providence, that God serves the needs of all His creations in due measure and in due time (Reif 2010). God, accordingly, should be able to create peace where human beings have found discord, imparting *shalom* from on high per the eschatological hopes of past Jewish generations.

But while prayer might have sufficed in an age when the Jewish people had neither cause nor recourse to pursue peace through positive action, this is not the case today. Both in Israel and in the Jewish Diaspora, Jews possess the right to voice their desires for positive social change in their own countries and across the globe. As a result, many have devised proactive agendas for peacemaking and reconciliation attuned less to the prospect of divine aid than to confronting the mundane challenges to their respective ideas of social justice.

Here is where the classical Jewish concept of *tikkun olam* is advantageous to the contemporary interpreter. As previously noted, the traditional Jewish notion of 'restoring the world' generally functions in contemporary Jewish discourse as an order for social justice. Since the world of the modern Jew encompasses more than only the Jewish people, the task of *tikkun olam* has lent itself to missions of charity, humanitarian aid, and active efforts at peacemaking in the world at large. It is not without reason, therefore, that Jewish activists attuned to the ongoing conflict between the Israelis and the Palestinians often seek to justify their efforts on the theological ground of *tikkun olam*. Indeed, peace in the Middle East would benefit not only the Jews but all peoples of the world prone to partake of it.

Of course, the pliable nature of the concept lends the peacemaking aspect of *tikkun olam* to a range of interpretations. The Anti-Defamation League (ADL), an arm of the international Jewish service organization B'nai B'rith, understands *tikkun olam* as a commission to combat bigotry against Jews and all persons subjected to hatred, whether in the United States, in Israel, or elsewhere. Striving for objectivity, the ADL deems all expressions of prejudice equally objectionable regardless of context. Another well-known vehicle of *tikkun olam* is the magazine *Tikkun*. Founded and edited by activist rabbi Michael Lerner, this journal features contributions by socially progressive commentators on Judaism, Israeli politics, and other subjects calculated to critique prevailing attitudes toward peace and social justice in our global society. As active voices of Jewish social conscience, both of these agencies legitimately strive for *tikkun olam*, albeit with different aims and to significantly different effects.

The objectives of the aforesaid agencies arguably are more reserved than those of organizations resolved to affect peace by influencing the policy decisions of the

State of Israel and her international allies. To that end, both of the major American Jewish lobbying organizations assert their objectifications of *tikkun olam* as guiding principles in their efforts. Yet one, the American Israel Public Affairs Committee (AIPAC), aligns itself with the more conservative camp of Israeli domestic politics, while the other, J Street, aligns itself with the more liberal camp. Where AIPAC, therefore, tends to prioritize Israel's domestic security in negotiation with the Palestinians, J Street tends to promote diplomatic negotiation as a necessary prerequisite for Israel's security. Clearly, the common pursuit of peace professed by these agencies lends itself to disparate peacemaking agendas.

Other Jewish-sponsored nongovernmental organizations prioritizing peace exhibit more overtly conciliatory agendas. A few examples will suffice to illustrate. In Israel, Peace Now (Hebrew: *Shalom Akhshav*) is a prominent advocacy group urging the state's immediate concession to the Palestinians' most urgent need for political independence. Among its more visible efforts is its advocacy for Israeli citizens identifying as conscientious objectors wishing to forgo their compulsory military service or, alternatively, refusing to serve in or at the borders of the Palestinian territories. Similar organizations operating in the Jewish Diaspora include Jewish Voice for Peace in the United States and the members of the continental consortium European Jews for a Just Peace. The Jewish Peace Fellowship, a group dedicated to pacifism on all fronts, cites Judaism's heritage of nonviolence in decrying any and all military efforts in the names of the Jewish state and Jews the world over.

Figure 3.2   A Peace Now demonstration in Israel. Source © jcarillet / iStockphoto

To their critics within the Jewish community, these liberal advocacy groups often seem to prioritize Judaism's ethical obligations to the Palestinians over Israel's obligations to her citizens. In contrast, the progressive American Zionist group Ameinu tends to favor a more balanced agenda, stressing the needs of both the Israelis and the Palestinians in its call for a negotiated peace. Other American Jewish agencies espousing similarly centrist views include the charitable American Jewish Committee and the Jewish Federations of North America. Yet despite their philosophical differences with the more left-wing organizations cited above, each applies the same healing principle of *tikkun olam*, envisioning its namesake "world" to extend well beyond the boundaries of the Jewish community.

Finally, I would be remiss not to acknowledge the many and worthy grassroots efforts in Israel and the Palestinian territories to forge pathways to peace through simple cooperation (Chaitin 2011). Arguably the most notable effort to this effect is Neve Shalom (Arabic: *Wāhat al-Salām*), or "Oasis of Peace," a cooperative settlement in Israel's Ayalon Valley region. (Feuerverger 2001). Founded in 1969, the village's charter calls for half of its population at any given time to be half Israeli Jews and half Palestinian Arabs of either Muslim or Christian persuasion. Though relatively few in number, the residents of Neve Shalom exemplify the principle of *tikkun olam* on a daily basis, living together in a community serving the diverse needs of all its inhabitants. The children of Neve Shalom learn in Hebrew and Arabic, engaging their own cultures and the cultures of their neighbors. Each of the village's constituencies worships in their nondenominational house of prayer, Muslims on Friday, Jews on Saturday, and Christians on Sunday. While Neve Shalom's model of harmonious coexistence might not offer a practical solution for all in its contested land, its ongoing success serves as a vital reminder that Judaism can succeed in the State of Israel without its adherents having to compromise their people's timeless pursuit of a better world.

Conclusions and Future Prospects

The classical traditions informing the theology of modern Judaism are diverse enough to support multiple agendas for contemporary peacemaking. Although tempered by the harsh realities of human conflict, the ideologies of peace embodied in the concepts of *shalom* and *tikkun olam* serve much the same needs of spiritual fulfillment as they have since their respective inceptions centuries ago. Yet where the authors of these terms typically imagined peace as an object beyond human reach, the foresight of the Israelite visionaries who dared to look beyond their present realities has yielded dividends in the contemporary Jewish pursuit of peace as a moral imperative for our own day.

As we have seen, contemporary Jewish visions of peace incur both Judaism's religious qualities and its national qualities. The current worldwide Jewish preoccupation with the ethical governance of the State of Israel speaks to this basic duality of Judaism's ethnic constitution. Regrettably, the invention of Jewish political theology demanded by the Zionist project also has served to complicate the common Jewish agenda for peace now and for the foreseeable future. One can only hope that the conciliatory efforts continually being made in the name of Judaism's multiple objects of *shalom* will provide the agents of Israel's ultimate peace with the moral guidance they will need to see their restorative project to its completion.

Questions for Discussion

1. What does the Hebrew word *shalom* mean? How did the circumstances of Israel's early history affect its range of meaning? How does the biblical language of *shalom* and its ideologies of peace compare to your preconceptions of what "peace" entails?
2. Do the Hebrew Scriptures articulate a coherent stance on the relative values of war and peace? How would you reconcile the Torah's legislation on just warfare with its expressions of hope for peaceful relations between Israel and the nations?
3. What events prompted the rabbinic sages to retreat from the insurgent ways of their Jewish predecessors? How do you think the reality of their political subjugation helped to condition their attitudes toward peace and nonviolence?
4. What is the meaning of *tikkun olam*? How and to what effect did the modernization of Jewish social consciousness serve to expand the traditional meaning of this moral principle?
5. What were the challenges to peaceful living that faced the Jewish people in the years leading up to the creation of the modern State of Israel? What kind of challenges has this development posed to traditional Jewish ethical discourse as it relates to the pursuit of peace?
6. What are some of the key Jewish needs at stake in the Israel–Palestine conflict? How do these needs compare to those of the Palestinians? Do you consider the needs of both parties to the dispute compatible with one another? What do you think must change in either or both of their approaches to peacemaking for reconciliation to occur?

References

Adwan, Sami, Dan Bar-On, Eyal Naveh, and PRIME (eds). 2012. *Side by Side: Parallel Histories of Israel-Palestine*. New York: New Press.

Batnitzky, Leora. 2011. *How Judaism Became a Religion: An Introduction to Modern Jewish Thought*. Princeton, NJ: Princeton University Press.

Buber, Martin. 1948. *Israel and the World: Essays in a Time of Crisis*. New York: Schocken.

Carr, David M. 2010. *An Introduction to the Old Testament*. Malden, MA: Wiley-Blackwell.

Chaitin, Julia. 2011. *Peace-building in Israel and Palestine: Social Psychology and Grassroots Initiatives*. New York: Palgrave Macmillan.

Chazan, Robert. 1987. *European Jewry and the First Crusade*. Berkeley, CA: University of California Press.

Cohen, Shaye J. D. 2014. *From the Maccabees to the Mishnah*, 3rd ed. Louisville, KY: Westminster John Knox.

Collins, John J. 2003. "The Zeal of Phineas: The Bible and the Legitimation of Violence." *Journal of Biblical Literature* 122: 3–21.

Feuerverger, Grace. 2001. *Oasis of Dreams: Teaching and Learning Peace in a Jewish-Palestinian Village in Israel*. New York: Routledge.

Firestone, Reuven. 2012. *Holy War in Judaism: The Fall and Rise of a Controversial Idea*. Oxford: Oxford University Press.

Goldenberg, Robert. 1998. *The Nations That Know Thee Not: Ancient Jewish Attitudes toward Other Religions*. New York: New York University Press.

Goldin, Judah. 1955. *The Fathers According to Rabbi Nathan*. New Haven, CT: Yale University Press.

Gopin, Marc. 2003. "Judaism and Peacebuilding in the Context of Middle Eastern Conflict." In *Faith-Based Diplomacy: Trumping Realpolitik*. Edited by Douglas Johnson, 91–123. Oxford: Oxford University Press.

Hershman, Abraham M. 1949. *The Code of Maimonides, Book Fourteen: The Book of Judges*. New Haven, CT: Yale University Press.

Heschel, Abraham Joshua. 1955. *God in Search of Man: A Philosophy of Judaism*. New York: Farrar, Straus & Cudahy.

Idel, Moshe. 2003. "Jewish Apocalypticism, 670–1670." In *The Continuum History of Apocalypticism*. Edited by Bernard J. McGinn, John J. Collins, and Stephen J. Stein, 344–379. New York: Continuum.

Kiel, Yishai. 2012. "The Morality of War in Rabbinic Literature: The Call for Peace and the Limitation of the Siege." In *War and Peace in Jewish Tradition: From the Biblical World to the Present*. Edited by Yigal Levin and Amnon Shapira, 116–138. London: Routledge.

Niditch, Susan. 1993. *War in the Hebrew Bible: A Study in the Ethics of Violence*. Oxford: Oxford University Press.

Nongbri, Brent. 2013. *Before Religion: A History of a Modern Concept*. New Haven, CT: Yale University Press.

Prawer, Joshua. 1988. *The History of the Jews in the Latin Kingdom of Jerusalem*. Oxford: Clarendon Press.

Rosenthal, Gilbert S. 2005. "*Tikkun ha-Olam*: The Metamorphosis of a Concept." *Journal of Religion* 85: 214–240.

Reif, Stefan C. 2010. "Peace in Early Jewish Prayer." In *Deuterocanonical and Cognate Literature Yearbook 2010: Visions of Peace and Tales of War*. Edited by Jan Liesen and Pancratius C. Beentjes, 377–399. Berlin: Walter de Gruyter.

Satlow, Michael L. 2006. *Creating Judaism: History, Tradition, Practice*. New York: Columbia University Press.

Schiffman, Lawrence H. 2006. "Messianism and Apocalypticism in Rabbinic Texts." In *The Cambridge History of Judaism, Vol. 4: The Late Roman-Rabbinic Period*. Edited by Steven T. Katz, 1053–1072. Cambridge: Cambridge University Press.

Schofer, Jonathan Wyn. 2005. *The Making of a Sage: A Study in Rabbinic Ethics*. Madison, WI: University of Wisconsin Press.

Shavit, Yaacov, and Mordechai Eran. 2007. *The Hebrew Bible Reborn: From Holy Scripture to the Book of Books. A History of Biblical Culture and the Battles over the Bible in Modern Judaism*, translated by Chaya Naor. Berlin: Walter de Gruyter.

Talmon, Shemaryahu. 1997. "The Signification of *shalom* and Its Semantic Field in the Hebrew Bible." In *The Quest for Context and Meaning: Studies in Biblical Intertextuality in Honor of James A. Sanders.* Edited by Craig A. Evans and Shemaryahu Talmon, 75–115. Leiden: E. J. Brill.

Tessler, Mark. 2009. *A History of the Israel-Palestinian Conflict.* 2nd edition. Bloomington, IN: Indiana University Press.

Wilkes, George R. 2012. "Religious War in the Works of Maimonides: An Idea and Its Transit across the Medieval Mediterranean." In *Just Wars, Holy Wars, and Jihads: Christian, Jewish, and Muslim Encounters and Exchanges.* Edited by Sohail H. Hashmi, 146–164. Oxford: Oxford University Press.

Further Reading

Broyde, Michael J. 1996. "Fighting the War and the Peace: Battlefield Ethics, Peace Talks, Treaties, and Pacifism in the Jewish Tradition." In *War and Its Discontents: Pacifism and Quietism in the Abrahamic Traditions.* Edited by J. Patout Burns, 1–30. Washington, DC: Georgetown University Press. Surveys classical Jewish sources on war and wartime ethics.

Eisen, Robert. 2011. *The Peace and Violence of Judaism: From the Bible to Modern Zionism.* Oxford: Oxford University Press. Presents an evenhanded overview of Jewish ideologies of peace and violence and their practical ramifications upon the Jewish experience in history.

Firestone, Reuven. 2004. "Judaism on Violence and Reconciliation: An Examination of Key Sources." In *Beyond Violence: Religious Sources of Social Transformation in Judaism, Christianity, and Islam.* Edited by James L. Heft, 74–87. New York: Fordham University Press. A short introduction to the subjects of violence and peacemaking in classical Jewish sources.

Gopin, Marc. 2002. *Holy War, Holy Peace: How Religion Can Bring Peace to the Middle East.* Oxford: Oxford University Press. Outlines approaches to mediating Israeli–Palestinian conflict in view of the Jewish and Muslim religious traditions.

Landau, Yehezkel. 2009. "The Religious Dimension of Israeli-Palestinian Peacemaking." In *Resolving the Israeli-Palestinian Conflict: Perspectives on the Peace Process.* Edited by Moises F. Salinas and Hazza Abu Rabi, 263–285. Amherst, NY: Cambria Press. Relates the author's experiences addressing the religious sensitivities of Jews and Muslims in reference to the Israeli–Palestinian conflict.

Lerner, Michael. 2012. *Embracing Israel/Palestine: A Strategy to Heal and Transform the Middle East.* Berkeley, CA: North Atlantic Books. Offers a contemporary, socially progressive Jewish theological argument for peaceful resolution of the Israeli–Palestinian conflict.

Milgrom, Jeremy. 1998. "'Let Your Love for Me Vanquish Your Hatred for Him': Nonviolence in Modern Judaism." In *Subverting Hatred: The Challenge of Nonviolence in Religious Traditions.* Edited by Daniel L. Smith-Christopher, 115–139. Maryknoll, NY: Orbis Books. Presents a brief introduction to classical Jewish sources on peacemaking and nonviolence.

Walzer, Michael. 1998. "War and Peace in the Jewish Tradition." In *The Ethics of War and Peace: Religious and Secular Perspectives*. Edited by Terry Nardin, 95–114. Princeton, NJ: Princeton University Press. An overview of classical Jewish sources on war and peace emphasizing the philosophical dimensions of their respective religious values.

Zakheim, Dov S. 2007. "Models of Reconciliation and Coexistence in Jewish Sources." In *War and Peace in the Jewish Tradition*. Edited by Lawrence H. Schiffman and Joel B. Wolowelsky, 497–531. New York: Yeshiva University Press. Presents classical Jewish sources useful in the promotion of peace and peaceful coexistence between Jews and other peoples.

Glossary

Diaspora: The term diaspora, Greek for dispersion, refers to the settlement of a people outside the region of their ethnic origin. The Jewish Diaspora began in 597 B.C.E. with the Babylonian conquest of the Kingdom of Judah, when many of its former subjects were deported to Mesopotamia or otherwise compelled to flee their ancestral homeland. Although the former territory of Judah was rehabilitated for Jewish settlement within 60 years of its conquest, the diaspora communities founded in the interim flourished in their new environments. Even today, as through the greater part of their history, diaspora Jews outnumber Jews in the State of Israel.

Israel: In its ancient context, Israel refers to a historical nation originating in the Levantine region of the Middle East during the second millennium B.C.E. The Jewish people trace their beliefs and their lineage to ancient Israel during the era when Jerusalem was its seat of governance and center of worship. In its modern context, Israel also refers to the modern Jewish commonwealth founded in 1947, also known as the State of Israel. Its citizens are known as Israelis regardless of their religious or ethnic backgrounds.

Jerusalem: Jerusalem was the capitol and cultic center of the original Kingdom of Israel and its local successors, the Kingdom of Judah and the province of Judea. A site of religious significance to Jews, Christians, and Muslims, it has seen centuries of nearly continual conflict as various political powers and religious constituencies struggled for its control. Today, Jerusalem is the administrative capital of the State of Israel and home to large Jewish and Arab populations. Many Palestinian nationalists assert the need to make Jerusalem the capital of their proposed state as well. As a result, the city's future political landscape remains uncertain.

Judea: Judea was the name of a Babylonian imperial province succeeding the Kingdom of Judah upon its conquest in 597 B.C.E. It was likely then when its former residents began to identify as Jews (Hebrew: *yehudim*) in addition to their ancestral ethnic designation Israel. The territory's name endured its transfer to Persian rule, then to Greek rule, briefly back to Jewish rule, and, finally, to Roman rule. Judea was erased from Rome's political map in 135 C.E., when it was officially renamed Syria-Palestine as a punitive measure in response to a failed but costly Jewish rebellion led by Simon bar Kosiba.

Palestine: Palestine is a historical name for the region today comprising the State of Israel, the Palestinian territories, and lands in adjacent countries. It originally referred to the Philistines, a Greek people who colonized the south-eastern Mediterranean coast during the twelfth century B.C.E. The archaic name was revived in 135 C.E. as Syria-Palestine, a decision meant to defeat the nationalistic ambitions of the Jews following the second of two costly revolts against Rome. Palestine or, in Arabic, Filastin, remained the common designation for the region until the declaration of the State of Israel in 1947. Indigenous Arabs displaced during the ensuing wars of Israeli independence have maintained the name Palestine as an alternative mode of geographical reference, an object of ethnic identification, and part of a cultural legacy worthy of their own designs for political independence.

Rabbi: Rabbi is a Hebrew word meaning "my teacher." It originated in ancient Judea as an honorific title for learned individuals or sages. Following the disastrous Jewish revolt against Rome of 66–70 C.E., an ideological movement emerged in Judea under the ordinance of self-professed rabbis emphasizing study of the Torah as the key to winning God's favor. Over the next several centuries, the rabbinic movement would gradually win popular influence to become the predominant model of Jewish practice and belief. In view of its ancient legacy, rabbi remains the preferred clerical title for Jewish religious leaders of all denominations.

***Shalom*:** *Shalom* is a Hebrew word meaning "completeness" or "wholeness" but conventionally translated as "peace." It also serves as a traditional Jewish salutation equivalent to "hello" and "goodbye." Classical Jewish texts use *shalom* for a variety of purposes including, but no limited to, the desire for peaceful relationships between individuals and nations. Today, the term is often invoked as a Jewish ethical ideal and a theological imperative for peacemaking.

***Tikkun Olam*:** *Tikkun olam* is a Hebrew term meaning "restoration of the world." Rooted in the language of medieval Jewish mysticism, it is typically understood today as an agenda for Jewish peacemaking through constructive action. The contemporary ideology of *tikkun olam* assumes the responsibility of the socially conscientious Jew to restore the world to the state of wholeness embodied in the principle of *shalom*.

Zionism: The term Zionism refers to an ideology of Jewish nationalism conceived during the nineteenth century in reference to the efforts of Jewish and non-Jewish individuals to establish a Jewish political state in Palestine. The name alludes to Mount Zion, a location in Jerusalem that has served as a poetic metonym for the city since ancient times. Although the Zionists achieved their immediate goal in 1947 with the birth of the modern State of Israel, their success served to alienate many Palestinian Arabs living within its border who did not wish to be Israeli citizens. Even, therefore, as it remains a symbol of national pride for many Jews throughout the world, the term Zionism has since become a derisive byword among its critics for perceived social injustices on the part of the Israeli government.

3.1

A Christian Response

Michael K. Duffey

Joshua Burns has explained very well the evolving understanding of war, peace, and nonviolence in the Jewish tradition. He began with the rich meaning of *shalom*. He places war making, peacemaking, and nonviolent resistance in their particular historical contexts: the Israelites' wars to gain the "promised land"; then their awareness of God's preference for negotiating for peace; and the embrace of pacifism by some Jews when more powerful nations conquered them. The prophet Isaiah exhorted the Jews to "study war no more." The rabbis did too. During the Crusades many Jews suffered martyrdom when they offered only nonviolent resistance. This is the first time in 2600 years that as a people they have realized the goal of having state power.

But we should return to the imperative of *tikkun olam*, "repair of the world," that the early rabbis urged. This was and is the hinge on which the Jewish commitment to working for peace and justice turns. Its original meaning as Burns explains was the command to repair broken relationships among Jewish kinfolk. But *tikkun olam* was gradually expanded to embrace the relationship between Jews and non-Jews. The Covenant God made with the Israelites was not exclusive: "others" and "outsiders," were not to be regarded so.

Judaism is today deeply divided regarding Israel and the Palestinian people. Burns reflects on the complexity and moral ambiguity of the Israel–Palestine conflict. He empathizes with the stateless Palestinians and urges Israel to work to "repair" Arab–Jewish relations. For more than half a century the world that Jews and Palestinians are destined to share has been a world of suffering and death, mostly for Palestinians.

One is grateful for the peace activism of Jewish organizations such as Peace Now that work for a negotiated peace. But a dark cloud hangs over Israel, a cloud of paralyzing fear. Such a fear eclipses realistic hopes for peace that can only happen if the Palestinian people are liberated from oppression and occupation. As long as fear paralyzes the spirits and psyches of Israelis there will be no peace. As long as

Peacemaking and the Challenge of Violence in World Religions, First Edition.
Edited by Irfan A. Omar and Michael K. Duffey.
© 2015 John Wiley & Sons, Ltd. Published 2015 by John Wiley & Sons, Ltd.

Palestinians do not have land and sovereignty there will be no peace. Repair of the world must take concrete forms: land for peace and defense of Palestinian human rights. Israel's concrete peace initiative is not a matter of *giving up* land but of *giving back* land that belongs to the Palestinians as recognized by the international community. Michael Lerner, a Jewish American peace activist, calls for:

> a new form of discourse [recognizing that] we are presented with two peoples who are equally entitled and equally in error. With that foundation in place, we will be able to move to the next stage, requiring the Jewish people to recognize that it is our responsibility to take the most decisive step to rectify the current situation, not because we are more wrong but because we are more powerful. (Lerner 2000, 27)

The prophet Isaiah continues to speak to all the "peoples of the book." Certainly it is applicable to how Christians behave in the world, being righteous doers of justice or doomed for their injustices. But Isaiah's vision is timely today as Israel considers the urgency of peace. Isaiah speaks Yahweh's demand to Jerusalemites:

> Seek justice and rescue the oppressed, defend the orphan, plead for the widow. ... Afterward you shall be called the city of righteousness, the faithful city. Zion shall be redeemed by justice, and those in her who repent, by righteousness. (Isaiah 1:15–17; 26–27)

To recognize and choose inclusiveness and to live justly are central elements of peacemaking within contemporary Judaism.

Reference

Lerner, Michael. 2000. "Current debate." *Tikkun* 15, 4.

3.2

A Native American Response

Tink Tinker

Joshua Ezra Burns has written a very engaging account of Judaism, tracing its roots from ancient israelite traditions. Since I spent considerable energies a half century ago trying to learn a little of the biblical hebrew language, reading Burns' text took me back to my own academic roots in no small measure.

The jewish emphasis on *shalom* as the key ingredient in spiritual existence is something that must necessarily touch every American Indian heart. My insistence that notions of balance and harmony are foundational for any American Indian cultural expression resonates with *shalom* in interesting ways. There is something else, however, in the jewish traditions as Burns outlines them that raises questions for any traditional American Indian, and perhaps my critique is endemic in the nature of any corporate expression that might merit the category appellation "world religion." Namely, it cannot, it seems, be escaped that these religious traditions called world religions change repeatedly through time. In the case of Judaism, Burns describes a dramatic shift, due to changing historical contexts, from an emergent ancient israelite ideology of a God who guides the people into repeated conquests that eventuate in the conquest of the lands held by the canaanite peoples,[1] situated generally where the modern state of Israel locates itself today. He then traces israelite and jewish trajectories of history through periods of conquest of Israel and then Judea that result in less aggressive and even pacifist periods of jewish religious theologies. Today, following the tragedy of the nazi holocaust perpetrated against jewish peoples in Europe, Burns notes the renewed theological investment in secular jewish notions of conquest related to the formation of the state of Israel in a territory wrested from palestinian peoples. If I might be allowed a simplistic mapping of these historical sequences, it seems the trajectory runs from historical periods of political/military ascendency to periods of historical change due to conquest and subjection, and back again to a position of some ascendency; each turn accompanied by somewhat predictable shifts in theological thinking.

Peacemaking and the Challenge of Violence in World Religions, First Edition.
Edited by Irfan A. Omar and Michael K. Duffey.
© 2015 John Wiley & Sons, Ltd. Published 2015 by John Wiley & Sons, Ltd.

American Indian folk play things out quite differently, and the german "conceptual" historian, Reinhart Kosselleck, might be useful in spelling out the difference. Historical change in the world of the Middle East and Europe has tended to be much more global than shifts on the North American continent. There were no sweeping campaigns of conquest in north America (and we could argue the same for south America, although euro-christian interpretations of the Aztecs, Inca, and Maya make that a more complex project). Sure, peoples moved from one territory to another at times, but there are no stories of conquest, per se. Indeed, what we know about inter-community conflicts is that there was very little in the way of killing or bloodshed – despite christian colonialist tales of such.

On the one hand, modern folk tend to forget history and to presume that their "present" (Kosselleck) is the only reality; while at the same time, these same folk have become so accustomed to the constant flow of change in their world that they are nearly inured to change as the normal condition of their present. When *will* the newest iPhone be released? I recall one of my sons seeing his first "rotary dial" telephone a few years back and not knowing at all how to use it. Yet for traditional indigenous folk, for what Kosselleck helpfully calls nonmodern societies (rather than temporally constructed as "pre" modern), a slow rate of change allows for the passing on of expectations of the future more consistently from one "present" (or from one generation) to the next. This does not mean that no change occurred in these nonmodern societies, but rather that change occurred, Kosselleck argues, "slowly and in such a long-term fashion that the rent between the previous experience and an expectation to be newly discovered did not undermine the traditional world."[2] For American Indians, part of this slow rate of change is a direct result of our cultural investment in ideals of balance and harmony and the constant need (from daily to yearly need) to mitigate violence in all of its forms.

We should not assume, then, that all is well in Native America. Under the military imperialism of euro-christian colonialism, european modernity became a sudden eruption – as a total disruption – among each colonized indigenous peoples of the world. Indeed we American Indians are today suffering all the rough edges of progress, change, colonialism, and conquest, particularly missionary conquest. We have been dragged into modernity and its Westphalian-state hegemonic demonry, dragged into notions of progress and constant change, against our will. The toll of missionary pressure on Indian people is huge, measured in the US government–christian collusion evidenced in social engineering projects like the intentional destruction of Indian languages (the original english-only movement); imposing fee-simple private ownership of property; negating Indian self-governance and imposing US citizenship; the coerced conversion to Christianity; and particularly in the removal of children from their families to contexts of incarceration called boarding schools.[3] The community-wide incidence of post-traumatic stress disorder in every Indian community today is a direct result of genocidal practices such as these resulting in poverty, self-destruction, low self-esteem, and a host of self-defeating behaviors. As a result, we have, as Memmi so aptly describes it, internalized our own colonialism to the point where we believe too much of what the colonizer taught us in those schools (Memmi 1991). Too many Indian young men and women are dressed in american uniforms, handling american weapons, killing the identified enemies of the US government, and counting them as their own enemies. And because they have some residual memory of the wrongness of what they are doing, they come home even more unbalanced than most other military returnees. It seems that they no longer (except for a few) remember where to turn for that ancient traditional ceremony that promotes healing after a conflictual military engagement with a neighboring people.

Notes

1   It should not go without notice that the earliest english invaders of this continent used the ensuing metaphor of "promised land" to speak of themselves and their own mission of conquest. The pilgrim and then puritan invasion used the metaphor explicitly; Church of England preachers early in the Jamestown years used the metaphor as well to exonerate their own adventure of land theft. Since the puritan experience continues to fuel the emerican narrative, the metaphor finds continued use even in our own time. See Taylor Saito (2010).
2   See Kosselleck (1985). I was initially pointed to Kosselleck by reading Scott (2004).
3   See Churchill (2004), especially my preface to that volume: "Tracing a Contour of Colonialism: American Indians and the Trajectory of Educational Imperialism," pp. xiii–xli. Also note Prucha (1973).

References

Churchill, Ward. 2004. *Kill the Indian, Save the Man: The Genocidal Impact of American Indian Residential Schools.* San Francisco, CA: City Lights Press.
Kosselleck, Reinhart. 1985. *Futures Past: On the Semantics of Historical Time.* Translated by Keith Tribe. Cambridge, MA: MIT Press.
Memmi, Albert. 1991. *Colonizer and Colonized.* Boston, MA: Beacon Press.
Prucha, Francis Paul, ed. 1973. *Americanizing the American Indian: Writings by the "Friends of the Indian" 1880–1900.* Lincoln, NE: University of Nebraska.
Scott, David. 2004. *Conscripts of Modernity: The Tragedy of Colonial Enlightenment.* Durham, NC: Duke University Press.
Taylor Saito, Natsu. 2010. "City on a Hill: America as Exception." In *Meeting the Enemy: American Exceptionalism and International Law.* 54–75. New York: New York University Press.

4

From Sincerity of Thought to Peace "All Under Heaven"(*Tianxia* 天下)

The Confucian Stance on Peace and Violence

Sin Yee Chan

Confucianism's Religious Texts

The Analects: A collection of the sayings and anecdotes of Confucius, his disciples, and contemporaries.

The Mencius: A collection of the sayings and anecdotes of Mencius. It probably was compiled during the Warring States Period.

Zhongyong (Doctrine of the Mean): An essay concerning how to achieve moral cultivation through adhering to the centrality and the harmony of the Way of Heaven and preserving one's innate moral nature.

Daxue (The Book of Great Learning): An essay including a text and commentaries on the passages in the text. It focuses on the process and the aim of moral cultivation and delineates the relationships between individuals and the social and the political world. The author is unknown and the essay was probably composed in the third century B.C.E.

The Xunzi: A collection of essays attributed to Xunzi written during the Warring States Period, though some passages of the essays were believed to be antecedent to Xunzi.

Liji (The Book of Rites): A collection of discussions on rituals drawn from materials written between the Warring States Period and Early Han Dynasty (206 B.C.E. – 220 C.E.). Authors are unknown.

Xiao Jing (The Classic of Filial Piety): A short book expounding the meaning and the prescribed behaviors of filial piety. The book was probably written in the second or third century B.C.E.

Peacemaking and the Challenge of Violence in World Religions, First Edition.
Edited by Irfan A. Omar and Michael K. Duffey.
© 2015 John Wiley & Sons, Ltd. Published 2015 by John Wiley & Sons, Ltd.

Introduction to Confucianism

Confucianism had been the state orthodoxy of China starting in 136 B.C.E. (during the early Han dynasty) until the overthrow of the Qing dynasty in 1911. Its influence has also spread widely throughout Asia. It reached Korea first during the Three Kingdom period (220–280 C.E.), and spread from Korea to Japan around 285 C.E. and then to other regions. It arrived lastly in Vietnam in 1070. However, since the middle of the nineteenth century, its influence in China has gradually declined as many conceived it as an obstacle to modernization and a major reason for Chinese political weakness. One of the major slogans of the May Fourth Movement[1] of 1919 was "Down with Confucius and his followers." The movement turned to "Mr. Science" and "Mr. Democracy." Since the establishment of the People's Republic of China in 1949 Marxism–Leninism has been upheld as the state orthodoxy and Confucianism suffered further decline as the Marxist idea of class struggles replaced Confucianism's value of harmony. The denunciation and rejection of Confucianism as a "feudalistic" philosophy eventually culminated in a brutal assault on Confucianism during the Cultural Revolution (1966–1976). Confucianism has had a kind of revival since the 1990s (Spence 2012). Jiang Qing, a scholar, founded a Confucian based educational institution and Confucianism was further popularized by a recent television series on the Confucian classic text, the Analects. Confucianism again made its way into the school curriculum. Confucius Institutes sponsored by the government have been established in campuses overseas to promote the learning of Chinese language and culture. Nevertheless, fearing the power of religious influence, the state's support of Confucianism is only half-hearted. Certainly, as a long-lived tradition, Confucianism still has a strong hold on the Chinese psychology, but now it has to compete with multifarious forces such as Marxist thoughts, capitalistic values, and Western democratic ideals to influence the Chinese culture. Also, as an enduring ancient philosophy, it unsurprisingly contains substantial sexist elements both in its language and its major ideas. For Confucianism to speak to modern minds, those elements need to be re-examined and critiqued.[2]

The following famous passage from the Confucian classic *The Great Learning* provides the key to the understanding of the Confucian ideal of peace as well as its stance on war and violence:

> Their thoughts being sincere, their hearts were then rectified. Their hearts being rectified, their persons were cultivated. Their persons being cultivated, their families were regulated. Their families being regulated, their states were ordered. Their states being ordered, all between heaven and earth became peaceful. From the Son of Heaven down to the mass of the people, all must consider the cultivation of the person the root of everything besides. (*The Great Learning*)

Two things can be noted from this passage. First, the stages of development from personal cultivation to the final stage of attaining peace of the whole world testify to the fundamental Confucian belief that social and political order rest on personal virtues – morality is the fabric of the world. Global peace per se without a moral component could not be the ultimate goal, nor would violence be justified for mere instrumental reasons. Second, integral to the social and political order is the element of personal relationships, especially familial relationships. Hence the ideal of peace is structured along the ideal of familial harmony, and violence is justified when the moral order of proper relationships is disrupted.

Before we examine the Confucian stance on the issues of violence and peace in detail, a brief introduction to the central concepts of Confucianism is in order. The cardinal concept in Confucianism is *ren*, which is often translated as benevolence, goodness, or humaneness. The Chinese character of benevolence (*ren*) is a combination of the two characters meaning "person" and "two." In the Analects, the term has two meanings. The first refers to love or benevolence and includes both familial sentiments as well as caring and benevolent sentiments toward anyone in the world. Many interpreters therefore see benevolence as being about human relatedness (Tu 1985). The second meaning refers to an ideal, perfect virtue, which includes various specific virtues such as wisdom, honesty, courage, etc.[3] A gentleman (*junzi*) is someone who is committed to moral cultivation in acquiring the virtue of benevolence and has attained a certain level of accomplishment in doing so. Confucius (551–479 B.C.E.) himself, however, claimed that he had not achieved this virtue. A sage is someone who has attained the highest level of the virtue. In Confucianism, personal moral cultivation is connected to the fulfillment of one's worldly obligations. This is the Confucian political ideal of "inner sage, outer king." Someone who is morally cultivated has the moral obligation to bring benefits and peace to the world. The most common way to do this is through political participation: either as a ruler or as a government official.

The term rites (*li*) originally refers to religious ritual rules but then expands to include moral rules and etiquette rules (social propriety governing all relationships – parents and elders, ancestors, society),which are seen by Confucius as the expression of the virtue of benevolence. Confucius believes that following rites has the effect of making a person act in a civil, refined, and aesthetically pleasing manner. More importantly, following rites contributes to the acquisition of the virtue of benevolence and brings about social harmony: "To return to the observance of the rites through overcoming the self constitutes benevolence" (Analects 12:1) and "Of the things brought about by the rites, harmony is the most valuable" (Analects 1:12).Besides practicing the rites, learning and thinking are also important requirements for acquiring the virtue of benevolence. When one has the virtue of benevolence and follows the rites, often one does what is morally proper, or achieves moral rightness (*yi*).

The Analects suggests that benevolence develops from familial sentiments:

> The gentleman devotes his efforts to the roots, for once the roots are established, the Way (*dao*)[4] will grow from it. Filial piety and fraternal obedience constitute the basis of benevolence. (Analects 1:2)

Proper familial sentiments are seen as the core of the virtue of benevolence. This is perhaps because the family is viewed as an essential training ground for love and kindness, and the sentiments toward members of the family can be extended outward to other fellow human beings. Family is treated as the paradigm for all social orders in Confucianism.

These basic ideas of Confucius were further developed by two other eminent early Confucians – Mencius (372–289 B.C.E.) and Xunzi (312–230 B.C.E.). Mencius believed that humans are born with four moral minds – minds of commiseration, shame, deference, and right/wrong – which, if cultivated, can develop into the four virtues: benevolence, moral rightness, rites, and wisdom. In other words, the capacity to have benevolence is an innate endowment that every human possesses. Mencius also rendered a more concrete illustration of how to extend familial sentiment to people outside the family: "Treat the aged of your own family in a manner befitting their venerable age and extend this treatment to the aged of other families" (Mencius 1A:7). The idea of a social order modeled after the family as a nexus of personal relationships is articulated in Mencius's idea of the Five Relationships: ruler–minister, father–son, older–younger brother, husband–wife, and friend–friend relationships. This social order should also be understood as a moral order in that each individual person is an occupant of various relationship roles and incurs the related role duties. One of the duties of a ruler, for example, is to serve as a moral role model for his subjects.

> In administering your government. … Just desire the good yourself and the common people will be good. The virtue of the gentleman is like wind; the virtue of the small man is like grass. Let the wind blow over the grass and it is sure to bend. (Analects 12:4)

In this way, Confucianism can be understood as a kind of relationship role ethics.[5] Since the Five Relationships consist of relationships that are hierarchical (with the exception of the friend–friend relationship), with reciprocal duties between the related parties, and bonded by ties of personal affection, the ideal Confucian social/moral order embodies these elements as well.

Xunzi does not share Mencius's optimism about human nature. On the issue of moral cultivation he emphasizes following the rites. To Xunzi, the rites are the device invented by the past sages to preempt human conflicts and social chaos by coordinating and regulating people's desires. The rites can serve this function because of their inherent hierarchism. Hierarchism distinguishes clearly the roles and duties of the superior and the inferior and regulates their desires and behaviors accordingly:

> The Ancient Kings abhorred such disorder; so they established the regulations contained within ritual and moral principles in order to apportion things, to nurture the desires of men, and to supply the means for their satisfaction. (Xunzi 19:1)

Figure 4.1   Temple of Heaven (Beijing). Source: Irfan A. Omar

> When the gentleman has been nurtured by these things, he will also be fond of ritual
> distinctions. What is meant by "distinctions"? I say that these refer to the gradations
> of rank according to nobility or baseness. (Xunzi 19:3)

Confucianism believes in the idea of Heaven not as a state of being or a place.
Instead Heaven sometimes is referred to as a deity that has preference, desire,
and intention. Sometimes Heaven is described not so much as a deity, but as a
source of orders, including natural and moral order, of the cosmos. The word
also refers to the physical sky, which is where the transcendental realm is. The
idea of Heaven's Mandate mainly refers to the sanction to rule given by Heaven
to the ruler (son of Heaven). The ruler's mandate presumably is based on his virtues and he can lose it if he lacks virtue. Heaven's mandate also refers to the
imperative to be moral issued by Heaven to every person. Confucius expresses
reverence to Heaven but the term rarely occurs in the Analects. As human nature
is moral according to Mencius, Heaven's mandate or the command to be moral
is already inherent in one's nature. Therefore to be sincere – to be true to one's
nature – is to follow Heaven's mandate. Mencius also portrays a moral cosmos.
He refers to the special kind of qi^6 – the vapor energy – that fills the space between Heaven and Earth as the flood-like-qi, which he describes as uniting with
rightness and the way. In contrast, Xunzi downplays the moral and the metaphysical nature of Heaven and naturalizes it, reducing it to patterns of regularity
and hierarchism.

Despite the different emphases of these three philosophers, we can conclude
that all of them prize benevolence as the highest virtue that all humans should
strive for. They all see the rites both as the embodiment of and the means to attain
benevolence. Carrying out the roles and duties pertaining to personal relationships,

Figure 4.2 Confucius. Source: © destigter-photo / iStockphoto

especially familial relationships, constitutes an essential part of benevolence. Morality is the foundation for human orders, whether it has metaphysical underpinnings or not.

With this basic understanding, we can now proceed to examine the Confucian position on the issues of violence and peace. I shall base my analysis primarily on the writings of ancient Confucianism, especially the Confucian classics of the Analects, the Mencius, the Xunzi, and the Liji (the Book of the Rites) as the later Confucian thinkers essentially follow the ancient thinkers on the issue of war and peace.

Meanings of Peace

The Chinese translation of the word "peace" is *heping* (harmony-levelness). The original usage of the word "*he*" has to do with sounds or how sounds interact with each other. *Shouwen*, the first Chinese dictionary, defines "*he*" as "mutual responsiveness of sound" (Li 2006). "*Ping*" originally means the unobstructed, smooth flow of air. It resembles the English word "peace," which also means having no disturbance or the absence of war and fighting. *Heping* therefore connotes both harmony and a lack of disturbances.

According to Li Chenyang, "harmony presupposes the existence of different things and implies a certain favorable relationship among them" (Li 2006).[7] Harmony implies diversity and contrasts with sameness (*tong*). Harmony pertains to both human and cosmic relationships: the function of the rites is to bring harmony to society (Analects 1:12). The *yin-yang* forces can harmonize and everything is in its right place (Liji 11:6). Li believes that because harmony implies differences and diversity, strife is inherent within it. Consequently, "disharmony is necessarily present during the process of harmonization" (Li 2006), which, he claims, is equivalent to harmony. Harmony is explained as a process.

While Li's observation that harmony implies diversity and differences is correct, his conclusion is debatable. Differences need not imply strife. Instead, they can be mutually compatible and complementary. If so, harmony need not involve a process of harmonization of conflicting elements and there is no textual evidence for thinking that it does. I shall therefore take harmony to refer to a condition in which different things interact in a mutually responsive and positive way such that it may, but need not, involve any conflict. The analogy of sounds responding to one another in an appropriate way represents the core meaning of this notion of harmony.

Incorporating this notion of harmony into the Chinese idea of peace, we can observe important differences between the Western and the Chinese ideas of peace. The Chinese notion implies diversity, co-existence, and interactions among different elements. It is a dynamic process that is positive and appropriate, resulting in patterns, or meaningful and valuable conditions. In contrast, the Western notion of peace is defined largely in a negative way as the absence of war, fighting, or disturbances.

Besides harmony, the Chinese notion of peace has another component – levelness (*ping*). As levelness denotes a lack of obstacles and disturbances, it can extend to include the psychological condition of feeling tranquil and safe. In this way, levelness is akin to the Western notion of peace. The Chinese notion of peace, *heping*, therefore can be seen as encompassing the Western notion of peace while adding the element of harmony. I would use "harmony and peace" instead of just "peace" as the translation for *heping*.

The notion of *heping*, however, is not yet equivalent to the Confucian ideal of harmony and peace. Besides stability and a lack of disturbance, the latter also requires a moral order that has the family as its paradigm. Recall the passage from *the Great Learning*. Bringing peace to the world (*pingtianxia*) has its basis in personal moral cultivation. A harmonious moral order consists of parties related to each other in personal ways, bonded with personal affection, obligated with reciprocal duties, and governed by a hierarchical structure.[8]

According to Confucianism, harmony and peace are to be achieved domestically by having virtuous rulers and ministers educate the people, practice the rites, the Five Relationships, and benevolent policies so as to ensure the people's economic wellbeing and develop their moral characters. Penal punishment is used only sparingly as a secondary measure.

Interstates-wise, the Confucian ideal state of peace and harmony is *tianxia*, in which the whole world is unified under a true king because of his virtues. Short of this ideal condition, powerful leaders are trusted to strive to achieve harmony and peace for their people via either the kingly way or the hegemony way.

The kingly way is to be led by a true king who aims to strengthen his own state, amass talents, and ensure the state is opposed to violence. "One who truly understands how to use force does not rely upon force. ...With a fund of good will to rely on, he cannot be reduced to insignificance" (Xunzi 9:8). Basically, it is believed that a true king's benevolence and moral rightness will naturally attract others to submit to him.

> Since his benevolence is the loftiest in the world, there is no one in the world who does not draw close to him ... there is no one who dares to oppose him ... he gains victory without battle and acquires territory without attack. (Xunzi 9:11)

The hegemony way is to be led by a hegemon who aims for government efficiency and the satisfaction of the people. Lacking the required benevolence and moral rightness, a hegemon devotes more efforts to maintaining the international order and winning allies' respect and trust.

> He restores states that have perished, protects ruling lines that are in danger of dying out, guards the weak, and restrains the violent. If he treats them as friends and equals and is respectful in his dealings with them, he will win their favor. (Xunzi 9:9)

Either way a powerful leader should not use aggression and aim at territory acquisition. "The true king works to acquire men, the hegemon works to acquire allies, and the ruler who relies on force works to acquire territory ... he who acquires territory incurs their enmity" (Xunzi 9:6).The success of a powerful leader, however, depends ultimately on a trust in their morality. The kingly way presumes a voluntary submission to a moral authority; the hegemony way presumes respect for the hegemon.

There are other less preferred but practical means to attain peace. One can try to buy peace with materials goods or to act in a neighborly manner by giving material assistance and encouragement (Mencius 1B:15). King Tang repeatedly offered food and labor to encourage and assist the ruler of his neighboring state to carry out sacrificial duties (Mencius 3B:5). Other means that were practiced in Chinese history include diplomacy, sending official envoys, missions, keeping hostages, formation of leagues of states with occasional meetings and agreements, building bonds through marriage, and signing detente and covenants (Kierman and Fairbank 1974). Since these practices are not commented on in the texts, I will not further analyze them in this chapter.

Peace on the Ground

In considering some Confucian nongovernmental efforts for peace, I shall focus on the roles of the intelligentsia and the clans. But we need to first examine the background of the Confucian stance on nongovernmental associations.

In traditional China, because of the role-relationship orientation of Confucianism, the state was seen as a family writ large. The ruler played the role of a parent to his subjects, including his ministers. Consequently, the interests of society and those of the state were seen as identical. To serve a (virtuous) ruler was to serve public interests, which were contrasted with the interests of individuals or private interests. Pursuing the former was laudable, seeking the latter contemptible (Fewsmith 1983). Moreover, in addition to being the intellectual and moral foundations of the state, Confucianism was also seen as the source of superior guidelines and solutions to practical problems. Expert knowledge and occupational associations were denigrated. Consequently, organized activities outside the state bureaucracy were treated with suspicion as they were seen as not serving important purposes and, even worse, pursuing private interests. On the other hand, to maintain the centralization of authority and restrict local influence, the state bureaucracy was kept relatively small and its officials were rotated on a regular basis. Consequently, groups, especially those at the local level, had ample social and political space for operations. That being said, groups still had only limited political power and exerted little impact on state policies.

The most common groups in traditional China were charity associations, guilds, study associations, associations of people from the same regions, and clans. The charity associations were for welfare relief purpose only. They were often small, local associations under the patronage of wealthy local gentries. Associations of people from the same native province were most active in cities. They provided an arena for socializing and networking and helped newcomers to integrate into urban communities (Sangren 1984). Compared with these two, guilds had more influence. All members of a trade were required to join a guild and adhere to its regulations. The guilds were given considerable judicial authority and sometimes even had a policing function in the enforcement of their regulations. Still their political power was very limited. They were not mentioned in the law and there were few commercial codes. They only had authority along functional lines and no territorial authority. Basically, they were seen as having delegated authority conferred by the state, rather than being an independent or alternative authority (Fewsmith 1983). The guilds were replaced by trade and labor unions in modern Chinese society, which still have little political power in the People's Republic of China.

While the above associations contributed somewhat to the maintenance of social order and thereby to peace, the group that made the most important contribution in traditional China was the clans, which have been well established since the Song dynasty. A clan can be defined as a patrilineal group of people sharing the same ancestry and a common surname. After the founding of the People's Republic of China, clans underwent a period of decline but have been growing again since the economic modernization in the late 1970s. In traditional China, clans owned land, and sometimes were even the province's largest landowners. Revenues generated from the fields owned by a clan were often spent on providing relief for the needy clan members as well as supporting students in the clan to study or to travel to take the Imperial examination. Clans were also responsible for organizing religious events relating to the worshipping of ancestors and cultural events such as festival celebrations. At times of political instability, the clans might also undertake the training of a militia to protect the clan members (Fei 1982). In brief, clans provided a safety net, facilitated access to the society's power structure (through their support of young clan members taking the civil service examination), and nurtured social bonds and cooperation among its members. All these had a significant impact on the maintenance of peace in local areas.

However, clans were a double-edged sword. Clan wars were common in traditional China as land rights and resource use disputes were rampant and often local magistrates were corrupt and could not effectively arbitrate. Intra-clan relationships also had tension. The rich members could be landlords and money lenders to their poor kinsmen. Though the tension rarely led to violent conflicts, social harmony could be hampered.

The prevalence of the Imperial examination system from which most officials were recruited started during the Song Dynasty (960–1279 C.E.).[9] The passing of this examination, that is, obtaining a degree, was determined by one's moral (Confucian) virtues as well as mastery of the Confucian canons and other literary accomplishments. Through this examination system, Chinese intellectuals have been closely connected to the government as either officials or aspiring officials. They were thereby able to achieve the Confucian ideal of "inner sage, outer king"; that is, to undertake the obligations of morally cultivated persons to bring benefits and peace to the world through political participation. Their closeness to the political center together with their subscription to the ideal of "inner sage, outer king" led the intelligentsia, especially the degree holders, to identify themselves as the protectors of the Way (*Dao*) and make it their duty to remonstrate against problematic policies or behaviors of the ruler. They could risk their careers, incur severe punishments, and even lose their lives when they did so. In addition, the role of remonstrance was formally institutionalized in the position of Remonstrating Censor.[10] In this way, the elites of the society were both participants in and the watchdog of the government. The famous saying of the Neo-Confucian Fan Zhongyan was the guiding motto of many intellectuals, "To worry before everyone under the Heaven gets worried, to rejoice after everyone under the Heaven has rejoiced."[11]

In traditional China, members of the intelligentsia were sometimes organized into study associations that provided lessons to candidates sitting for public examinations and even served as forums for political discussion and mobilization.

However, since the intelligentsia were highly respected and influential as the van-guard of Confucianism and with members being officials or potential officials, the state was wary of them forming factions, which historically had been sources of conflicts and disruption of governance. Therefore, their organization was forbidden outright by the state most of the time. This, together with the faith in the guidance of their own moral heart-mind, explained why the dissidents were always unorganized individuals.

It was therefore no coincidence that the groundbreaking May Fourth Movement (1914) and the Tiananmen Square protest for democracy (1989) were both spear-headed and sustained by the overwhelming participation of young idealistic uni-versity students who saw themselves as inheriting the roles of the intellectuals in the tradition – being the conscience of society. The picture of the three university students kneeling in front of the Great Hall of the People, carrying a petition on top of their heads and begging to meet with the then Premier Li Peng at a very early stage of the Tiananmen movement vividly recalled the Chinese intellectuals' remonstrance tradition. Similarly, the Nobel Peace Laureate Liu Xiaobo (who called for political reform and the end of the single-party rule of the Chinese Communist Party), the world-renowned dissident artist Ai Weiwei (who exposed government corruption and cover-ups in the Sichuan corruption scandal), as well as the predominant majority of the human rights activists in contemporary China are all intellectuals. These modern intellectuals are no longer fighting for many of the traditional Confucian values, but they are as committed as their predecessors to the obligations of bringing peace and benefits to society. Instead of fighting for individual's rights (such as lesbian, gay, bisexual and transgender (LGBT) rights) or procedural justice as activists in the West often do, they focus on issues that have major impact on people's basic livelihoods and on issues affecting the political participation of intellectuals such as anti-corruption, transparent political processes, and freedom of the press. Owing to the political repression of the Communist regime of the People's Republic of China, they also share their prede-cessors' lack of organization. Acting largely on an individual basis, they adopt non-violent means (such as hunger strikes), and conceive of their chief responsibility in terms of expressing, promulgating, and promoting the right ideas, which they believe are the cornerstone of positive changes.[12]

Violence and war

Many scholars see the history of imperial China, for better or worse, as the evi-dence of Confucianism in action. Specifically, many interpret Imperial China as expressing a history of pacifism and attribute this to the influence of Confucianism.[13] The peaceful tributary system was often cited as evidence for the Chinese paci-fism. Under the tributary system, China refrained from conquering and annexing its lesser, weaker, and less developed neighboring states. In return, these states consented to become China's tributaries and regularly paid homage as well as sending letters and tribute goods to China. China itself was supposed to exert cultural influence on these states to help advance their moral and cultural development. This prevalent view, however, has been under much scrutiny lately. Historians and political scientists contest that the foreign policy of imperial China was indeed dictated instead by realpolitik and pointed out how China alternated between peace and territorial aggression depending on its military strength (Wang 2011). It is beyond the scope of this chapter to settle the dispute. My aim here is to examine the philosophical aspect of the issue of war and violence from the Confucian standpoint.

The Chinese term "*baoli*" is often translated as violence. It consists of two words, "*bao*" (violent/brutal) and "*li*" (power/force).The original meaning of "*bao*" was a rain ritual performed by a ruler or an official with the person exposing himself to the scorching sun in order to obtain rain from heaven (ter Haar 2011). The character "*li*" originally takes after the shape of a rake, operation of which requires the use of strength. The word therefore denotes the use of physical force. The term "baoli" therefore connotes injury or bodily damage associated with the use of physical force and resembles the meaning of the English word "violence." My discussion of violence below refers to two broad categories. The first concerns violence issued from or toward a state or a government. This includes war and penal punishment. The second is about violence engaged in by private individuals. This includes acts of vengeance, suicide, and bodily mutilation. My most expansive discussion on violence will be on the topic of war as a Confucian just war can be seen as a paradigm of the use of state violence in Confucianism.

Violence from/toward a state: War

Let us first look at the background dichotomy of *wen* (civil/refined) and *wu* (martial/military). *Wen* refers to culture, civilization, refinement, and the associated cultural activities of religions, arts, morality, conventions, writings, etc. To appeal to *wen* is to use nonviolent means such as morality, rituals, and dialogues to seek a solution. *Wu* refers to the use of force, and is often associated with martial activities issued from a government or an authority. The two founding rulers of the second historical dynasty, the Zhou dynasty (1046–256 B.C.E.), were named as King Wen and King Wu. *Wen* and *wu* were seen as two reciprocal and equally important ideals required for attaining cultural equilibrium before the Warring States period (475–221 B.C.E.). Early Chinese mythical heroes and sages such as Shen-nung and the Yellow Emperor were seen as excellent civil and military leaders. Justified *wu* sometimes is seen as the expression of the natural emotion of anger of the sages toward the unruly. *Wu* also serves to display the awe-inspiring prowess of the kings and their virtues, hence augmenting their power of *wen*. This in turn strengthens the sage's power of *wu*. *Wen* and *wu* are in a reciprocal relationship. This belief in the reciprocity and parity of *wen* and *wu* changed during the later Zhou dynasty when the disastrous effects of pervasive wars led to a general aversion to war, resulting in an ascendancy of *wen* over *wu*.

Confucianism inherits many of the earlier ideas about *wu*, but it no longer esteems *wu* as an ideal. Some commentators even suggest that war has no place in the ideal Confucian political order. For example, Daniel Bell points to the Confucian ideal of *tianxia* (all-under-Heaven), a condition in which the national boundaries disappear and the whole world, sharing the same Confucian values, is unified and peaceful under the sovereignty of a virtuous ruler. Bell claims that there is no room for coercive force in this condition as governing is based solely on the ruler's virtues.[14]

This conclusion, however, is debatable. We need to distinguish between an ideal state and a utopia. *Tianxia* is an ideal state as it refers to an aspired but not yet real- ized condition. But it is not a utopia because the state that it refers to need not be perfect. Hence, a military campaign by a virtuous ruler to crush a sporadic war instigated by an unruly leader is still a possibility.

Whether my objection is valid or not, most scholars agree that Confucianism does not follow pacifism when addressing the imperfect reality. Confucius unam- biguously endorses certain kind of wars: "When the Way prevails in the Empire, the rites and music and punitive expeditions are initiated by the Emperor" (Analects 16:2). He even specifies armaments as a required part of a government, though not as important as trust: "Zigong asks about government. The Master said, 'Give them enough food, give them enough arms, and the common people will have trust in you'" (Analects 12:7). A ruler is responsible for having the troops trained well before sending them off to fight. Failure to do so is to abandon them, "To send the common people to war untrained is to throw them away" (Analects 13:30). Use of force is indeed a serious matter to Confucius. It, along with fasting and illness, is something he treats with great caution (Analects 7:13) and therefore is not something he frequently talks about (Analects 7:21).

Mencius and Xunzi provided more elaborate discussions on topics similar to that of *jus ad bellum* (justification for waging war) and *jus in bello* (just warfare conduct) in the Western philosophy. To them, just war (*yi zhan*) is equivalent to punitive expedition, which is also mentioned by Confucius, as we have just seen (Analects 16:2).We therefore need to examine this notion of punitive expedition more carefully.

> In the *Spring and Autumn Annals* there were no just wars. There were only cases of one war not being quite as bad as another. A punitive expedition is a war waged by one in authority against his subordinates. It is not for peers to punish one another by war. (Mencius 7B:2)

Indeed it is emphasized that punitive expedition is to be distinguished from war. "In the rule of a true king there are punitive expeditions (*zhu*) but no warfare (*zhan*)" (Xunzi 15.5). The Chinese character that is often translated as punitive expedition is *zheng^a* (going to war). The original meaning of *zheng^a* is to make a long trip with a clear destination. The meaning of *zheng^a* as "going to war" certainly derives from this original meaning.

Punitive expedition, *zheng^a*, is no ordinary warfare. Mencius specifies *zheng^a* as "a war waged by one in authority/superior position against his subordinates. It is not for peers to *zheng^a* each other" (Mencius 7B:2). He also interprets *zheng^a* by using its homonym – the word *zheng^b* (correct/rectify): "To zheng^a is to Zheng^b" (Mencius 7B:4). Therefore, *zheng^a* implies the notion of a party in a superior position to use military force against an inferior in order to correct the latter. Besides "rectify" the original meaning of *zheng^b* (correct) includes "being at the center, not lopsided or biased."[15] One corrects by moving the strayed person or object (back) to the center, that is, the right position. In sum, punitive expedition is a moral mission conducted by means of a superior deploying military to bring about correction.

In Confucianism, punishment can be related to *zheng^b* (correct) in the following ways.

- To *correct the behavior* of a *guilty* person. However, in the case of punitive expedition, the tyrant who has caused so much suffering does not deserve a second chance. Hence correction in this sense is inapplicable: "In the past when King Wu attacked the 'possessor of Shang' and condemned Zhou Xin to execution, he had his head cut off and suspended from a crimson banner" (Xunzi 18:3).
- To remove tyrants and deter potential offenders, hence effecting or restoring the *right (correct) social/moral order*: "The military principles of which I spoke are just the means whereby to prohibit violent and aggressive behavior and to prevent harm to others" (Xunzi 15:2). In this way, war of self-defense is also justified as it is to protect the right order against aggression. War of self-defense, however, is only permissible and not required. A ruler can choose to abdicate instead of fighting (Mencius 1B:13).[16]
- To *express or demonstrate the correct (moral) order of retributive justice*. Punitive expedition is sometimes described as (justified) vengeance. "When an army was sent to punish Ge for killing the boy, the whole Empire said, 'This is not coveting the Empire but avenging common men and common women'" (Mencius 3B:5).
- To *educate or "correct" the common people* – correct in the sense of leading people to the right position. Punitive war displays the virtues of a true king such as his benevolence in caring about people's wellbeing and his righteousness in hating evildoing. Such a display would sway people's morality. "Therefore, where the soldiers of the benevolent man encamp they command a godlike respect; and where they pass, they transform the people" (Xunzi 15:6). Other virtuous emotions such as valor and righteous rage are also expressed in punitive expedition:

If there was one bully in the Empire, King Wu felt this to be a personal affront. This
was the valor of King Wu. Thus, he, too, brought peace to the people of the Empire
in one outburst of rage. (Mencius 1B:3)

To sum up, the Confucian conception of punitive expedition is a moral mission to
correct – to restore social/moral order, express moral rightness, and display virtues – thereby affecting the moral characters of the people. It is therefore different
from a judicial conception of punishment that is based solely on criminal law. It is
also dissimilar from the prevalent form of just war in contemporary Western
society – war of humanitarian intervention aiming to provide humanitarian relief
and assistance.

But to be a moral mission, punitive expedition needs to meet certain conditions.
First, a moral authority is required to launch the war. While sages and great
teachers are also moral authorities in Confucianism, only political leaders
command military force. Therefore, it makes sense to require the moral-political
authority of a true king (*wang*), or, second best, a hegemon (*ba*), to undertake the
expedition. "If there happens to be no true king ruling the world, he (a hegemon)
will invariably triumph" (Xunzi 9:8). Defined further, "A true king is someone who
honors rites and promotes worthy men. A hegemon is someone who relies upon
laws and loves the people" (Xunzi 17:12). A true king has virtues and Heaven's
mandate to rule. "Who has the right to march on Yen? ... A Heaven-appointed
officer has the right to do so" (Mencius 2B:8). Lacking both qualities, a hegemon
instead has power, efficiency, and the capacity to oversee interstate order. He may
also derive moral authority from the trust and consent given to him by the other
state rulers.

Second, the launcher of war must have moral intent. Otherwise a war may be a
mere self-serving action. Third, there must be justifiable causes such as aggression
and tyranny. Fourth, the moral dimension of punitive expedition requires it to
take an extremely cautious stance toward war and be wary of the immense human
and social costs incurred in warfare. War should wait until other attempts to
address the critical condition have failed. "When Dai Wang was in Bin, the Di
tribes invaded the place. He (King Tang) tried to buy them off with skins and silks;
he tried to buy them off with horses and hounds; he tried to buy them off with
pearls and jade; but all to no avail" (Mencius 3B:5). Finally, war launched for the
purpose of cultural or religious conversion is prohibited.[17] In this framework of
punitive expedition, the moral transformation of the people is a subsidiary effect
of the display of the ruler's virtues, not any deliberate measures targeting their
beliefs.

In sum, punitive expedition requires the right intent, the right cause, it should
be launched by the right authority, the moral cost should be taken seriously, and it
should not be undertaken for the purpose of cultural or religious conversion.

Punitive expedition underscores the Confucian belief that it is one's moral
character rather than nonmoral factors such as laws, rewards, resources, or luck

that holds the key to the maintenance of the social, moral, and political order. The success of this moral mission is believed to depend entirely on the virtues of the commander of the expedition. A true king unifies the people by his virtues (Mencius 1A:7). He inspires people's dedication and valor, attracts volunteers for military intelligence as well as military and administrative talents. "The basis of all aggressive warfare and military undertaking lies in the unification of the people" (Xunzi 15:1).

Punitive expedition also highlights relationship-role ethics. The chain of command in an army is modeled after a family. "Subjects will serve their lord and inferiors will serve their superiors like a son serving a father or a younger serving an elder brother" (Xunzi 15:2). Similarly, people of the invaded states treat the invading true king "as a father or mother" (Xunzi 15:2). They look up to him respectfully and long for his protection and care.

My discussion of the Confucian position on just warfare conduct will be brief since the rationale is quite clear. Xunzi lays out detailed rules (Xunzi 15:5):

Do not punish the common people; punish only those who lead the common people astray. If any of the common people fight with the enemy, they become enemies as well. People who submitted to the leaders of the Zhou army were allowed to live and were cared for the same as the people of Zhou.

Do not lay siege to a city that is firmly guarded. Do not attack when the soldiers resist strongly. Do not massacre the defenders of a city.

Do not move the army in secret. Do not keep the forces long in the field. Do not allow a campaign to last longer than one season.

Mencius also condemns warfare conduct such as "to kill the old and blind the young, destroy the ancestral temples and appropriate the valuable vessels of the enemy state" (Mencius 1B:11).[18] These regulations seem to be based on the virtues of benevolence and moral rightness: punishing only the guilty, keeping destruction and interruption of people's livelihood to the minimum, humane and lenient treatment of the people of the enemy country, and respecting their culture and property.

Violence from the state: Penal punishment

Confucianism holds that penal punishment alone is insufficient and needs to be subordinated to the rites in order to achieve social order:

Guide them by edicts, keep them in line with punishments and the common people will stay out of trouble but will have no sense of shame. Guide them by virtue, keep them in line with the rites, and they will, besides having a sense of shame, reform themselves. (Analects 2:3)

Nevertheless punishments are necessary: "The basic principles of order are rituals and punishments" (Xunzi 25:18). Basically, punitive expedition and penal punishment are seen as belonging to one single category: "The first grade punishment is warfare, the second grade is sword and saw, the third grade is whip and bamboo" (Guoyu Jijie 2002). The two indeed have many features in common. First, they share the same basic justification of *zheng*[b] (correct). Penal punishment is also about retributive justice. Confucius disputes repaying an injury with kindness: "What, then, do you repay a good turn with? You repay an injury with straightness, but you repay a good turn with a good turn" (Analects 14:34). The retributive attitude is described as natural:

> "to reward where there is achievement and punish where there is fault."… It is the natural response of treating well what is good and of despising what is evil, out of which the principles of government necessarily grow. (Xunzi 16:3)

Penal punishment is also a means to maintain social order. It can discipline people (Xunzi 9:9), change those who have committed crimes and deter others from attempting wrongdoing (Xunzi 9:24), help to prohibit acts of violence, and instill hatred of evil acts (Xunzi 18:3).

Second, penal punishment also needs to be issued from the appropriate authority:

> Suppose a man killed another, and someone were to ask, "Is it all right to kill the killer?" I would answer, "Yes." But if he further asked, "Who has the right to kill him?" I would answer, "The Marshal of the Guards has the right to kill him." (Mencius 2B:8)

Penal punishment also requires virtuous rulers and officials for its effective execution. For example, it requires faithfulness (*xin*) or certainty of punishment to ensure it is being taken seriously: "It is desirable that reward and punishment must be carried out faithfully" (Xunzi 15:4). Clarity (*ming*) of the penal laws enables people to know how to follow the laws: "So chaotic is the instruction and so abundant are the punishments that the people are led astray and bewildered and they fall into error" (Xunzi 28:3). Displaying authoritativeness (*wei*) instills respect and fear in people and makes them cautionary about punishment. "This is to let the people know that why they dreaded and feared lay with the king, that is why the penalty is awe inspiring" (Xunzi 10:12). Wisdom is required to mete out proportionate punishment.

Third, the use of penal punishment also needs to be minimized.

> In ancient times, when Yao ruled the world, he executed one man, punished two others, and after that the whole world was well ordered. This is what the old text means when it says, "let your authority inspire awe, but do not wield it; set up penalties but do not apply them." (Xunzi15:24)

Violence from private individuals: Vengeance, suicide and self-inflicted harm

Vengeance follows the principle of retributive justice, which as seen earlier, is endorsed by Confucianism. Sometimes, vengeance is even treated as a mandatory moral obligation. The Confucian classic, Liji (Book of Rites), claims:

> One should not bear the same Heaven as the murderer of one's father. One should never turn aside one's weapon if one encounters the murderer of a brother. One should not dwell in the same state with the murderer of a friend. (Liji 1:70)

Apparently, endorsing private vengeance contradicts Mencius's requirement for punishment to be issued from a proper authority. But there is no real contradiction as Confucianism believes that familial ties can override legalistic requirement. Confucius asserts the permissibility to cover for one's father's wrongdoing: "Fathers cover up for their sons, and sons cover up for their fathers. Straightness is to be found in such behavior" (Analects 13:18).[19]

Suicide and self-inflicted harm are also violence undertaken by individuals. Avoidance of both is a Confucian duty given the emphasis on filial piety. The opening chapter of the Confucian classic, Classic of Filial Piety (Xiao Jing) underscores the imperative of preserving one's body: "We receive our body, including our skin and hair, from our parents. We dare not to bring injury to it. This is the beginning of filial piety" (Xiao Jing 1:1). However, self-harm done for the sake of moral rightness is permissible and even praiseworthy. "Life is what I want, moral rightness is what I want. If I cannot have both, I would rather take moral rightness than life" (Mencius 6A:10). Confucius also praised loyal officials who died for their ruler (Analects 16:12). The popular book *Twenty-four Filial Exemplars* in the late Imperial period is a collection of stories about filial piety. Many of the stories allude to violent sacrifice by filial pious children. For example, a son used his naked body to melt an area in a frozen lake in order to harvest fish for his father; a daughter-in-law cut her own flesh to make broth for her mother-in-law. Such behaviors were praised as "dying-for-the-dao" (*xun dao*) (Mencius 7A:42).

In sum, violence can be justified and sometimes even required in Confucianism. Often justified violence is both a means to achieve some worthy goals and an expression of virtues. As such, it is always a response to something undesirable, whether it is tyranny, wrongdoing, or suffering. It is thus a necessary evil and its use should be minimized.

Conclusion

The ultimate Confucian ideal of peace is the ideal of *tianxia*, the condition in which the whole world shares the same Confucian moral values and submitsto a virtuous ruler. Recognizing the reality as being short of this ideal, Confucianism accepts the justified use of violence, of which punitive expedition is its paradigm. Punitive expedition is a moral mission to correct/punish. Morality furnishes its basic justification, authority, and goals, and is believed to account for its victory as well. The Confucian idea of peace incorporates the idea of harmony, which implies diversity and interactions among different elements. But this notion of harmony and peace also includes morality as its essential element. Hence the most effective means to secure peace, according to Confucianism, is to have a powerful leader heading a hierarchy that is based on personal virtues. The efforts from the people to attain and maintain peace are also premised on the importance of morality. The intellectuals' self-assumed role as the conscience of society is based on the Confucian ideal of "inner sage, outer king." The functioning of the clan system is based on the Confucian valuing of the family and thereby the lineage. Therefore, either from the ground or from the top, whether by means of violence or nonviolence, the ultimate aim is to establish a moral order relying on the virtues of the social superiors and embodying the Confucian values, especially the paramount importance of the familial relationships.

Questions for Discussion

1. Do both military success and peace require morality as their basis as claimed by Confucianism?
2. Does the Confucian ideal of *tianxia* imply cultural uniformity or does it allow cultural diversity?
3. The Confucian idea of a just war – a punitive expedition requires it to be issued from a moral authority. Is this requirement a realistic requirement for a just war in our contemporary world?
4. The early Chinese view about the parity of the *wen* (the civil) and the *wu* (the martial) is later replaced by the Confucian idea of prizing the *wen* over the *wu*. Yet Confucianism still assumes a reciprocal relationship between the two. For example, a virtuous ruler who practices *li* has the strongest army and punitive war demonstrates/expresses the ruler's virtues and its success enhances his influence and power. Are military and civil power reciprocal in that a strong civil power also requires a strong military power and vice-versa in our contemporary world? (We can also think about economic power as a kind of military power and rephrase the question to be about economic power and civil power.)
5. The Confucian idea of punitive expedition assumes that war can have an educational function, especially in the sense that the leader of the punitive expedition displays his virtues and thereby sways people's morality. Is it true that a war can have a positive educational influence?
6. Confucianism allows self-inflicted violence including suicide to be enacted for the sake of morality. Sometimes it means that suicide is permissible for the

sake of personal relationships. Are personal relationships such as filial piety and loyalty to one's ruler an adequate justification for giving up one's life?

Notes

1   The May Fourth Movement was a mass student movement that had significant impacts on the cultural and political development of China, especially in the respect that it nurtured the development of communism in China.

2   See, for example, Chan (2000); or Rosenlee (2007).

3   For the discussion of the meanings of "*ren*," see Shun (1993).

4   The Way (*dao*) refers to the universal, proper way in which things should be done.

5   This is the very heart of Confucianism, around which many other aspects turn. It is discussed further in Chan (1993). See also Ames (2011).

6   *Qi* in ancient China was believed to be a kind of vapor energy or vital energy that fills Heaven and Earth and its balance affects both humans and nature. *Qi* therefore also fills the body of humans and lack of balance of *qi* causes upset in an individual's physical and psychological wellbeing, as well as disorder in the human realm. Mencius describes one special kind of *qi* – the "flood-like *qi*" and gives it moral qualities.

7   Alan Chan (2011) distinguishes two notions of harmony: one consists of having a subordinate party submitting to a superior party in a hierarchical relationship; another is about blending possibly conflicting elements. He agrees that the idea of diversity underlies both notions and that the second notion is the prevalent one in Chinese philosophical tradition.

8   Another related term is *taiping*, often translated as "greater peace" or "highest peace." The term first appeared in *Lushi Chunqiu*, an eclectic book under the influence of early Chinese philosophical schools of Confucianism, Daoism, Legalism, and Mohism. The term connotes "a kind of entropy in nature and society, which would automatically lead to universal peace by the elimination of all inequalities." Throughout the imperial history, *taiping* has been associated with radical thoughts and rebellions aiming at social and political equality and it was not endorsed by Confucianism. For example, the Yellow Turban Rebellion (184 C.E.) and the Taiping Rebellion (1850–1864 C.E.) explicitly referenced the term in their doctrines and their description of an ideal kingdom. The *Classic of Taiping* (*Taping Jing*) was written by Daoists who believed in equality and it incorporated ideas from the Yellow Turban rebels. The idea of equality has not been important in Confucianism, but the chapter *liyun* in the Confucian classic Liji does portray an ideal state in which social equality prevails and people are public-spirited rather than focusing on their own families.

9   The system itself was introduced in the Sui dynasty (589–618 C.E.).

10   This position was created in the eleventh century, but there were remonstrance officials before that.

11   My translation.

12   For the discussion of the role of intellectuals as conscience of society, see Goldman (1981).

13   It is important to recognize the role of pacifism in Confucian history. For further elaboration see Fairbank (1968).

14   Bell (2008).
15   Xinbian Shuowen Jiezi daquanji bianweihui (2011).
16   James Stroble (1998) contends that a punitive expedition is used to express legitimacy
     rather than to establish the correct social order. He points to a "paradox of authority":
     "the authority to use military means comes from the ability to unify the empire …
     since this implies that the social order which is the aim of the deployment of coercive
     violence is already achieved before there can be authority, or that the order and the
     authority is coeval, it cannot be the case that the use of violence is necessary to achieve
     that order" (Stroble 1998). Stroble is right about punitive expedition as an expression
     of moral authority, but the paradox of authority can be dissolved by distinguishing two
     different kinds of order. The first one is the moral order based on virtues and moral
     correctness. The second is the social order or the orderly functioning in a society.
     Tyranny clearly disrupts the latter and the punitive expedition aims to restore it. But
     tyranny cannot disrupt the moral order that is exemplified in the rule of a true king. A
     true king therefore commands the moral authority to restore the social order.
17   I therefore disagree with Don Wyatt's (2011) comment that Mencius's idea of a unified
     world would incline him to expect the aggregation of the world.
18   The Confucian Dong Zhongshu (179–104 B.C.E.) of the Han dynasty (206 B.C.E. –
     220 A.D.) adds further conditions for proper warfare conduct such as declaration of
     war before the fighting, prohibition of sudden attack, war only in remote areas. It is
     also wrong to wage a war against a country that is mourning the loss of its ruler.
19   Mencius has a similar story of how the sage Shun would abandon his throne to escape
     with his father if his father were convicted of murder (Mencius 7A:35).

References

Ames, Roger. 2011. *Confucian Role Ethics*. Honolulu, HI: University of Hawaii Press.
Bell, Daniel. 2008. "Just War and Confucianism." In *Confucian Political Ethics*. Princeton,
     NJ: Princeton University Press.
Chan, Alan. 2011. "Harmony as a Contested Metaphor and Conceptions of Rightness (*yi*)."
     In *How Should One Live*. Edited by Richard King and Dennis Schilling. Boston, MA:
     DeGruyter.
Chan, Sin Yee. 1993. "An Ethic of Loving: Ethical Particularism and the Engaged Perspective
     in Confucian Role-Ethics." PhD dissertation, University of Michigan.
Fairbank, John K. 1968. *The Chinese World Order: Traditional China's Foreign Relations*.
     Cambridge, MA: Harvard University Press.
Fei, John and Liu, Ts'ui-jung. 1982. "The Growth and Decline of Chinese Family Clans,"
     Journal of Interdisciplinary History 12, 3: 375–408.
Fewsmith, Joseph. 1983. "From Guild to Interest Group: The Transformation of Public
     and Private in Late Qing China." *Comparative Studies in Society and History* 25, 4:
     617–640.
Godehardt, Nadine. 2008. "The Chinese Meaning of Just War and its Impact on the Foreign
     Policy of the People's Republic of China." German Institute of Global and Area Studies
     Working Paper, no. 88, September 2008. http://www.giga-hamburg.de/en/system/
     files/publications/wp88_godehardt.pdf (accessed January 20, 2014).

Goldman, Merle. 1981. *China's Intellectuals: Advise and Dissent*. Cambridge, MA: Harvard University Press.

Guoyu Jijie (ed.). 2002. *Xu Yuangao*. Beijing: Zhonghua Shuju, 4, 6a.

Johnston, Alastair. 1995. *Cultural Realism*. Princeton, NJ: Princeton University Press.

Kierman, Frank, and John K. Fairbank (eds) 1974. *Chinese Ways in Warfare*. Cambridge, MA: Harvard University Press.

Knoblock, John. 1988. *Xunzi* Vol. I. Stanford, CA: Stanford University Press.

Knoblock, John. 1990. *Xunzi* Vol. II. Stanford, CA: Stanford University Press.

Lau, D. C. 1979. *The Analects*. New York: Penguin.

Lau, D. C. 2005. *The Mencius*. New York: Penguin.

Li, Chenyang. 2006. "The Confucian Ideal of Harmony." *Philosophy East and West* 56: 583–603.

Spence, Jonathan. 2012. *The Search for Modern China*. New York: W.W. Norton & Company.

Shun, Kwong-loi. 1993. " 'Jen' and 'Li' in the 'Analects.' " *Philosophy East and West* 43, 3: 457–479.

Stroble, James. 1998. "Justification of War in Ancient China." *Asian Philosophy* 8, 165–190.

Ter Haar, Barend. 2011. "Violence in Chinese Religious Culture." In *The Blackwell Companion to War and Violence*. Edited by Andrew Murphy. Indianapolis, IN: Wiley-Blackwell.

Turner, Karen. 1993. "War, Punishment and the Law of Nature in Early Chinese Concepts of the State." *Harvard Journal of Asiatic Studies* 53: 285–324.

Wang, Yuan-Kang. 2011. *Harmony and War: Confucian Culture and Chinese Power Politics*. New York: Columbia University Press.

Wyatt, Don. 2011. "Confucian Ethical Action and the Boundaries of Peace and War." In *The Blackwell Companion to Religion and Violence*. Edited by Andrew Murphy. Indianapolis, IN: Wiley-Blackwell.

Tu, Wei-ming. 1985. *Confucian Thought*. Albany, NY: SUNY.

Xinbian Shuowen Jiezi daquanji bianweihui. (ed.). 2011. *Shuowen Jiezi daquanji*. Beijing: Overseaschin Press.

Further Reading

Kuan, Feng. 1971. "A study of Sun Tzu's Philosophical Thought on the Military." *Chinese Studies in Philosophy* 2: 116–157. A paper on the thoughts of Sun Tzu, the greatest master of Chinese war and strategic thinking.

Lo, Ping-Cheung. 2012. "The Art of War Corpus and Chinese Just War Ethics Past and Present." *Journal of Religious Ethics* 40: 404–446. The paper examines the Art of War corpus of which the Seven Military Classics have been seen as the military bible in China since the eleventh century.

Rand, Christopher Clark. 1994. *The Role of Military Thought in Early Chinese Intellectual History*. PhD, Harvard University. An analysis of military thought in the pre-Han and early Han period looking at the moral goals and cosmic significance of war.

Shaughnessy, Edward. 1996. "Military Histories of Early China." *Early China* 21: 159–182. A review article of some significant monographs on early Chinese military histories.

Ter Haar, Barend J. n.d. "Violence in Chinese Culture: Bibliography." Accessed December 4, 2014. http://faculty.orinst.ox.ac.uk/terhaar/violencetext.htm.

Ter Haar, Barend. 2011. "Violence in Chinese Religious Culture." In *The Blackwell Companion to War and Violence*. Edited by Andrew Murphy. Indianapolis, IN: Wiley-Blackwell. A paper arguing for the importance of violence in Chinese religious culture.

Yung, Cheng. 1976. "A Tentative Discussion of Legalist Military Thought during the Warring States Period." *Chinese Studies in Philosophy* 7: 40–56. The paper examines the military thoughts of the school of legalism in pre-Chin China.

Zhang, Ellen. 2012. "Weapons Are Nothing but Ominous Instruments: The *Daodejing*'s View on War and Peace." *Journal of Religious Ethics* 40: 473–502. The article discusses Lao Tzu's views on war and peace.

Glossary

Heping (peace): Often translated into English as peace, in Chinese the term consists of two characters meaning, respectively, harmony and levelness (or lack of disturbances).

Junzi (gentleman): someone committed to moral cultivation in acquiring the virtue of *ren* who has attained a certain level of accomplishment in doing so.

Li (rites): The rites, which originally refers to ritual rules, but then expands to include moral rules and etiquette rules, are seen by Confucius as the expression of the virtue of *ren*. The rites are often associated with music as a means of educating and refining people's minds.

Qi (vapor energy): The material that fills the space between Heaven and Earth as well as constituting human bodies.

Ren (benevolence): Often translated as benevolence, goodness, or humaneness, the most important virtue in Confucianism.

Tianxia (all under Heaven): A political ideal in which national boundaries disappear and the whole world is united under a virtuous ruler.

Wen (civil/refined): Denotes culture or practices that have the effect of civilizing and refining people's behaviors and characters.

Wu (martial/military): Denotes the use of force or military deployment.

Yen: A state in ancient China.

Yi (moral rightness): A source of guidance for one's behavior.

Zhan (war): To conduct or be engaged in a war.

Zheng[a] (war): To make a military conquest.

Zheng[b] (correct): To correct, rectify, or make something right.

Zhu (war): To launch a war.

Zhi (wisdom): the intellectual virtue of wisdom.

4.1

A Buddhist Response

Eleanor Rosch

It is fortunate that Confucianism is included here among the world's religions. It raises deep questions about the relation of the religious and moral life to society, to governance of society, and to the norms for behavior of people in all aspects of social life. Confucianism avoids easy classification as either religious or secular – our conceptual distinction after all – and thus provides a playing field for modern sensibilities of many types. If humanity is ever to find a way out of continued warfare, planetary degradation, and the possible destruction of civilization on a massive scale, we will need to take questions about moral virtue and the social order seriously.

Although Buddhism began as a teaching seemingly antithetical to Confucianism, its latest manifestation, the Shambhala path, has many Confucian elements, even a distinctly Confucian flavor. According to the Shambhala origin story, the present Shambhala root texts appeared at this time in history because of the needs of a world in crisis that traditional Buddhism alone could not meet. Buddhism began as a religion of wandering ascetics seeking personal liberation from samsara. According to the legend of the Buddha's birth, the sage Asita predicted that the child would become either a *Chakravartin* (a world ruler) or a great sage (meaning a religious leader in that cultural context). The Buddha's father, king of a small principality, understandably wished him to become the former. The canonical story of the Buddha's upbringing and escape from his father's palace are based on this kind of assumption of incompatibility between the life of a temporal ruler and that of a spiritual seeker.

Early Buddhism was further divided on whether the role of king or government official could even be considered right livelihood.[1] For example, in one Jataka tale[2] a prince who remembers a past life when he was a king and then spent eons in hell for meting out punishments to criminals, decides to act deaf and dumb rather than assume the throne, even knowing he will be put to death for such disabilities. On the other hand, there was the Indian ideal of the Chakravartin who, like the

Peacemaking and the Challenge of Violence in World Religions, First Edition.
Edited by Irfan A. Omar and Michael K. Duffey.
© 2015 John Wiley & Sons, Ltd. Published 2015 by John Wiley & Sons, Ltd.

true king in Confucianism, is so virtuous that he rules a world empire where there is neither crime nor warfare. More realistically, there was an ideal of the righteous king who possesses the 10 royal virtues: morality, liberality, alms-giving, honesty, mildness, self-restriction, nonanger, nonviolence, patience, and nonoffensiveness (a somewhat milder portrait than that of the Confucian hegemon). These 10 are essentially lay virtues in early Buddhism; they can bring the king good karma but not liberation. It is a higher calling to be a monk, and higher yet to be a monk who can practice as a forest ascetic.

In Mahayana, there is also a split between those who denigrate the role of king[3] and the more frequent argument that a good king should rule for the benefit of his subjects and practice compassion in all that he does. Like a father caring for his children, a king should keep his kingdom secure from invaders, and he should punish his subjects to reform them not to cause them irreversible harm. It is only in Vajrayana and Shambhala that kingship and the role of power in general comes into its own as a potentially enlightened and necessary moral force.

The Confucian ideal of "inner sage, outer king" is a central tenet of Shambhala. Each person is seen as ruler of the kingdom of his own life and world, and the ideal for a human being is to bring together the two divergent paths given in the sage's prophesy for the infant Buddha. And how should that Shambhala everyman king rule? In Shambhalian terminology, when a person can "touch and trust" his own "primordial goodness and worthiness," that person can "relax with his senses and relationships," and begin to "rule his world." His living energy, his "windhorse," is aroused and his "natural power," as well as natural "caring for the world around him," will start to manifest (Mipham 2005).

Like Confucianism, Shambhala organizes many of its teachings around the "Heaven, Earth, and man" principle. Here Heaven represents the vast space and wisdom beyond the mind, Earth is a grounded presence in the here and now, and man the conduit that brings them together. This is represented in many activities from flower arranging to a newly developing specifically Shambhala meditation in which the man principle is represented by the human capacity for feeling. The Heaven, Earth, and man principle also represents a natural hierarchy, an anathema to the hippies who were the first students of the founder of Shambhala.

Shambhala differs most from its parent Buddhism in that its purpose is not just to awaken realization in its students but also to create an enlightened society – and these two goals are considered inseparable. The logic is that humans are not separate from the society around them nor is it separate from humans.[4] Like the Confucian gentleman, although the Shambhalian might develop his wisdom and virtue by training in solitude, he is expected to manifest what he attains in the public sphere in some fashion.

In Shambhala, society is considered to be the relationship between two people and also the network of all relationships.[5] Thus humans have the power to change society. But change it into what? Now we come to the great and difficult questions that study of Confucianism raises and that Shambhala is currently experimenting with on a practical level. As a group undertakes to work toward an enlightened society, it needs to develop an idea of what that is. Knowing that you don't like the way things already are is not enough; that is how social activist groups turn to infighting and fall apart as soon as their objective of overcoming some wrong is accomplished. Likewise, knowing that people in the enlightened society will be in touch with basic goodness and will manifest enlightened awareness is not quite enough. The question is: how should a peaceful, harmonious, virtuous, enlightened society be structured? Below are some of the issues with which the Shambhala community is dealing; note the resonances with Confucianism.

Hierarchy. Natural hierarchy begins internally with individuals. Surely anyone would want his or her mind to be a flourishing kingdom ruled by wisdom not a dysfunctional chaos in which every random thought and insane impulse gets an equal vote. And in society, wouldn't it be refreshing to have leaders, even kings, who were moral, trustworthy, compassionate, and well trained enough in both wisdom and the reality of conditions in the world that they could be given genuine power? But how can such leadership be trained? Plato wrote that his philosopher kings were to be taken from their homes and educated with a focus on mathematics. In Confucian China, aspiring government officials were trained by memorization of the Confucian classics. How should training of leaders be done in the contemporary world so that hierarchy does not become despotism?

Education. Complex societies require specialized institutions for education. But it is easy to quash a child's natural curiosity and desire to learn with regimentation. How to balance creativity and control? The Shambhala community has founded schools at all levels from Alaya Preschool through Naropa University. Students in schools of education looking for research topics might wish to study this naturally occurring experiment.

The arts, culture, and the artistry of living. In a manner reminiscent of the Confucian concepts of *li* (rites) and *wen* (civil, refined), Shambhala has emphasized the arts from its inception: poetry, calligraphy, painting, storytelling, music, food, conversation, and decorum. Shambhala further teaches that in daily life, when the deep mind is present with an action, every move that a person makes with his body, speech, or mind is a work of art (Trungpa 1996). It can also be viewed as a ceremony. "Life is a ceremony. The power of ceremony is that through the rituals of our day, we understand who we are. ... The shared ceremony of society creates the layout and design of everything from homes and businesses to cities and countries."[6] Such layout and design is also not separate from the energies of the natural world. With "true perception" one sees that the world is alive with the "tangible, elemental" energies that our scientific worldview denies (Hayward and Hayward 1998). Shambhala incorporates elements of the Chinese art of placement *Feng Shui* and also has its own recommendations for how to organize and use the rooms in a home or business.

In short, it may be time for Western culture to pay more attention to the ancient teachings of Confucianism and to consider the details of its recommendations for the organization of society and of a human life. There may be treasures there that would prove useful in developing a wiser, more civilized, and more peaceful world.

Notes

1 For a summary of both the early Buddhist and Mahayana sources on this issue see (Zimmerman 2006).
2 The Jatakas are folkloric accounts of past lives of the future Buddha.
3 For example, "Somebody [who is] not a fool does not gain a kingdom;/A fool, however, does not have empathy.../Without empathy, there is no *dharma*" (Zimmerman 2006, p. 221).
4 In Buddhism this is the principle of the interdependence of all things of the phenomenal world, an aspect of shunyata.
5 "The dynamic between two individuals is the source of secret and invisible power. ... Just you and me really means the whole world" (Mipham 2014).
6 Mipham (2014), p. 74.

References

Hayward, Jeremy and Karen Hayward. 1998. *Sacred World: The Shambhala Way to Gentleness, Bravery, and Power*. Boston, MA: Shambhala.
Mipham, Sakyong. 2005. *Ruling Your World: Ancient Strategies for Modern Life*. New York: Doubleday.
Mipham, Sakyong. 2014. *The Shambhala Principle: Discovering Humanity's Hidden Treasure*. London: Harmony Books.
Trungpa, Chögyam. 1996. *True Perception: The Path of Dharma Art*. Boston, MA: Shambhala.
Zimmermann, Michael. 2006. "Only a Fool Becomes a King: Buddhist Stances on Punishment." In *Buddhism and Violence*. Edited by Michael Zimmermann, 213–242. Lumbini: Lumbini International Research Institute.

4.2

A Jewish Response

Joshua Ezra Burns

Sin-Yee Chan addresses the description of political leadership in the Confucian tradition and draws comparisons between the hegemon and the kings of Israel as keepers of the peace. She describes the Confucian ideal of civic leadership as the *wang*, the true and virtuous king mandated by Heaven. The hegemon derives his mandate neither from his innate virtue nor from his royal ancestry but from the prudence of his actions. He must prove himself worthy of the power invested in him through his leadership in war and in peace. The hypothetical king must always guide the policy decisions of the actual king, to serve the best interests of the people under his leadership. If the hegemon manages to uphold this moral standard, even his more aggressive actions are deemed just and necessary inasmuch as they stand to maintain order in the 'all-under-Heaven' or *tianxia* that is the ideal, harmonious state.

It seems to me that Confucius and his followers felt compelled to respond to the gap between the ideal and the real. Acknowledging, in other words, that the perfect state of affairs is not always tenable, they urge those in power to overcome the imperfections of their people's circumstance by emulating the ideal king even at the cost of disturbing the local peace which the true king already will have established or confirmed. This, I believe is the essence of the realpolitik to which Chan refers.

One observes a strikingly similar relationship between the real and the ideal in the ancient Jewish political tradition. Rooted in the legislation of the Torah, the Jewish concept of kingship denies the sovereign his prerogative so much as to raise an army. According to the book of Deuteronomy, the king of Israel must be chosen by God. That must be his only distinguishing quality. In all other respects, the king must not exalt himself above other members of the presumably law-abiding subjects. He is allowed neither to acquire many wives nor to amass great material wealth. The only thing he actually is permitted to do is read the Torah all the days of his life, which, the author alleges, surely will lead him to fear God and to abide

Peacemaking and the Challenge of Violence in World Religions, First Edition.
Edited by Irfan A. Omar and Michael K. Duffey.

by His divine commandments. Only his high morals will ensure his succession by righteous descendants to sustain Israel's sovereignty in perpetuity (Deut. 17:14–20).

Clearly, these are not practical instructions. One wonders how effective a king can be as a protector of his people's peace when he does nothing but contemplate God's law. In fact, the king depicted in this legislation resembles no king in Israel's documented history. He is an ideal type drawn from that very history, his negative qualities reflecting those of Israel's past rulers recalled to have failed in their commands by doing just what the Torah supposedly said they ought not have done: submitting to foreign kings, launching misguided military offensives, consorting with women, and generally offending God.

Let's recount a bit of Israel's history. By most critical accounts, the book of Deuteronomy was written at the behest of King Josiah of Judah, who in the seventh century B.C.E. sought to preserve his kingdom's independence from the neighboring empires of Assyria and Egypt. But Josiah was not self-serving in his portrait of the ideal Israelite king as man of his own heart. His aim in commissioning Deuteronomy was that of a reformer enjoining his subjects to join him in serving God's will. Only in view of the propensity of Israel's past leaders to upset the peace did Josiah think to cast the ideal king as one whose rule is so virtuous as not to incur the need for war to begin with. By his reckoning, war arises only when God means to show His displeasure with Israel on account of their disobedience of His laws. Consequently, Josiah reasoned, the ideal king should neither tempt fate by neglecting those laws nor allow his subjects to do the same. Serving as his people's moral exemplar, the devout king would never have cause to take up arms. War simply would not occur.

Regardless of one's cultural orientation, it is easy to see that the truly just king is an impossible ideal. In a world plagued with conflict, one cannot govern a nation without expecting to have to defend that nation. In that sense, peace is also an impossible ideal. In casting the hegemon as a legitimate alternative to the true king, Confucius and his followers accepted the inevitability of violence or the breach of social protocol as a means toward achieving the *tianxia* of their idyllic imaginations. The author of Deuteronomy also acknowledged the reality of violence. An entire chapter of the book is devoted to the ethics of warfare (Deut. 20). But even in the heat of conflict, the author urges the offering of peace, *shalom*, as the first line of offense (Deut 20:10). Just like in the Confucian tradition, the ideal Israelite leader is urged only to go to war when the enemy leaves him no viable alternative.

Yet within just a few generations of the book's composition, Deuteronomy's legislation on war and peace and the responsibilities of the divinely appointed Israelite king were rendered obsolete. The fall of the Kingdom of Judah to the Babylonian Empire in 597 B.C.E. spelled the end of the institution of Jewish kingship that Josiah and his literary executor worked to refine. The new political reality of the Jewish people was one of subjugation – not uniformly oppressive, but subjugation nonetheless. Over the next several centuries, Deuteronomy's quaint portrait of the ideal king as a devout Torah scholar gradually ceded to a more ambitious portrait of a Messiah, a supernatural agent anointed by God to establish a new world order with Israel at its helm. In this scenario, the arrival of the Messiah would signal a war to end all wars to be followed by a divine judgment, and, finally, lasting peace for the Jewish people and for all the nations on earth ready to submit to God's will.

The removal of the Jewish people from the global political arena thus transformed the Jewish model of virtuous governance from a tenable objective to one achievable only through divine intervention. In the process, it turned the object of true peace for Israel from merely an unlikely prospect into an eschatological hope. Today, Jews are divided over the issue of how best to define the objective of peace in view of the current political dispensation. I wonder, therefore, if Judaism in all its diverse modern expressions can learn from the Confucian tradition. Much of what divides Jews today has to do with differences of opinion over what constitutes peace. Does the promise of *shalom* mean peace for the Jewish people or peace for all the nations? Can it mean both? And how might the elected leader of a Jewish nation-state fashion himself or herself in the mold of the ideal Israelite king in whose place he or she stands in the sacred imaginations of religious Jews the world over?

In view of these concerns, I believe that the Confucian concepts of the hegemon, the *bawang*, and *tianxia* offer helpful ways to think about the present Jewish situation. Even in the absence of a true king, a Messiah, one might make the case that the actual leader of a Jewish state should nevertheless fashion himself or herself as a Messiah, if only in respect to those administrative offices of which he or she is capable.

As for the Confucian concept of *tianxia*, I see many parallels with the Jewish concept of *shalom*. As Chan explains, the idea of a harmonious peace for all under Heaven is rooted in the model of the family and its localized hierarchy of interpersonal relationships. The idea of world peace associated with the reign of the Messiah also traces to a more humble kind of *shalom* indicating agreement between individuals. And just as universal *tianxia* is a remote ideal, so has the arrival of a Messiah proven a remote possibility in the Jewish tradition, a divine incentive for which devout Jews continuously strive but never actually achieve. The great twentieth-century scholar of Jewish mysticism Gershon Scholem famously characterized Jewish Messianic belief as fostering "life lived in deferment" (*leben in aufschub*) forever guided by unrealized expectations and an impossible dream of spiritual fulfillment. One wonders whether his disappointment might have been tempered by a concept of *shalom* closer in its ambition to that of *tianxia*, a local, temporal peace attainable not through supernatural means but through conscientious governance within the Jewish body politic.

I am encouraged by Chan's enlightening treatment to know that our cultural values converge in certain respects on the realities of war and peace.

5

"Peace is the Strongest Force in the World"[1]
Buddhist Paths to Peacemaking and Nonviolence

Eleanor Rosch

Better than a thousand pointless speeches
Is one word that brings peace.

The Dhammapada[2]

A lone saffron robed monk enters the dusty squalor of a Cambodian refugee camp on the Thai border. It is 1979, and the camp contains thousands of Cambodians, war-torn and broken from the horrors of the Khmer Rouge killing fields. The monk enters at risk of his life, since Khmer Rouge members still dominate the camps. As he walks slowly toward the center of the camp, excitement spreads, and refugees come out, many fearfully, for a glimpse of this long forbidden symbol of the Buddhism that had once been a pillar of their society. What message does the monk (the Venerable Maha Ghosananda) bring them? As he walks, his voice rings out with an ancient teaching from the *Dhammapada* (Sayings of the Buddha):

> Hatred never ceases by hatred
> But by love alone is healed.
> This is the ancient and eternal law. (Kornfield 1991, viii)[3]

This is the kind of peacemaking narrative offered in the talks and writings of contemporary Buddhists as a natural (even if not always implemented) outcome of the Buddhist vision. In Buddhism, peace is spoken of as fundamental and powerful. This includes internal peace of mind, peace between people, and peace in the societal and natural worlds. Over the long arc of Buddhism's historical development, the meaning of peacemaking and nonviolence have changed

Peacemaking and the Challenge of Violence in World Religions, First Edition.
Edited by Irfan A. Omar and Michael K. Duffey.
© 2015 John Wiley & Sons, Ltd. Published 2015 by John Wiley & Sons, Ltd.

with changes in Buddhist teachings and practices, arguably becoming increasingly socially oriented over time. A specialty of Buddhism as it is presented in contemporary Buddhist discourse is an emphasis on meditative/contemplative practices and the realizations that come from these as the basis for both knowledge and actions. Buddhist doctrines and the nature of those realizations and practices have interacted with each other in complex ways, changing as Buddhism evolved.

It is my intention in this chapter: (1) to describe briefly the primary teachings and meditative/contemplative practices of the major historical forms of Buddhism; (2) to connect the teachings and practices to peacemaking and nonviolence, indicating examples of particular social movements that have resulted; (3) to examine what in Buddhism might encourage and provide the means needed for nonviolent peacemaking; and finally (4) to ask what peacemakers (of any kind) might learn from that.

Overview of Buddhism

There are presently three major world forms of Buddhism with a fourth perhaps forming contemporaneously. These forms are called *yanas* (paths) by Buddhists and by some scholars of Buddhism. They are Theravada, Mahayana, Vajrayana, and Shambhala. All are actively growing in the West. A characteristic of the evolution of Buddhism is that each of the later forms incorporated some of the basic teachings of the earlier ones, added understandings of its own, and reinterpreted the earlier teachings in light of the additions. Although there is a core of kinship between the forms, each has its own texts, teachings, revered teachers, characteristic practices, and modern adaptations. A contemporary phenomenon is that each of the forms has given rise to social activist and peacemaking groups; these are being called Engaged Buddhism (or Socially Engaged Buddhism). I will describe each form in turn.

A word about reading the following sections: Buddhists tend to view Buddhist teachings as instructions for how to see the world, live one's life (as a lay person or monastic), and as pointers and conduits for contemplative realization, rather than as doctrines in the Western sense. Thus any description of Buddhism purely in terms of a conceptual system of doctrines and beliefs, as is typically done for Western religions, is likely to sound somewhat off base in a Buddhist context. Although there is scholarly dispute concerning what, if any, of this was true historically (McMahan 2008; Sharf 1995), and, indeed, whether any generalizations at all can be made about Buddhism across time and cultures (Faure 2009), in the following descriptions I have attempted to honor the Buddhist modes of presentation as much as possible, bringing in scholarly deconstruction when clearly warranted, for example in questioning correspondences between Buddhist texts and behavior.[4]

Figure 5.1   Woodcut 1 - The Buddha. Source: Michael K. Duffey

Theravada (speech of the elders)

Buddhism arose approximately 2500 years ago in India in an era that was anything but peaceful. Technological advances, such as the smelting of iron had affected virtually all aspects of society, and had led to increased warfare, dislocation of populations, and social and cultural upheaval. With that came religious ferment, seekers wandering the continent in search of wisdom and liberation from suffering. The canonical story of the Buddha's life occurs in such a context. Born the son of the king of a small principality, he is described as growing up having everything that anyone could possibly want, yet is still discontent. Venturing away from his sheltered palace, he encounters a sick man, an old man, and a dead man and is moved to go forth to find answers to life's basic issues. What does he find?

Theravada Buddhism is the one surviving school of early Buddhism, and is now the primary Buddhism of Southeast Asia: Thailand, Myanmar (Burma), Sri Lanka, Laos, Cambodia, and parts of Vietnam. It contains the basis of Buddhist psychology: an account of why we are not already peaceful and happy, and the initial

Buddhist practices to remedy that. The format in which this is often presented is that of the Four Noble Truths: life is marked by *dukkha* (suffering/unsatisfactoriness); there is a cause of suffering; by extinguishing the cause, suffering will cease; and there is a path by which this can be accomplished. It sounds simple and optimistic, but there is a catch. To see any of this personally – the pervasiveness of suffering as well as its cause and cure – requires looking deeply into one's experience. In the words of the Dhammapada, "The master sees with deep wisdom" (403). This is something that we cannot do with a wild "monkey" mind; thus it is in taming that mind that both Buddhist contemplative practices and Buddhist morality enter and where we find the initial introduction of personal peacefulness through meditation and/or through a life of restraint and kindness.

There are two aspects to early Buddhist meditation: peaceful abiding (*shamatha*) and clear seeing (*vipassana*). Shamatha is usually performed by holding the mind to a single object of meditation such as the breath. Its purpose is to calm and stabilize the mind sufficiently so that the meditator is able to direct his attention to moment-to-moment mental occurrences in order to see into their nature.[5] What does he see?

Early Buddhism speaks of the Three Marks of Existence: impermanence, egolessness, and suffering. *Impermanence* points not only to obvious changes such as that people die (called gross impermanence), but to the subtler moment-to-moment arising and falling, birth and death, of one's perceptions and thoughts. Impermanence is usually the first thing the beginning meditator notices, albeit in the form of an active, wandering mind. *Egolessness* raises the question: who is it that observes that mind? What the meditator notices is that the *I/me* who he assumes is the observer is illusive, never in direct sight, and never quite in control. What the more experienced Buddhist meditator also sees is that this illusive supposed self is the center of his motivation, emotions, and actions. *Suffering* is understood in Buddhism to be inherent in a life of struggle to grasp what is felt to be good for that imagined self, to avoid or attack what is felt bad for it, and to ignore all else. One is trapped in the struggle because getting what one wants increases rather than assuages desire (watch what happens the next time you bite into something delicious). Similarly acting out fear, aggression, or ignoring will not relieve one of these emotions as one might wish, but only serves to augment them. In short, in people's usual mode of being, there is no contentment or peace.

This constant cycling from one unsatisfactory mode of being to another is called *samsara*. Samsara was traditionally thought of as composed of actual realms into which a sentient being could be born, but in the West it is usually treated as a succession of mental states (also a traditional option). The realms are states of desire, aggression, or ignorance. The most painful states (called hell realms) are characterized by intense anger, hatred and aggression; the least painful are states of drugged-like ignorance (called god realm) in which beings waste their potential and eventually crash. The most fortunate birth, either for a lifetime or a moment

of experience, was considered to be human realm where intelligent desire generates both enough pain and enough wisdom that people might be led to seek a way
out of their habitual patterns, thus potentially entering a path of realization and
liberation (Trungpa 1976).

The goal of meditation – and of life – was to be liberated from samsara. How? In
early Buddhism, the logic was that since it is desire, aggression, and ignorance in
the mind that forge the chains of cause and effect (*karma*) that keep one impris-
oned, those "three poisons" need to be eliminated from the mind. There were two
basic methods: (1) One could allow one's mind states to rise and fall without
response. This eliminates karmic seeds but requires meditation and an ascetic life
and so was the province of monastics. (2) One could also counter unwholesome
states such as greed, hatred, and aggression with other more wholesome mind
states such as nonviolence, generosity, or loving kindness (*metta*). This method creates good karma, and was appropriate for both monastics and the lay community.
Actions consonant with these wholesome states were the basis of Buddhist morality.

The ultimate goal in early Buddhism and in present Theravada is to attain nirvana (*nibbana*), a state from which, after death, one would not again be reborn.
Although the Buddha refused to elaborate on this state on the grounds that it
would lead to distracting speculation (for example in The *Malankyaputta* Sutta,
Warren 1977), comments in the Dhammapada indicate that the master practitioner who, with great gladness, knows that he has come to the end of the way is
now pure, free, and has found peace.

Mahayana (great vehicle)

Mahayana Buddhism is estimated to have begun around 100 C.E. in India. It eventually spread throughout East Asia: China, Korea, Japan, and parts of Vietnam.
Mahayana added two major teachings to early Buddhism: emptiness (*shunyata* –
see Further Reading and Glossary) and compassion (*karuna*), which are said to be
inseparable "like the two wings of a bird." This is a vast topic, but what is relevant
for present purposes is that in Mahayana there is a type of functioning of the mind
beyond the motivations of samsara. Experientially, emptiness may be interpreted
as a sense of openness, vastness, experience-as-dreamlike, interdependence/unity
with the universe, unfathomability, or sudden release. With that arises the enlightened attitude that cherishes all sentient beings with warmth and compassion.

From the vantage point of emptiness and compassion, the Mahayanist can live
with his senses and thoughts in an enlightened way in this life. In fact, Mahayana
practitioners may take Bodhisattva[6] vows to be reborn in life after life in order to
be of benefit to others. The following fragments from Mahayana liturgies give a
flavor of the vow:

> Sentient being are numberless/I vow to serve them… [typical beginning of a Soto
> Zen Bodhisattva vow]

May I become a light for those in need of light ... a servant for those in need of
service ... a protector of the unprotected. (Santideva 1995, 21)[7]

With such an attitude, lay life can be as valuable and potentially enlightening as
monasticism because of the opportunities and challenges it presents for compassion. In short, in the Mahayana, liberation from samsara does not mean escape
from this life but a transformation of what it means to be in this life.

In later Mahayana, Buddha Nature schools of thought arise; they assert sentient
beings already have an enlightened nature, and the goal of practice is to break
through to the full realization of it. This may be accomplished by fierce concentration,
for example on a koan – a paradox to be meditated upon in order to confound the
conceptual mind of samsara and attain realization (Loori 2006) – and/or by "just
sitting" (*shikantaza*) with a "beginner's mind" (Suzuki 1970). The realized practitioner gains not only peace, but also the inscrutability and power to purvey it,
attributes magnified in the Vajrayana.

Vajrayana (the diamond vehicle)

The Vajrayana began c. 800 C.E. in India. Early forms of it moved into China and
Japan, later ones to Tibet. Because it is the Tibetan forms that are most known and
practiced in the West, I will limit discussion to those. Vajrayana adds two new
teachings to the Buddhism that came before it, as well as a variety of methods originating in Indian Tantra and in pre-Buddhist Tibet. The new teaching is that there
is wisdom awareness (*rigpa*) beyond samsara and beyond emptiness that knows
the primordial ground of being: peaceful, pure, timeless, complete, and all-good.
From that ground radiates the phenomenal world of experience. Known with pure
vision (*dagnang*), the ordinary world of experience – samsara with its grasping,
aggression, ignorance, and suffering – is seen to actually consist of the wisdom
energies of that radiance. Put in the simpler language of the newly emerging
Shambhala path (Trungpa 1984), existence is basically good, and the human body,
senses, mind, society, and world are sacred expressions of that goodness. The
purpose of meditation is to uncover and live from that understanding.

Shambhala

Shambhala is sometimes considered the social activism aspect of Vajrayana. It was
founded by the Tibetan lama Chogyam Trungpa in the United States in the
mid-1970s from terma (received texts), a Tibetan tradition in which texts that are
particularly relevant to the circumstances of a specific time and place will appear
when needed, usually in the mind stream of a suitable receiver. A core Shambhala
teaching is that a peaceful enlightened society is necessary as the container for and
manifestation of personal wisdom and compassionate action. In contrast to present societies that are seen as built on the motives of samsara, an enlightened

society is possible because it can be built on the underlying mind that knows basic goodness directly and is thus fearless, powerful, wise, and loving. Establishing an enlightened society is crucial at this juncture of human history because otherwise the world is headed into a dark age in which human civilization, if it survives at all, will be much diminished. Shambhala society is to be inclusive (like the contemplative mind itself), existing to serve and nourish all facets of society: other religions, families, schools, the environment, businesses, the arts, medicine, government, leadership, and all the other institutions and expressions of human life.

With this, Buddhism comes full circle. In early Buddhism the senses and the activities of ordinary lay life are considered dangerous because they can evoke the three poisons of passion, aggression, and ignorance, and further enmesh one in the prison of samsara. But in these most recent developments of Buddhism, it is believed that when seen with the eye of enlightened awareness beyond the mind of samsara, all of that is none other than awake, sacred, living wisdom itself; the prison is the garden.

Buddhist Sacred Texts

Theravada – the Tripitaka (the Pali Canon): The texts of the Pali Canon are divided into three categories: the Suttas (the Dharma teachings), the Vinaya (rules for monastics), and the Abhidharma (a later systemization sometimes called "Buddhist psychology"). The Suttas are further subdivided into the long, medium, and short discourses (Pande 1967). Theravada citations in this chapter are from the Suttas. The Dhammapada, the most widely read work from the Pali Canon, is a collection of pithy verses from the short discourses.

Mahayana – the Mahayana Sutras: There are many extant Mahayana-like sutras and much scholarly debate about which of them should be classified as canonical Mahayana texts (Warder 1970).

Vajrayana – the Tantras and Terma texts: The Buddhist Tantras (no relation to the sex therapy called "Tantra" now being practiced in the United States) are the basic source material, but since the texts of the tantras themselves are technically not publicly available, it is best to go to the references given for Vajrayana. For Terma texts, see the Glossary.

Perhaps the most important point for Westerners to realize about Buddhist texts is that no text has the status of the Bible or the Qur'an. Most contemporary Buddhists consider Buddhism to be a living transmission tradition. In Mahayana and particularly Vajrayana, it is the teacher (combined with the student's own practice) who is most important in the transmission. Thus the primary sacred texts that tend to be studied by practicing Buddhists are the transcribed talks, writings, and transmissions of their own teacher, later the writings of earlier commentators and teachers in his lineage, and at some point other contemporary teachers. Only the scholarly and those training as teachers would be likely to go to the original sutras or tantras. Thus the works of contemporary Buddhist teachers as well as those of historical commentators that I have cited are considered sacred texts and treated as such, at least by those in the relevant communities.

Finally, one must realize that, in much contemporary Buddhism, the ultimate sacred text is the reality that underlies the medium in which it is presented whether that medium is a text, a teacher, or anything else. Here are two examples of teachings that show this in action:

> Clinging always brings suffering. This is a natural law, like the law of fire. It does not matter whether you believe that fire is hot. When you hold fire, it will burn you. (Ghosananda 1991, 36)

> The ...Vows [Bodhisattva] as we chant them can be traced to the Sixth Patriarch's Platform Sutra. But where do these vows really come from? They arise from our very own life. (Egyoku Nakao 2008)

Historical Development of the Meanings of Peace, Nonviolence, and War

Peace is so central to Buddhism that it is necessary to start with this topic since the other aspects of peace and peacemaking flow from it. In all the forms of Buddhism, the goal of having "a precious human birth" is to find and manifest the true, fundamental, and unconditional state of being that is beyond samsara and is the birthright of sentient beings. "Perfect peace" is one aspect of that state. Even in the later *yanas* of Buddhism, the full flowering of human life has a peaceful (as well as a radiant and expressive) base. By the "ancient and immutable" karmic laws of causality, one cannot approach or reach a state of peace by violent or other nonpeaceful means, whether of thought or action. For example, anger, hatred, ill will, and all the actions that stem from them will only replicate themselves and never lead to freedom from such negativity. It is thus the responsibility of anyone on the path to practice peace, in fact to "be peace" in order to be of benefit to oneself and others (Nhat Hanh 1987a). That said, beyond these commonalities, the meaning of peace and peacemaking changes as the Buddhist understanding of the fundamental state of being and thus the goals of its realization in the ordinary relative world change through history.

In early Buddhism, peace is defined and taught primarily as the peace of mind of individuals. While ultimate peace is achieved only in nirvana after death, relative peace of mind in this life can be attained to the extent that a person can tame his mind and let go of the desires, fears, and aggressions of samsara. "Suffering follows one with an untamed mind as surely as a cart follows an ox. /Peacefulness follows one who has mastered the mind as surely as his own shadow" (Ghosananda 1991, 36 – he is teaching on the opening verse of the Dhammapada).

Nonviolence also begins as a state of mind in which one does not react to the aggression in one's own thoughts or to the attacks of others:

> Oh how he abused me and beat me/How he defeated me and robbed me/Bind your-self to such thoughts and you live in hate. … Cut the bonds to such thoughts, and live in peace. (Dhammapada 3–4).

The peace that comes from mastering the inner war also gives power. For one who does not react to abuse, "The power of forbearance is his mighty army" (Dhammapada 399). Such a one also gains the ability to act for the good, "Like a garland made out of flowers/Make your life out of good deeds" (Dhammapada 53). We will see how both power and good deeds play out in subsequent yanas and subsequent topics.

In Mahayana, increasing glimpses of *shunyata* (emptiness) are understood to be the sword that cuts through the bonds of aggression, that is, that severs allegiance to the thoughts, stories, ambitions, and presuppositions about how things are that keep the mind from being peaceful. And the Bodhisattva ideal speaks to peace between people; if one's intention and purpose in life is to help other people, one will not normally be abusive or violent toward them.

In Vajrayana, peace is considered the fourth mark of existence. Within every experience, if one can penetrate to it, one will find a core of peace and strength; it is like reaching the still (yet potent) center of a hurricane. Paradoxically, according to Vajrayana, it is this peace that people are actively trying to avoid when they make the turn toward aggression; peace undercuts one's fantasies of egohood, whereas it is the emotions of samsara, such as greed and aggression that keep the fantasy world spinning. But for this very reason, one can always turn the other way and "choose peace" (Chodron 2007). Beyond that, there is an emphasis in Vajrayana on the fundamental peace that includes and embraces both peaceful and nonpeaceful states of mind and of the world.

One of the meanings of *shunyata* in Mahayana and Vajrayana is that nothing in the relative world arises independently. In the vast web of interdependence, personal peace of mind and interpersonal and social peace are not actually sepa-rate, nor is there a true separation between minds and the natural world. Thus in Vajrayana and Shambhala, the practitioner has an increasing responsibility toward the interdependent world as a whole, since his states of mind and his actions affect it.[8]

War in Buddhism meant armed conflict between politically separate states as it does now in the West. However unlike the West, war in early Buddhism was seen

Figure 5.2 Woodcut 2 - Four Bodhisattvas. Source: Michael K. Duffey

as the external manifestation of a lack of moral perfection and meditative realization in kings, their ministers, and, through them, the population of their countries as a whole. In the ideal state, ruled by a perfectly righteous *Chakravartin* (universal monarch), it was believed there would be neither crime nor warfare. A more democratized and universal version of this view is taught today; for example, the Tibetan lama Chagdud Tulku speaks of "the space of inner peace from which you recognize with great clarity that war and suffering are the outer reflections of the mind's inner poisons" (Tulku 1988, 94).

Moral Teachings Regarding Violence and Nonviolence

There are two kinds of teachings in Buddhism that Westerners would recognize as moral: precepts that either forbid or bind a person to particular behaviors, and general instructions for how to live one's life. In early Buddhism, five basic precepts apply to lay people as well as monastics; these are injunctions against killing, stealing, lying, intoxication, and sexual misconduct. In their earliest form such directives refer to specific behaviors and are stated in the negative. As Buddhism evolves, prescriptions in the later yanas come increasingly to refer to intentions and may be stated in the positive or have a positive subtext. For example, "Do not kill" has added to it, "Foster life," and then, "Do not let others kill. Find whatever means possible to protect life and prevent war" (Nhat Hanh 1987b, 19).

Instructions for living one's life include nonviolence as part of a total context. In early Buddhism and present Theravada, this context is the Eight-Fold Path: right view, intention, speech, action, livelihood, effort, mindfulness, and concentration. Right view and intention come from one's understanding of the basic Buddhist teachings as explained earlier; right effort, mindfulness, and concentration contain the instructions on how one is to meditate; and right speech, action, and livelihood are the actions that result from understanding the teachings both mentally and at the level of meditative realization. Naturally, the meaning of "right view" and the others change to incorporate changes in the teachings. For example, a right intention in Theravada might be to liberate oneself from samsara; in Mahayana and Vajrayana, it might be to liberate all sentient beings (including oneself); and in Shambhala it could include the intention to establish an enlightened society in which all beings would flourish.

In Mahayana and in the Mahayana instructions given as part of the Vajrayana and Shambhala teachings, morality is more often taught as the six *paramitas* (that which get you to the other shore). These are generosity, discipline, patience, exertion, meditation, and wisdom. Ideally these are to be practiced in a way that transcends the mind of samsara. For example, patience is natural to one who touches into the timelessness of the ground of being; generosity is truly generous when practiced without duality between giver and receiver, and so on.

In the Mahayana sutras, there is additional instruction about what the would-be bodhisattva should do with respect to war. The *Vimalakirti Nirdesa* Sutra tells us that in a time of war (an "era of the sword"), a bodhisattva teaches kindness and peace to beings, and when armies line up for battle, he uses his powers (given him by his great wisdom and compassion) to stop the combat (Luk 1972; Thurman 2003). The Vietnamese peace activist Thich Nhat Hanh translates this famous passage of the sutra, normally rendered in the third person and thus kept somewhat abstract, into a direct instruction to his students and readers who, by implication, are now the bodhisattvas: "Wherever there is furious battle/Use all your might/To keep both sides' strength equal/And then step into the conflict to reconcile them" (Nhat Hanh 1999, 95). This was in fact the kind of activity undertaken

Figure 5.3 Thich Nhat Hanh. Source: Used by permission of Parallax Press (www.parallax.org). Photo by Karen Hagen-Liste

by his organization the School of Youth for Social Service in Vietnam during the Vietnam War – despite great danger and loss to its members.

Vajrayana inherits all of the moral injunctions that preceded it and adds the explicit responsibility to become sufficiently wise and enlightened that one can follow, not just the words, but the meaning of these teachings. It is one's teacher who is the conduit for such wisdom and power, and in accepting a teacher the student becomes bound to him (*samaya*), and should follow his instructions. Thus it is said that when a student has renounced samsara, is acting out of the intention to help others, and has opened himself to his teacher, he will then have the clarity to see what needs to be done and will have the power to carry his actions through to fruition.

How all of these instructions for living come together for peace in ordinary life may be shown by one of the few Pali texts in use by all three of the yanas, the *Karaniyametta* Sutta. It begins, "This is what should be done by the man who is wise, who seeks the good, and who knows the meaning of the place of peace." The text goes on to list attributes of such a man: he is upright, easily contented, not submerged by the things of the world, his senses controlled, not conceited, not desirous of great possessions even for his family, and he does nothing mean or that the wise would reprove. Such a man cultivates the wish that all beings in whatever state be happy, at ease, safe, joyous, and free from deceit, anger, or ill will.

> Even as a mother watches over and protects her child, her only child, so with a boundless mind should one cherish all living beings, radiating friendliness over the entire world, above, below, and all around without limit. (Conze 1951, 185–186)

History of Buddhism's Responses to Violence

As we have seen, the recommendation to individuals in early Buddhism is largely pacifist. The master meditator should not respond to insult or injury even when being cut into pieces by an aggressor. If a monk killed or seriously injured someone, he was expelled from the order and, short of radical reformation, assured of far less fortunate rebirths. But what of larger-scale social violence such as wars and the need to deal with criminals? In the India of the time of the Buddha, such matters were the provenance of kings, and the Brahmanic codes were clear: it was the king's duty to protect his subjects from invasion by enemies through courageous battle and to keep civil order through (horrendously harsh by modern standards) impris-onment, mutilations, and/or executions of criminals (Zimmerman 2006). Where does Buddhism stand on these matters? I will first recount some passages from the Suttas and historical events related to Buddhist peacemaking that are canonical in the discourse of contemporary Buddhists, particularly those in Socially Engaged Buddhist organizations, and then move to a more sociological overview.

The Pali Suttas relate how the Buddha responded on three occasions to situa-tions of potential warfare between neighboring states. In the first instance he placed himself between the two armies and stopped the attack by convincing the attacking king that his reason for the attack, a dispute over water rights, was less important than the lives of the young warriors that would be lost. In the second case, he stopped the conflict by some tricky diplomacy. In the third instance, he judged the conflict unstoppable and did not intervene.

The Buddha's advice to kings also covered matters of internal peace and social order. The king should govern for the welfare of his people and, to prevent social disruption, should care for the needs of all his subjects. Otherwise, as is warned in the *Cakkavatti-Sihanada* Sutta,

> from the not giving of property to the needy, poverty became rife, from the growth of poverty, the taking of what was not given increased, from the increase of theft, the use of weapons increased, from the increased use of weapons, the taking of life increased. (Walshe 1987, 399–400)

And what should the ruler do when the country does become plagued by petty thefts and violent robberies? The *Kutadanta* Sutta counsels that rather than levying more taxes or trying to suppress the wrongdoers by imprisonment or capital punishment, the king should "provide peasants with food and young seedlings, merchants with capital, and government employees with reasonable salaries" (Minh Chau 2006, 221).

The next iconic political figure in Buddhist history is the Indian King Ashoka, who reigned some 300 years after the death of the Buddha. In his youth, Ashoka was warlike, conquered widely, and established the first empire on the Indian subcontinent. According to legend, one day as Ashoka roamed his most recent conquest, he became horrified by the carnage and suffering he had inflicted, renounced warfare, adopted Buddhism as the state religion, and thereafter ruled in what we today would call an enlightened manner, establishing hospitals, forbidding animal sacrifice, decreeing that honor and respect be given to all religions, and ceasing to invade neighboring states (Thurman 1985, 115). The reign of King Ashoka was an important turning point in the relations between ruler and the community, particularly the monastic community, in Buddhist countries. Thereafter, the validation for kingship became how well the king treated the Buddhist monastic establishment, granting them land and other resources and taking monks as advisors, while the role of the monastic sangha was to support the king in his domestic and foreign governance – even when he engaged in aggressive warfare or other violent actions.

Monasticism was also the backbone of civil society in early Buddhism as far as historians can glean from records. Each village of any size had a temple, and the monks of the temple served the community in its secular as well as religious needs. Not only were the monks tasked with teaching the Dharma, setting a moral example, and providing the villagers with the opportunity to gain merit by bringing them food and other necessities; they were also the doctors and schoolteachers; they settled disputes, advised the elders, and acted as counselors (and probably what we now call therapists) for the villagers. Such a structure offered at least the potential for the moderation, forbearance, nonviolence, and loving kindness enjoined in the Pali texts to be taught at the local level and thus serve as a counterbalance to whatever warfare, tyranny, or injustice the rulers, bandits, or bands of rogue monks might impose. This basic system remained in effect in Southeast Asia until the period of colonization by Western nations.

Buddhism encountered a different situation both culturally and politically as it moved eastward into China where it changed structurally in a number of ways (Chen 1964; Dumoulin 2005 vol. 1) and changed yet again as it moved into Korea (Buswell 2005), Japan (Dumoulin 2005 vol. 2), and Tibet (Snellgrove 1987). What remained constant was the monastic establishment as the basic carrier of the teachings and its need for royal support in order to flourish. Again we see examples of the Buddhist establishment actively supporting or at least remaining silent in the face of aggressive warfare and tyranny. We also see periods of social breakdown and chaos in which Buddhist monks themselves take up arms, lead rebellions, or just run wild (see the books listed under Buddhist warfare in the

Buddhist peacemaking organizations and resources section). And in all these instances we see Buddhist teachings interpreted to support violence, the case most disturbing to Westerners being that of Japan during World War II (Victoria 2006). (But note that history, like news, deals primarily with what goes wrong.) As Buddhism entered the West it lost its monastic basis. It is transmitted by individual teachers to their (primarily) lay students who now perform activities such as meditation, study, and retreats that were once the province of monks. Within the Western sociopolitical and cultural context, there are, to date, no Buddhist groups that have espoused violence in principle.

What should we make of the history of Buddhist violence? When learning of it, contemporary Buddhist practitioners are often distressed but seldom surprised. The pull of samsara with its passion, aggression, and ignorance is very strong, they say. The later yanas add that fear of the groundlessness of the more awake states of awareness can further derail practitioners. And Vajrayana warns that there is psychological and spiritual materialism as well as the more familiar material materialism (Trungpa 1973). The usual contemporary Buddhist antidote (which Buddhists also recommend to other religions) is deeper religious practice in which experience of the actual teachings replaces mere words.

Contemporary Buddhist studies scholars, on the other hand, are wont to conclude that history shows Buddhism is actually a violent religion (Faure 2010) or that there is no Buddhism, only Buddhisms, and thus that cruel and violent behavior is as legitimate a form of Buddhism as any other (Jerryson and Juergensmeyer 2010 and Zimmerman 2006 argue for this point of view, whereas Victoria 2006, argues against it.) Anthropology might weigh in with the viewpoint that culture (ideals, morality, myths, views of reality, etc.) and social structure are two different things (Geertz 1973). When these become misaligned, as when a peaceful Buddhist worldview is under pressure from an aggressive society, there will be a breakdown, and people will strive to bring the two into greater cohesion, either by reinterpreting Buddhist teachings to support aggression, or, as in the case of the modern rise of socially engaged Buddhism, to change social structures to more closely fit ideals.

Permissible violence and restrictions on its use

In Theravada Buddhism, strictly speaking there is no permissible violence. Any aggressive response either to one's own thoughts or to the provocations of another person will create bad karma. On the other hand, it is the responsibility of rulers to protect the country from invaders and maintain civil order. What if these two conflict? This has been the situation for the Sinhalese Buddhists in Sri Lanka during the protracted insurgency of the Tamil Tigers. The young Sinhalese soldiers are worried about the karmic consequences of fighting and potentially killing. The monks counseling them, although themselves conflicted over this issue, bless the men and assure them that it is their intention (*cetana*) that matters; if they can feel no anger or hatred toward the enemy and instead concentrate on feeling loving kindness, then they can avoid the karma (Kent 2010).

A similarly complex situation exists in southern Thailand where, due to repeated attacks on Buddhist villagers and monks by the local Muslims, Thai soldiers have been moved into the monasteries, and even some monks carry guns (Jerryson 2010). In contrast to the sympathy generally engendered by these two situations, recent Buddhist mob violence against members of the Muslim minority in Burma incited by the vitriolic hate speech of a young monk, generally elicits rejection from Buddhists, at least those outside the conflict zone, as "un-Buddhist."

In Mahayana and Vajrayana teachings, acting with kindness, compassion, and for the greater good supersedes rules. Thus killing in order to save a greater number of people is honored – as in a canonical tale in which the captain of a ship kills one man who is going to kill the other 499 on board. Sacrificing one's own life for another is modeled in the Jataka tales,[9] the most famous of which is when the future Buddha gives himself as food to a starving tigress. However, self-immolation for a cause, particularly the recent spate of it among Tibetans, is controversial. Killing is also debatable in the case of an assassination where the arithmetic is hypothetical or where it is a matter of saving the Dharma (or the true Dharma) rather than lives. And Buddhists, certainly Western Buddhists, tend to react with horror to the use of Dharma reasoning to justify bald faced aggression, for example, proclamations by Japanese Buddhist leaders during World War II that there was no harm in killing as long as one understood that no real self exists to kill or be killed. This said, it should be noted that the canonical recommended Buddhist response to all such actions is to send compassion, not judgment, equally to perpetrator and victim – even as one may take steps to ensure it does not happen again.

The specialty of Vajrayana is to confront and deal with inner aggression directly so that it may be transmuted into the energy of skillful means (*upaya*) needed to perform Buddha activity. Thus in Tibetan rituals and myth, there is much use of imagery in which aggressive energy is turned against itself. For example, a three-sided dagger (*phurba*) may stab passion, aggression, and ignorance in one blow. A favorite metaphor is that of the peacock who is believed to be able to eat poison and thus transform it into the rainbow colors of its feathers. In principle, a highly realized teacher who acts directly from the wisdom beyond mind has license to do anything, but that is because he is believed to be bound by vows and cosmic laws more demanding than human custom. For example, the tragicomic mythic hero Gesar of Ling fights and kills an army of demons, but he is then responsible for getting them all out of the hell realms, which takes eons (David-Neel 1934).[10] The one case I know of in which a nonmythic contemporary person seriously overstepped the bounds (an American Dharma heir of a lama brashly endangered many lives), that gentleman was promptly removed from his position by the head of his lineage and ordered into indefinite retreat.

Emerging Innovative Peacemaking Practices

Social activism as we know it is a modern development, and, given a political climate in which it is possible, activist peace and justice movements have sprung up in all of the forms of Buddhism. I will touch here only on the largest and most visible. (For more material on these see the Socially Engaged Buddhism subsection under Further Reading in the Resources section.)

In Sri Lanka as early as the 1950s, the Buddhist layman Dr A. T. Ariyaratne, partly influenced by Gandhi, founded Sarvodaya Shramadana as a means of fostering Buddhist-inspired economic development at the village level. Ariyaratne uses the logic of the Four Noble Truths (suffering, its cause, its cessation, and the path to cessation) as a format for analyzing the causes and cures for specific worldly types of suffering. As conflict between the Tamils and Sinhalese increased, Sarvodaya organized a series of peace walks and meditations in which Sri Lankans on both sides practiced *metta* (a loving kindness meditation) and pledged to work toward removing hatred and violence from their hearts and actions. Here is an example of the coordination of individual and societal peacefulness. Approximately two million people participated in these peace gatherings, 10% of the population of Sri Lanka, and this work has been credited with helping forge the initial 2-year ceasefire between the Tamils and Sinhalese. (Imagine the effect if 10% of the population of the United States, 30 million people, were to join in a peace march.)

In Thailand, the foundations for Buddhist activism were laid by the monk Buddhadasa and are presently carried on by his student Sulak Sivaraksa. Buddhadasa taught that the spiritual and social were not separate, that the social goal of Buddhism was world peace, and that the key to accomplishing it is the unselfishness and purity that comes from realizing there is no actual self. Sulak works for the transformation of Thai society, and is the founder of the International Network of Engaged Buddhists (INEB). A hallmark of Buddhist activism in Thailand is the ingenious ways it has found to make use of existing cultural customs. For example, to counter the ongoing deforestation of the countryside by foreign logging companies, senior monks ordain trees, thus making whole tracts of forest inviolable. In already deforested areas, villagers are requested to give seedling fruit trees to the monks in lieu of their usual offerings; thereby the land is protected from erosion, and the villagers receive both merit for the gift and fruit from the trees. Such activities illustrate what is generally striven for, at least in theory, in contemporary Buddhist activism; not only is it nonviolent but it seeks a win–win solution to conflicts.

The reconstruction of Cambodian society and government after the decimation of the country by the Khmer Rouge illustrates perhaps the most difficult aspect of Buddhist peacemaking for Westerners to understand. The Cambodian monk and meditation master Maha Ghosananda was instrumental not only in re-inspiring the country by his presence, teachings, and vast month-long peace walks, but by his role in negotiating the peace agreement and brokering the four-party interim government that formally terminated the Khmer Rouge dictatorship. The Khmer Rouge was allowed a place in the government as one of those parties, and members of the Khmer Rouge were never brought to justice for their crimes. There is Buddhist logic to this; dwelling on the past and revenge for wrongs is not what brings peace.

In Myanmar/Burma, the long, patient wait under house arrest of democratically elected Aung San Suu Kyi and the images, in the 2007 uprising, of vast assemblies of monks walking peacefully, despite reprisals, in protest against actions of the military junta provide evidence of Burmese Buddhist nonviolent activism. This may have had a hand in bringing about the present easing of restrictions in Burma.

Thich Nhat Hanh, the Vietnamese monk, meditation teacher, and poet, is one of the best-known Buddhist peace activists in the West. It is he who gave Socially Engaged Buddhism its name. During the Vietnam War, he founded The School of Youth for Social Service, members of which worked throughout the country to alleviate the suffering caused by the war without taking sides with either North or South. For this they were considered enemies by both sides and summarily killed. Now in his 80s and still exiled from Vietnam, Thich Nhat Hanh travels widely giving teachings. He has founded the Community for Mindful Living (CML), the interfaith Order of Interbeing, and several residential communities such as Plum Village in France. His first principle is that in order to work effectively for peace, one must "be peace." Thus his followers are enjoined to meditate, study, and train themselves using the method of *mindfulness*, a term that he uses quite broadly. He considers social involvement a natural extension of meditation practice; that is, anything that one does to alleviate suffering such as working with the homeless, prisoners, abused women, or environmental causes is as much working for peace as marching in an antiwar protest. All of it should be done with a mind of compassion and empathy that does not take sides or judge people.

The Buddhist Peace Fellowship (BPF) was formed under the influence of Aitken Roshi, head of the Diamond Sangha in Hawaii, and Thich Nhat Hanh. It now includes members from a variety of Buddhist sanghas as well as non-Buddhist activists. It operates with a determinedly nonhierarchical structure, and local chapters involve themselves in the peace work to which they feel most drawn. BPF is the Buddhist chapter in the Fellowship of Reconciliation (FOR), a Christian led inter-religious peace organization. BPF has been a source of influence through its publications; their magazine called *Turning Wheel* has become an organ for engaged Buddhist writings, and books of edited collections of such writings sell widely.

The Peacemaker Order is a multifaceted innovative activist organization founded and headed by the American Zen teacher Bernard Glassman Roshi. It operates with three basic tenets: begin with the mind of not knowing; bear witness to the pains and joys of the world; and heal yourself and all beings in the universe. Glassman is best known for leading street retreats in lower Manhattan, meditation retreats at the crematoriums at Auschwitz-Birkenau, and for organizing the

Greyston Mandala, a network of for-profit businesses and nonprofit agencies that serve the poor and initiate community development in an impoverished area of Yonkers, New York. Greyston includes: the Greyston Bakery, a highly profitable gourmet confectioner that provides job training and employment to the homeless; Greyston Building, which renovates abandoned buildings into affordable housing; an AIDS hospice and walk-in clinic; a handicrafts company that recycles used clothing and provides employment, and the Greyston Family Inn. The Peacemaker Order is closely associated with The Interfaith Peacemaker Assembly and a network of Peacemaker local groups throughout the United States and abroad.

Based in Taiwan, the Tzu Chi (Compassionate Relief) Foundation is the largest humanitarian nongovernment organization in the Chinese-speaking world. Founded in 1966 by the Buddhist nun Cheng Yen out of pennies that local housewives pledged to save from their grocery money to donate to impoverished families, it has now grown to approximately 10 million members and works in 47 countries. Its Buddhism is of the late Mahayana Buddha Nature teachings, but it is content to offer a wide range of services wherever needed without either politics or religion. Through its strict adherence to its rules of noninterference and non-proselytizing and its skill in providing services, it has become the only foreign aid agency allowed into mainland China to help with disaster relief.

The present Dalai Lama serves as an icon of nonviolence and compassion for the Western world. His good humor and rejection of anger toward the Chinese who have devastated Tibet are an inspiration to his admirers. Although his efforts at negotiation with the Chinese have not been met with success, he has been able to bring together Tibetans, an accomplishment that requires explanation: Tibetan Buddhism is divided into four main lineages, each with a spiritual head. A Dalai Lama is the head of only one lineage the Gelug, which was founded in the fourteenth century as a fundamentalist reform movement in a time of strife. Its teachings are basically early Mahayana, distinguishable from the Vajrayana of the other lineages. In the seventeenth century the fifth Dalai Lama, in a massive military campaign, conquered the rest of Tibet and installed himself as the political head of the country. Thereafter, the Gelug lineage remained in suppressive political and doctrinal conflict with the other lineages. As late as the 1970s, teachers of other lineages would speak of the Gelugpas in terms reminiscent of our descriptions of the Borgias of Renaissance Italy. That has changed in the last 30 years. The present Dalai Lama has shared resources with the other lineages, allowed them their own doctrines, forbidden his lineage to continue activities that the other lineages perceived as persecutions, and in general won most Tibetans over with his goodwill – not always the case for governments in exile of fractured societies. He has also founded the Dalai Lama Center for Peace and Education in Vancouver and the Mind and Life Institute whose mandate is the (not uncontroversial) effort to bring science and Buddhism together.

Shambhala aims at systemic transformation of the institutions of society so that they will embody the "inherent peacefulness, goodness, and creativity" of existence. The Shambhala sangha – approximately 10 000 members spread over 62 countries with the largest concentration in North America – is the proving ground for such experimentation. How can a society create sane educational institutions that foster natural learning while still providing structure? Shambhala has founded Alaya Preschool, Shambhala School K-12, and Naropa University. How might someone run a successful business based on enrichment of the world rather than on earning money for a small number of stakeholders? How can we ensure leaders who are able to inspire, lead, and make wise decisions without falling prey to the corruption of power and self-inflation? Shambhala runs intensive leadership and business training programs for its own sangha and has founded related public institutes: ALIA, Sane Systems, and The Berkana Institute. Finally, what kinds of institutions can protect a society from violence (the task now charged to the military and police) without being violent in return? In Tibetan iconography, protector figures surround each mandala; their mandate is to confront any intruder meaning harm with such "authentic presence" that the troublemaker has a change of heart and enters peacefully. Shambhala is experimenting with this and is now partnering with groups in Chicago to see how it might help in reducing violence in the troubled areas of that city.

Conclusions: What in Buddhism Provides the Means for Nonviolent Peacemaking?

Buddhist teachings, meditation practices, and ways of living are understood to form the basis of Buddhist social actions, at least by contemporary Buddhist teachers. Such factors, it is argued, are what make possible renunciation of the violent mind of samsara as first taught in early Buddhism, discovery of the mind of loving kindness and compassion doctrinally emphasized in Mahayana, and surrender to what is beyond the mind of samsara brought to the fore in Vajrayana. Ideally such practices and realizations also provide the wisdom and confidence to remake the world for peace as striven for in Shambhala and in the various forms of Engaged Buddhism. There are a number of principles and methods in Buddhism that differ from social activism in the West; hopefully a discussion of these will serve to stimulate creative thoughtfulness in westerners.

1. The peacemaker needs to be peaceful. An angry, vengeful, or antagonistic peace worker might sometimes contribute to a short-term goal but will be sowing the seeds for the longer-term continuity of aggression. Virtually everything discussed so far about Buddhism can be used as a means towards inner peace. Basic meditation is intended to calm and stabilize the mind and the bodily energy system, and the development of the clear seeing that "penetrates ignorance," by revealing a relative world of impermanence, egolessness, and

suffering, should help to quell the extremes of greed, anger, hatred, and fear. (I have seen strongly provoked people calmed by being reminded of such truths.) Mindfulness provides the discipline of body and mind whereby a person is no longer blown about by every passing thought and impulse and can make considered decisions. In the later yanas, a glimpse of emptiness or basic ground can interrupt fixed ideas and negative habits. *Metta* and compassion practices, by shifting one's attitude toward serving others, also help create inner warmth and peace in oneself. Finally any glimpse of a ground, beyond the relative mind, that can hold both peace and turmoil without bias makes for a peaceful inclusiveness.

2. Relatedness to others and nonjudgmental empathy with them. As a practitioner becomes increasingly aware, through mindfulness, of the wildness, demands, and aggression of her own thoughts and emotions, she can begin to see her likeness in the maneuverings of other people and to feel kinship with them. And, ideally, as a person learns to be gentle with what arises internally, he can also cast a gentle eye on outward interactions. Contemplation of causal interdependence further helps to elicit such a frame of mind. If everything in the relative world is the product of causes and conditions, then had I been the subject to the same causes and conditions that produced that person with whom I disagree so violently, or who is causing so much harm, or who has committed such a horrendous crime, then I would believe and act just as that person does. Not only would I be walking in that person's shoes, I would be that person. *Metta* and compassion meditations help yet further to melt fixed judgmental attitudes about oneself or others. Notice that Buddhist descriptions of the realization of one's interrelatedness with other people and everything else that "arises in the world" often sound very close to the basic attitude of relatedness described for indigenous peoples by Tink Tinker.[11]

3. Going beyond "justice." In Western thought, it is almost impossible to separate the idea of justice from a judgmental attitude, even from the idea of revenge. If instead of payback for things done wrong in the past, one were to think, "What is the best outcome in the future for everyone involved, and how can that best be achieved?" then not only might daily interactions with people go differently, but prisons and the criminal justice system might be run in a less aggressive manner. This principle also encompasses political justice. A group that has held power in a country and done much damage, such as the Khmer Rouge in Cambodia, need not be fought into abject powerlessness or punished for their mistakes. Peace in Cambodia was made possible not by seeking reprisal, but by aiming to reconcile alienated parties and alleviate suffering swiftly.

4. Going beyond winning. At an even deeper level, the goal of Buddhist peacemaking is not to win while another loses. Gain versus loss, victory versus defeat, and success versus failure are said to be stumbling blocks

within the mentality of samsara. As is taught by the Thai Buddhist activist Sivaraksa:

> Victory creates hatred. Defeat creates suffering. … He who kills will be killed. He who wins will be defeated. … Revenge can only be overcome by abandoning revenge. … The wise ones desire neither victory nor defeat. (Sivaraksa 1996, 78)

5. Practicality and immediacy of action. One does what can be done rather than holding out for ideals. This begins with a mindfulness that can make discerning choices. In Mahayana and the later yanas, this immediacy is understood to be nonconceptual and to arise out of the mind of not knowing. The discipline is to stay with that state of not knowing and let the impetus toward action arise from it, rather than from the habits of samsara. There is faith that just as the well-trained martial artist will know what motion to make without thought, so the disciplined and sincere would-be bodhisattva will be moved to say and do what is best without strategizing.

6. Nonduality. The nondual can be experienced at different levels. First is the interdependence of phenomena; for example, a piece of paper does not self-exist in a vacuum but is dependent on the trees, the sun, the logger, the logger's parents, etc. This may lead to a sense of unity; we are part of the world, and thus our welfare and the welfare of the world are not separate.[12] The root and cutting edge of Buddhist nonduality in the later yanas is the nonduality of the subject and object of experience. All of the Buddhist practices already discussed, including Vajrayana mind-to-mind transmission, play a role in bringing a practitioner to this point. Nondual experience is naked and direct; it is the popping of the bubble of the seeming experiencer living in his cocoon of me-ness and spinning the dramas that create inner and outer warfare. The practitioner willing to abide in this nakedness gains intimations of the expanded world of beauty, brilliance, and peace available to him if he is willing to live thus.

7. Power. Power is the result of finally having let go and now being in touch with the energies of the world. It resembles the ideal of "nonaction" in some of the martial arts, such as aikido, as well as the Tibetan and Shambhala ideal of the enlightened warrior (*pawo*) who is beyond aggression. In the West we tend to think of peace and nonviolence as quiescent and weak. Not so in Buddhism, as is illustrated in the following teaching story, to which I will give the final word.

In a time of warring clans, the inhabitants of a small village, hearing that the enemy is approaching, flee into the forest, leaving behind only the Abbot of the village temple. As the enemy soldiers sweep into the village, the general struts into the temple and is startled to see a lone figure sitting unmoved. He strides up to the Abbot and shouts, "You! Don't you know you are looking at a man who can run you through in an instant without blinking?" The Abbot replies, "Ah, yes. And don't you know that you are looking at a man who can be run through in an instant without blinking?" The two lock eyes, and slowly the general sinks to his knees, bows his head to the floor, and requests the Abbot to become his teacher.[13]

Questions for Discussion

1. What are the primary teachings of Theravada Buddhism? What teachings does Mahayana add? What does Vajrayana add? Why do you think the different forms of Buddhism may have stayed together as one religion while other religions such as Judaism and Christianity split apart?
2. Name and describe three peace activist movements in contemporary Buddhism. How does each employ Buddhist principles?
3. What is a practitioner of Theravada Buddhism supposed to do with his anger or his aggressive impulses? What might a Mahayanist do with such impulses? What could an advanced Vajrayana practitioner supposedly do with them?
4. What role does meditative/contemplative practice have in the Buddhist understanding of peace and nonviolence? What implications might this have for contemplative traditions in Western religions?
5. How are Buddhist principles and practices being used in present Buddhist peace activism? Is any of that different from activism in other religions and/or different from secular activism? What in Buddhist activism might or might not be applicable on a larger scale?
6. If groups or members of a religion act violently and use teachings within the religion to justify their actions, does that mean that that religion is violent? What factors in the religion or its environment would lead you to say "yes" or "no?"
7. What in Buddhist teachings support the principle of not seeking vengeful or punishing forms of justice? Is this practical? When might it work and when not?
8. Vajrayana is sometimes accused by the earlier yanas of being covertly theistic with its all-good ground of being. How might it affect attitudes toward peacemaking and nonviolence to think of the basis of being and of creation in human-like terms as is done in Western religions or to refuse to use linguistic personification as is the case in Vajrayana Buddhism? What would count as evidence of such effects among religions?
9. What might a large-scale enlightened peaceful society be like? How might it institutionalize education, business, government, protection from invasion

and crime, child rearing, agriculture, urban planning, the arts, health care, and/or anything else you're interested in – and what role would religion(s) play in it? What kinds of religion?

Notes

1 The quotation in the title is from Ghosananda (1991), 30.

2 The Dhammapada is a collection of pithy verses from the Suttas of the Pali canon. Direct translations from the Dhammapada are my own. The number following the citation is the standard identifying number for that verse.

3 The incident related is an amalgam of a number of verbal reports with the written accounts provided in the Preface, Foreword, and Editor's Introduction to Ghosananda (1991).

4 More material on the topics in the following sections can be found in the books listed in the Buddhist peacemaking organizations and resources section, and expanded definitions of non-English words are provided in the Glossary.

5 *Shamatha* is the Sanskrit word for peaceful abiding, and *vipassana* the Pali word for clear seeing. I am giving these forms because they are what are generally used in North American meditation communities where they have come to be used as English words. Although the distinction between these two may be clear in principle, in actuality there is much dispute between Buddhist groups regarding which specific meditation practices should be classified under which label. Another English word in popular present use for these types of meditation is *mindfulness,* a term that tends to indiscriminately include not only shamatha and vipassana but also various Western therapeutic techniques along with their hypothesized effects (Rosch in press).

6 An aspiring Bodhisattva is someone who takes vows not to go into nirvana until all beings are enlightened, but instead to be continuously reborn in order to be of service. A realized Bodhisattva would be someone who actually is reborn, not because he or she is driven by "the fierce red winds of karma," but because of that vow (see also Glossary).

7 Phrases such as these from Santideva are often used in Mahayana and Vajrayana Bodhisattva vows.

8 Note how many of the practical Buddhist teachings on interdependence mirror the sense of relatedness in Native American and other indigenous cultures discussed by Tink Tinker's chapter in this volume.

9 The Jataka tales are folkloric stories of the Buddha's former lives as a self-sacrificing Bodhisattva. They are particularly popular in Southeast Asia where they serve as children's stories.

10 Here "hell realms" has the traditional meaning of a realm into which a sentient being can be born, not the meaning of a state of mind alone. Hell realms are states of aggression (see the explanation of samsara under Theravada).

11 You might wish to compare Tinker's description (see Chapter 7 in this volume) with Buddhist descriptions of interdependence in some of the works listed under "Further Reading," Socially Engaged Buddhism.

12   See Duffey, Chapter 2 in this volume, for an example of how Thich Nhat Hanh applies
      the interdependent sense of nonduality to American participation in the Vietnam war.
13   I have heard different versions of this story told several times by Vajrayana teachers,
      but the only written source appears to be Leggett (1977), 160. My account of the story
      is an amalgam of these sources.

References

Buswell, Robert E. (ed.) 2005. *Currents and Countercurrents: Korean Influences on the East
    Asian Buddhist Traditions.* Honolulu, HI: University of Hawaii Press.
Chen, K. K. S. 1964. *Buddhism in China: A Historical Survey.* Princeton, NJ: Princeton
    University Press.
Chodron, Pema. 2007. *Practicing Peace in Times of War.* Boston, MA: Shambhala.
Conze, Edward, trans. 1951. *Buddhist Scriptures.* New York: Penguin.
David-Neel, Alexandra. 1934. *The Superhuman Life of Gesar of Ling.* New York: Claude
    Kendall.
Dumoulin, Heinrich. 2005. *Zen Buddhism: A History, Vol. 1 India and China, and Vol. 2 Japan,*
    translated by James W. Heisig and Paul Knitter. Bloomington, IN: World Wisdom.
Egyoku Nakao, Sensei Wendy. 2008. Presentation for Dharma Nashville.
Faure, Bernard. 2009. *Unmasking Buddhism.* Chichester: Wiley Blackwell.
Faure, Bernard. 2010. "Afterthoughts." In *Buddhist Warfare.* Edited by Michael K. Jerryson
    and Mark Jeurgensmeyer, 211–225. Oxford: Oxford University Press.
Geertz, Clifford. 1973. *The Interpretation of Cultures,* 2000 edition. New York: Basic Books.
Ghosananda, Maha. 1991. *Step by Step: Meditations on Wisdom and Compassion.* Berkeley,
    CA: Parallax.
Jerryson, Michael. 2010. "Militarizing Buddhism: Violence in Southern Thailand." In
    Buddhist Warfare. Edited by Michael K. Jerryson and Mark Juergensmeyer, 179–209.
    Oxford: Oxford University Press.
Jerryson, Michael K. and Juergensmeyer, Mark (eds) 2010a. *Buddhist Warfare.* Oxford:
    Oxford University Press.
Kent, Daniel W. 2010. "Onward Buddhist Soldiers: Preaching to the Sri Lankan Army." In
    Buddhist Warfare. Edited by Michael K. Jerryson and Mark Juergensmeyer, 157–177.
    Oxford: Oxford University Press.
Kornfield, Jack. 1991. "Preface." In *Step by Step: Meditations on Wisdom and Compassion.*
    Maha Ghosananda, vii–viii. Berkeley, CA: Parallax.
Leggett, Trevor. 1977. *The Tiger's Cave.* London: Routledge & Kegan Paul.
Loori, John Daido (ed.) 2006. *Sitting with Koans: Essential Writings on the Zen Practice of
    Koan Introspection.* Somerville, MA: Dharma Communications Press.
Luk, Charles, trans. 1972. *The Vimalakirti Nirdesa Sutra.* Boston, MA: Shambhala.
McMahan, David L. 2008. *The Making of Buddhist Modernism.* Oxford and New York:
    Oxford University Press.
Minh Chau, Thich. 2006. "Buddhist Ethics and a New Moral Order." In *Buddhist Exploration
    of Peace and Justice.* Edited by Ronald S. Green and Chanju Mun, 215–224. Honolulu,
    HI: Blue Pine.
Nhat Hanh, Thich. 1987a. *Being Peace.* Berkeley, CA: Parallax.

Nhat Hanh, Thich. 1987b. *Interbeing: Fourteen Guidelines for Engaged Buddhism*. Berkeley, CA: Parallax.

Nhat Hanh, Thich. 1999. *The Miracle of Mindfulness: A Manual on Meditation*. Translated by Mobi Warren. Boston, MA: Beacon Press.

Pande, Govind Chandra. 1967. *Studies in the Origins of Buddhism*. Cambridge: Cambridge University Press.

Rosch, Eleanor. In press. "The Emperor's Clothes: A Look Behind the Western Mindfulness Mystique." In *Handbook of Mindfulness and Self-Regulation*. Edited by Brian Ostafin, Michael Robinson, and Brian Meier. Amsterdam: Springer.

Santideva. 1995. *The Bodhicaryavatara*. Translated by Kate Crosby and Andrew Skilton. Oxford: Oxford University Press.

Sharf, Robert H. 1995. "Buddhist Modernism and the Rhetoric of Meditation Experience." *Numen* 42: 228–283.

Sivaraksa, Sulak. 1996. "Buddhism in a World of Change." In *Engaged Buddhist Reader*. Edited by Arnold Kotler, 70–78. Berkeley, CA: Parallax.

Snellgrove, David. 1987. *Indo-Tibetan Buddhism: Indian Buddhists and Their Tibetan Successors*. 2 vols. Boston, MA: Shambhala.

Suzuki, Shunryu. 1970. *Zen Mind, Beginner's Mind*. New York: John Weatherhill.

Thurman, Robert A. F. 1985. "Edicts of Ashoka." In *The Path of Compassion: Writings on Socially Engaged Buddhism*. Edited by Fred Eppsteiner, 111–119. Berkeley, CA: Parallax.

Thurman, Robert A. F. trans. 2003. *The Holy Teaching of Vimalakirti: A Mahayana Scripture by Vimalakirti*. University Park, PA: Penn State University Press.

Trungpa, Chögyam. 1973. *Cutting Through Spiritual Materialism*. Boston, MA: Shambhala.

Trungpa, Chögyam. 1976. *The Myth of Freedom and the Way of Meditation*. Boston, MA: Shambhala.

Trungpa, Chögyam. 1984. *Shambhala: The Sacred Path of the Warrior*. Boston, MA: Shambhala.

Tulku, Chagdud. 1988. "The Power of Peace." In *The Path of Compassion: Writings on Socially Engaged Buddhism*. Edited by Fred Eppsteiner, 93–94. Berkeley, CA: Parallax.

Victoria, Brian Daizen. 2006. *Zen at War*, 2nd ed. Lenham, MD: Rowman & Littlefield.

Walshe, Maurice, trans. 1987. *The Long Discourses of the Buddha: A Translation of the Digha Nikaya*. Boston, MA: Wisdom.

Warder, A. K. 1970. *Indian Buddhism*. Delhi: Motilal Banarsidass.

Warren, Henry Clarke, trans. 1977. *Buddhism in Translation*. New York: Atheneum.

Zimmermann, Michael. 2006. "Only a Fool Becomes a King: Buddhist Stances on Punishment." In *Buddhism and Violence*. Edited by Michael Zimmerman, 213–242. Lumbini: Lumbini International Research Institute.

Further Reading

Early Buddhism and Theravada

Buddhaghosa, Bhadantacariya. 1976. *The Path of Purification (Visuddhimagga)*. 2 vols. Boston, MA: Shambhala. A comprehensive commentary written c. 430 C.E. that condenses and systematizes the theoretical and practical teachings contained in the Tripitaka.

Byrom, Thomas. 1993. Trans. *Dhammapada: The Sayings of the Buddha*. Boston, MA: Shambhala. A beautiful though not literal translation.

Kornfield, Jack. 1977. *Living Buddhist Masters*. Santa Cruz, CA: Unity. A highly readable collection of interviews and discourses from 12 contemporary Southeast Asian Buddhist teachers.

Rahula, Walpola. 1959. *What the Buddha Taught*. New York: Grove. A pioneering introduction to Theravada Buddhism for the English-speaking public.

Mahayana

Nhat Hanh, Thich. 1987. *Being Peace*. Berkeley, CA: Parallax. Contains many of Thich Nhat Hanh's teachings, poems, and fables on peace and meditation.

Shantideva. 1995. *The Bodhicaryavatara*. Translated by Kate Crosby, and Andrew Skilton. Oxford: Oxford University Press. A classic Mahayana Buddhist text written c. 700 C.E. as a guide to the way of life of a compassionate would-be Bodhisattva.

Sprung, Mervyn. 1979. *Lucid Exposition of the Middle Way*. Boulder, CO: Prajna. An introduction to Nagarjuna's *Madhyamika* philosophy through a pairing of Nagarjuna's verses with a later commentary by Chandrakirti in his work the *Prasanapada*.

Trungpa, Chogyam. 1993. *Training the Mind and Cultivating Loving-Kindness*. Boston, MA: Shambhala. Practical training in compassion provided by Trungpa's commentaries on a set of pithy Mahayana sayings designed to be helpful in difficult situations.

Vajrayana

Fremantle, Francesca. 2003. *Luminous Emptiness: Understanding the Tibetan Book of the Dead*. Boston, MA: Shambhala. A highly readable exposition of the Vajrayana understanding of life and death written as a commentary on *The Tibetan Book of the Dead*.

Ponlop, Dzogchen. 2003. *Wild Awakening: The Heart of Mahamudra and Dzogchen*. Boston, MA: Shambhala. Presentation of teachings considered the most difficult in Tibetan Buddhism in a readable direct style.

Sogyal. 1991. *The Tibetan Book of Living and Dying*. San Francisco, CA: HarperSanFrancisco, 1994. Bestselling overview of Tibetan Buddhism, combining folksy anecdotes, Dharma talks, and pointed instructions.

Trungpa, Chögyam. 2001. *Crazy Wisdom*. Boston, MA: Shambhala. Life of Padmasambhava written in a manner designed to transmit his profound wisdom.

Shambhala

Mipham, Sakyong. 2013. *The Shambhala Principle: Discovering Humanity's Hidden Treasure*. New York: Harmony Books. Implications of Shambhala principles of basic goodness and enlightened society for relationships, government, the economy, education, health, and human rights.

Trungpa, Chögyam. 1984. *Shambhala: The Sacred Path of the Warrior*. Boston, MA: Shambhala. The first presentation of Shambhala in a series of talks, now considered a classic.

Trungpa, Chögyam. 2001. *Great Eastern Sun: The Wisdom of Shambhala*. Boston, MA: Shambhala. Talks to students in a program called Shambhala Training that convey some of the power and bite of these teachings not usually publicly available.

Socially Engaged Buddhism

Eppsteiner, Fred (ed.) 1985. *The Path of Compassion: Writings on Socially Engaged Buddhism*. Berkeley, CA: Parallax. A collection of short essays by the major teachers and organizers who founded Socially Engaged Buddhism.

King, Sallie B. 2009. *Socially Engaged Buddhism*. Honolulu, HI: University of Hawaii Press. A coherent book on the foundations and principles of Socially Engaged Buddhism with engagingly written examples of how these principles are being put into practice

Kraft, Kenneth (ed.) 1992. *Inner Peace, World Peace: Essays on Buddhism and Nonviolence*. Albany, NY: SUNY. Interesting and at times surprising essays on various aspects of peacemaking – for example, how children apply nonviolent resistance with their parents.

Queen, Christopher S. (ed.) 2000. *Engaged Buddhism in the West*. Boston, MA: Wisdom Publications. Substantial essays on the major socially engaged Buddhist groups in North America and Europe.

Queen, Christopher S. and Sallie B. King (eds) 1996. *Engaged Buddhism: Buddhist Liberation Movements in Asia*. Albany, NY: SUNY. A series of essays well described by the title.

Buddhist Warfare

Jerryson, Michael K. and Juergensmeyer, Mark (eds) 2010b. *Buddhist Warfare*. Oxford: Oxford University Press. Eight case studies from antiquity to the present where Buddhist organizations have used religious rhetoric to support military activity.

Victoria Brian Daizen. 2006. *Zen at War*, 2nd ed. Lenham, MD: Rowman & Littlefield. Documents with hair-raising thoroughness the role of Buddhist leaders in supporting Japanese militarism during World War II.

Zimmermann, Michael (ed.) 2006. *Buddhism and Violence*. Lumbini: Lumbini International Research Institute. A set of thought-provoking case studies in which Buddhism has grappled with or supported violence.

Buddhist Peacemaking Organizations and Resources

Buddhist Peace Fellowship (BPF) www.buddhistpeacefellowship.org (accessed December 5, 2014).

The Community for Mindful Living (CML) http://www.uufr.org/community-life/friendship-and-fellowship/cml (accessed December 5, 2014).

The Dalai Lama Center for Peace and Education dalailamacenter.org (accessed December 5, 2014).

International Network of Engaged Buddhists (INEB) www.inebnetwork.org (accessed December 5, 2014).

International Women's Partnership for Peace and Justice: Buddhist Education for Social Transformation (BEST) http://womenforpeaceandjustice.org/courses-we-offer/best/ (accessed December 5, 2014).

The Order of Interbeing www.orderofinterbeing.org (accessed December 5, 2014).

The Peacemaker Order (and the Zen Peacemaker Order) zenpeacemakers.org (accessed December 5, 2014).

Sarvodaya Shramadana http://www.sarvodaya.org/about (accessed December 5, 2014).

Shambhala www.shambhala.org (accessed December 5, 2014).

Tzu Chi http://www.us.tzuchi.org/us/en/ (accessed December 5, 2014).

Glossary

Bodhisattva: An aspiring Bodhisattva is someone who takes vows not to go into nirvana until all beings are enlightened, but instead to be continuously reborn in order to be of service to others. A realized Bodhisattva would actually be reborn from his vow rather than from karma. The Bodhisattva vow was instituted in Mahayana and is considered a prerequisite for entering Vajrayana.

Egolessness: The fundamental Buddhist realization that the lasting and all-precious self we think we are is nowhere to be found. The early Buddhist meditator might be directed to see egolessness in impermanence (we arise anew each moment) and/or to find it in his observation that that self is not in any of the physical or mental components of which he is constituted. Mahayana adds that experiences of a self do not arise independently but only in interdependence with all other phenomena; in particular the sense of oneself as perceiver always arises interdependently with the object perceived. Vajrayana adds that each newly arising moment of nondual inter-dependent experience is actually the radiance of the pure, all-good ground of being.

Interdependence: The realization that neither oneself nor any of the objects in the world has an independent existence. All things arise in interdependence with other things.

Karma: The cause and effect of actions that are performed with intention. Each intentional action plants the seed for a result that will mature when the conditions are right. Karma is understood to apply to cause and effect in a single lifetime (where the observant meditator can see it in action) as well as from one lifetime to another. A wholesome intention plants a seed that will eventually bring a beneficial result; an unwholesome intention does the opposite. Karma is understood to be the driving force that keeps the wheel of samsara turning. Westerners tend to be agnostic about rebirth across lifetimes, but very interested in how they can use knowledge of causality gained by close *observation of experience in order to change their present lives for the better.*

Mindfulness: Being closely present with one's moment-to-moment experience over a period of time of reasonable duration.

Nirvana (Pali: nibbana): The undefiled, deathless, liberation from samsara from which, after death, a sentient being will no longer be reborn. Nibbana is striven for as the end of the path in early Buddhism and in present Theravada. In Mahayana the practitioner vows not to go into nirvana but to be reborn for the sake of benefitting others. In Vajrayana the teaching is that fully awake wisdom awareness has no bias toward either samsara or nirvana.

Nonduality: An advanced state of wisdom awareness in Vajrayana. In nondual perception and thought the mind is fully present but without the sense of a subject and an object of experience. In this kind of awareness the basis for ego-clinging is gone (which is why practitioners tend to flee from it when it is glimpsed), and the mind is made available to various wisdom energies. It is only in nondual awareness that a practitioner can remain lucid during dreamless sleep and, according to Vajrayana teachings, during one's transition into death.

Pure perception: In Vajrayana the awake wisdom awareness that sees all phenomena, internal and external, as the radiance of the all-pure and all-good ground of being.

Samaya: The bond that a student of Vajrayana enters into with his teacher.

Samsara: The constant cycling from one unsatisfactory state of desire, aggression, or ignorance to another driven by "the fierce red winds" of karmic causality. Samsara is traditionally described in terms of six realms/states of mind, a lower and an upper (in terms of pain) state of mind for aggression (hell realms are the lower, competitive jealous god realms the upper), for ignorance (animal realm the lower, drugged-like god realm the higher), and for desire (hungry ghost realm the lower, intelligent human realm the higher). It is only from human realm that a being is free enough to begin striving to get off the wheel of samsara.

Shamatha: peaceful abiding. Shamatha meditation is usually performed by the meditator holding his mind (or repeatedly returning his mind) to a single object of meditation such as the breath. Shamatha is seen as a prelude to vipassana or other forms of meditation.

Shunyata: Emptiness. One of the primary Mahayana realizations is that neither oneself nor any of the objects in the world have an independent existence. Beyond that the practitioner might realize that the whole of samsara has no fundamental existence behind the colorful façade of experience. In the Dzogchen (great perfection) school of Vajrayana, emptiness is understood to be purity.

Rigpa: the name in the Dzogchen (Complete Perfection) school of Vajrayana for the ultimate wisdom awareness as well as, in some teachings, the ground of that awareness.

Terma: Received texts, a Tibetan tradition in which texts that are particularly relevant to the circumstances of a specific time and place will appear when needed, usually in the mind stream of a suitable receiver.

Upaya: Skillful means, a term used in Mahayana and Vajrayana for the skill in dealing with life and benefitting people that a Buddhist practitioner is said to automatically develop in conjunction with developing wisdom.

Vipassana (Sanskrit: vipashyana): Clear seeing. In vipassana meditation, the meditator focuses his mind on moment-to-moment experience in order to see into its nature.

Yana: Path.

5.1

A Hindu Response

Kalpana Mohanty

It is enriching to read and listen to Eleanor Rosch's story of nonviolence and enlightenment. I come from India where Lord Buddha was born; in my own home state of Odisha, in Dhauli Giri, Bhubaneswar there is a beautiful Shanti Stupa (peace pagoda). This pagoda was constructed in a place where Kalinga war was fought and where Emperor Ashoka was converted from his warrior lifestyle to embrace the Buddhist tradition. Buddhism is very close to my heart; I have visited many Buddhist temples and participated in Buddhist meditations in India, Sri Lanka, Thailand, and Japan. I remember this famous chant:

BUDDHAM SHARANAM GACCHAMI (I take refuge in the Buddha)
DHAMMAM SHARANAM GACCHAMI (I take refuge in the *dhamma*)
SANGHAM SHARANAM GACCHAM (I take refuge in the *sangha*).

Rosch mentioned that Buddhism arose approximately 2500 years ago in India at a time of religious ferment. Perhaps many of us would have wondered what this religious ferment was. I would like to say a word about that. Here religious ferment means religious disorder or when religion loses its balance. What was this religious disorder or loss in balance? In the later part of the Vedic Hindu period, the religious life of India had lost its balance resulting in peacelessness and chaos. The popular Hindu tradition only consisted of rites and sacrifices for which they relied on the Brahmins. The teachings of the Upanishads had rejected all rituals and sacrifice and formulated a new system of Hindu religion based on an idealistic philosophy. The philosophical religion was interpreted by the higher castes who lived like ascetics. Finally, the caste system had become very rigid and the lower classes were isolated and were prevented from reading the Vedic literature. At that time of religious ferment (563–482 B.C.E.) came Gautama Buddha, who was born a Hindu, and who protested against the ritualism of the masses and the asceticism of the higher classes and against racial prejudice and social

Peacemaking and the Challenge of Violence in World Religions, First Edition.
Edited by Irfan A. Omar and Michael K. Duffey.

discrimination. Buddha who revolted against the Bramhanical tradition said: "A man does not become a *bramhana* (renunciant) by his plaited hair or birth: in whom there is truth and righteousness he is blessed and he is *bramhana*" (The Dhammapada 26:393). Gained through his experience, the Buddha delivered his message of compassion, love, and self-restraint. The challenge of Buddhism to the Vedic Hindu religion was a stimulating inspiration to the minds of Hindu thinkers who ventured along new paths of reasoning. The coming of Buddhism also diminished the importance of caste distinctions, which made the Buddhist sangha open its doors to all castes.

Another important effect of the Buddhist movement was that animal sacrifice was abandoned by many Hindus. Only the worshippers of Goddess Kali continued to observe them. Buddhism also exercised a great deal of influence on education, art, and architecture. That Buddhism spread far and wide in India is clear from the many remains of the Buddhist architectural achievements from that period.

A. T. Ariaratne, who pioneered the Sarvodaya movement in Sri Lanka after being influenced by Mohandas Gandhi and Vinoba Bhave noted many similarities between the teachings of the Buddha and Hinduism. Sarvodaya means "welfare of all," which Ariaratne upheld as a principle. He also spoke about the method to put this principle into practice as *satyagraha* (insistence on truth), which is to fight in a nonviolent and disciplined way against an injustice while anchored in truth. Ariaratne also emphasized that the objective of satyagraha was to always oppose the wrong but not be against the wrongdoer. The doer of evil should not be abused by word, or thought, or molested physically, but should be made aware of the wrong and injustice caused by him or her. Today, we must ask the question how can Buddhism, which is a dominant religion in Sri Lanka and Myanmar, can be instrumental in bringing peace to all the people in those countries irrespective of their religion and ethnic background.

5.2

A Native American Response

Tink Tinker

Buddhism has always had a certain allure for me as an American Indian scholar, even though a superficial comparison of the two traditions would suggest extensive differences. A significant part of the allure is Buddhism's core nontheistic character. In this late postcolonial moment, it is no longer clear to most Indian folk that our experience of the world was always nontheistic. Indeed most Indians today will gladly recite the liberal euro-christian aphorism that we all worship the same God – if by different names. One of my mentors, Vine Deloria, Jr, asked me more than a decade before his death to publish an essay describing the lack of a God figure in Indian traditional cultural/religious understanding. Unfortunately, I failed to accomplish that assignment in time for him to use the essay as a footnote (his acknowledged intention), but I have recently published an essay titled "Why I Do Not Believe in a Creator" (Tinker 2013).

I would like to comment on a couple of cardinal differences that might place Buddhism and American Indian traditions somewhat at odds with one another. As a long-lived world religion, Buddhism indeed does work itself out differently diachronically, across spatial geographic regions, and through different traditions. It is clear, from reading Eleanor Rosch, that each of these treats peace and nonviolence somewhat differently. While American Indian cultural traditions vary markedly from one community to the next, each community is preserving a tradition that is hundreds of generations in the making – in each disparate community. We continue to preserve these differences yet today even as we show respect for one another across those community lines.

In terms of social contexts, one persistent difference between Buddhism and these American Indian traditions that seems to push itself to the fore is that of resources. American Indian communities are almost universally desperately poor.[1] Buddhist temples tend to have much more access to the wealth of the communities around them, something that can result in relatively opulent temple constructions. Our ceremonies, of course, do not require the construction of buildings for temples

Peacemaking and the Challenge of Violence in World Religions, First Edition.
Edited by Irfan A. Omar and Michael K. Duffey.
© 2015 John Wiley & Sons, Ltd. Published 2015 by John Wiley & Sons, Ltd.

or churches, etc. Our meeting places tend to be either outdoors or in peoples' homes. As a result, the resources needed for a major ceremony like a green corn dance or a sun dance will require annually the intense involvement of physical labor to make sure that the annual temporary construction is in place – the building of large arbors for dances, lodges and small lodges for purification or "scratching" ceremonies, and the like – all constructed of materials gathered from the local landscape. The intense poverty of our communities, however, means that our key "interpreters" (so-called medicine men and women) are left in particular poverty – without having taken any vow of poverty. They are usually so busy with ceremonies helping people in their community that they could not possibly keep up with a 40-hour daytime job. One negative result of this dynamic is that they too often turn to euro-christian supplicants looking for a "neat" new Age experience. But the new-agers do have resources and can pay handsomely for their religious experiences. This takes our healers and spiritual leaders away from their communities and co-opts them in a euro-christian world of capital with its particular forms of bonding around the exchange of money.

Another difference is my clear sense from reading Rosch that Buddhism essentially works itself out as an inordinately individualist practice. American Indian traditions are equally nonindividualist but rather what I have called communityist. All of our cultures are oriented around maintaining the harmony and balance of the communal whole. While we do have ceremonies that put persons out from the immediate community for designated periods of fasting and communicating with the spirit realm, we always expect those people to return to the community within a few days – with new insights, new knowledge, new strength, and new skills to build up the harmony and balance of the community. Our strongest and most gifted spiritual people never enter into processes to gain spiritual power for themselves, but always in order to give back to the immediate community. This foundational ideal of balance is what caused the Colorado American Indian Movement (AIM) to persistently proclaim that its protests intended to be nonviolent – wherever possible (allowing for violence to be instigated by others that would call on AIM people to protect women and children).

And finally, Buddhist traditions play out in ways that are hierarchical. For instance, the relationship between a student and her or his teacher seems to be structured in formal hierarchies. Our American Indian world (at least prior to the Indian Reorganization Act of 1934) is non-hierarchical to the opposite end of the spectrum. As one contemporary spiritual and political elder recites persistently, "There are no bosses in the Indian world." This is a very complex statement and cannot be unpacked in just a few words. Essentially, however, it means that our communities traditionally were structured around a very different psycholinguistic model than are euro-christian cultures – and perhaps many others. In my essay disavowing any creator figure in our Indian traditional life, I describe the difference in terms of the distinction between an up–down (hierarchical) image schema and what I call an egalitarian–collateral image schema. While we have expectations of one another in any Indian community (something others may call mores), there are few fixed norms in the final analysis.

The old traditional elders were and are reluctant to use english imperative verb forms. Instead, they tend to use modal forms that point to kinds of possibility. When I asked an old medicine man for ceremonial help a quarter-century ago, he responded by suggesting that I "could" go get a stick of red willow; that I could strip the bark off of it; that I could paint it red; and that I could tie a red tobacco offering onto its end. While he left the choice entirely up to me, I was clear that if I expected real ceremonial help that it would begin with my doing the things he suggested. It would have crossed a line, however, for him to have used the imperative, delimiting a hierarchical relationship between the two of us. This would have created imbalance in the relationship between us, hyper-empowering one over the other. In the final analysis, the crucial relationship was not between me and this ieska (interpreter) but rather between me and the spirit energies that worked with this man. For him to have acted with any sense of hierarchical superiority at all would have thwarted the possibility of my relationship (through him in ceremony, albeit) with those spirit helpers.

I was certainly heartened that so many contemporary traditions of Buddhism have generated peace and nonviolence institutions, agencies, and consortial efforts. As a large global movement, then, Buddhism ought to provide a significant impetus toward creating a more nonviolent world – and more so than the more disparate (and often heavily colonized/read christianized) American Indian traditions. And yet, our ceremonial traditions continue to strive for personal, community, and cosmic balance.

Note

1 Of course, all will point to the exceptions among the few casino-rich communities. Yet, it is these casino-rich communities that will almost invariably have lost their cultural moorings in favor of huge per capita payouts of casino wealth.

Reference

Tinker, Tink. 2013. "Why I Don't Believe in a Creator." In *Buffalo Shout, Salmon Cry: Conversations on Creation, Land Justice, and Life Together*. Edited by Steve Heinrichs, 167–179. Harrisonburg, VA: Herald Press.

6

Peacemaking and Nonviolence in the Hindu Tradition

Kalpana Mohanty

The weak can never forgive, forgiveness is the attribute of the strong.
M. K. Gandhi

Hinduism's Sacred Texts

Rig Veda: The hymns of praise to the gods, and to the cosmic powers at work in nature and in man is the first and the oldest of the four Vedas. It has a collection of 1000 hymns developed over 1000 years between 1200 and 1000 B.C.E. The other three Vedas are Yajur Veda, Sama Vedas, and Atharva Veda.

Ramayana (Life of Rama): One of India's great epics, it is a classical story of Rama c. 2015 B.C.E. and Sita, whose lives are examples of high standards of dignity and nobility.

Mahabharata: The Great Epic of India, is the world's longest poem (180 000 lines) that revolves around the conflict between two kingdoms, of the Pandavas and the Kauravas, and the great battle of Kurukshetra (c. 1424 B.C.E.). The epic also contains many discourses on philosophy, religion, astronomy, cosmology, politics, economics, and many stories illustrative of simple truths and ethical principles.

Bhagavad Gita ("Song of the Lord"): This is a conversation between Lord Krishna and the warrior Prince Arjuna on the brink of a great battle.

Puranas: These are ancient folk stories containing ethical teachings.

Upanishads: Upanishad means "to sit devotedly." The Upanishads are Vedic Sanskrit texts composed and transmitted orally by teachers whose pupils sat devotedly around them in forest retreats. They are the philosophical

Peacemaking and the Challenge of Violence in World Religions, First Edition.
Edited by Irfan A. Omar and Michael K. Duffey.
© 2015 John Wiley & Sons, Ltd. Published 2015 by John Wiley & Sons, Ltd.

narratives expounding the nature of the soul and cosmos. General agreement among scholars is that there are 108 Upanishads.

Yoga Shastra: Yoga is a mental and physical discipline practiced for religious purposes. Shastra means science. Therefore, Yoga Shastra is the science of yoga.

Yoga Sutra: Written by Patanjali, this is a classic text on the discipline of yoga. As stated by Patanjali, it is not his own creation but only a summary of the tradition as transmitted from ancient times.

Introduction to the Hindu Tradition

Hinduism, the oldest of the world's religions, evolved from the Vedic religion of ancient India. Veda is a Sanskrit word that means knowledge and wisdom. The Vedas are regarded by the sages as "revelations" that comprise Hinduism's most authoritative scriptures. They were brought to India by Aryan (nomadic tribes) invaders after 1200 B.C.E. from northwest Persia, now part of Iran. Hinduism is an ancient system of knowledge known as Sanatana Dharma ("eternal religion" or "everlasting path"), which is also a traditional name of the religion (Mée 1995, ix). The fundamental beliefs of Hinduism include the existence of a cosmic principle or ultimate reality known as Brahman, and its identification with the individual soul, the *atman*. According to Vedanta (the concluding part of the Vedas) whatever exists in this cosmos is pervaded by one divine consciousness. All living beings go through a cycle of rebirth (*samsara*), which ends with self-realization leading to liberation (*moksha*) (*Britannica*, s. v. "Hinduism"). The principle of *karma* (actions) determines a living being's status with the cycle of rebirth. This means that a totality of actions, good or bad, are able to affect the individual's future destiny. A person's good karma would ensure a positive rebirth and bad actions would result in an adverse rebirth.

The main Hindu deities are Brahma, the creator, Vishnu, the preserver, and Shiva, the destroyer, who purifies human beings from their false egos. Other deities are viewed as incarnations of these three gods. Hinduism has a hierarchical social structure, a caste system: Brahmins are responsible for religious teaching and priestly duties; Kshyatriyas are law makers, law enforcers, and warriors; Vaishyas are landowners, merchants, and business people; and Shudras are skilled artisans and laborers. In addition there is a fifth group, the "outcastes" or "untouchables," who performed what are considered "polluting" jobs such as handling of the dead bodies for cremation.[1]

Satguru Sivaya Subramuniyaswamy, a contemporary American-born Hindu spiritual teacher, offers a simple point for understanding the Hindu tradition. There exists only one, all-pervasive Supreme Being, who is immanent and transcendent, creator and unmanifest reality. Sometimes this worldview is regarded as monistic, as in a belief that all reality is an emanation from the same one Supreme Being. The world constantly undergoes cycles of creation, preservation, and destruction. The reality of existence is cyclical rather than linear. The souls of each being are in a journey, moving ever so slowly toward God with an ultimate goal of *moksha* (liberation). This liberation from the cycle of rebirth will result in the attainment of spiritual knowledge. Every soul is eventually destined to reach liberation however long it may take. The principal law that governs each person's journey and point of liberation is karma. It is the law of cause and effect through which individuals chart out their path through their actions, speech, and thoughts. Each soul, through birth, death, and rebirth, reincarnates countless times until a karmic balance is achieved and moksha is realized.

Besides human beings, there are other forms of beings, such as gods and devas (spirit beings) who exist in an unseen plane or world. Human beings can interact with and relate to these beings, seek their help, and even collaborate with them in their common journey toward the goal of liberation. This is done through temple worship, *yagnas* (fire ceremonies), and personal devotion to these divine beings (*bhakti*). Many Hindus believe that a spiritual teacher (guru) is essential to achieve liberation, which is equated with the realization of the transcendent reality. With guidance from an accomplished teacher, one is able to properly undertake personal discipline, cultivate good conduct, and achieve purification through meditation and asceticism. Since all life is sacred, the practice of *ahimsa* (noninjury or nonviolence) is vital to reducing one's karmic baggage. This preference for nonviolence has historically made Hinduism a bit more tolerant of other religions and accepting of the idea that all genuine religious paths are various facets of God's pure love and light (Subramuniyaswamy 1993).

Peace, War, and Nonviolence

Aum (*Om*) *shanti* (silence), tranquillity of mind, listening to the inner voice, agreement, and amity have been used interchangeably in different contexts in the Hindu Tradition. In Yoga Shastra, the role of "*Om*" is a soothing, relaxing, and unbroken thought to meditate upon leading to a state of silence or peace ("Om Shanti"). This is the first step for maintaining inner peace. Peace is a reflection of spiritual consciousness. It begins within each person, and extends to the home, neighborhood, nation, and beyond.

There is a description of and discussion about war between the Pandavas and Kauravas in the Hindu epic, the Mahabharata. The Pandavas are five brothers who are the descendants of Pandu; the Kauravas were believed to be descended from Kuru. The two are fighting over ownership of a piece of land. The epic also discusses the meaning of peace and nonviolence. The war caused massive havoc and destruction within 18 days. It is like a dance of destruction of Lord Shiva (Vasudev 1990, 69).

In the Hindu tradition, the sky, earth, river, and sun are all considered sacred. Considering these and all things sacred requires the practice of nonviolence (*ahimsa*). The Vedas beseech, "peace to the earth and to airy spaces, and peace to heaven, waters, plants and the trees" (*Yajur Veda*, cited in Subramuniyaswami 1993, 204). The Vedic saints proclaimed ahimsa as the way to achieve harmony with our environment, peace between people and compassion within ourselves. Nonviolence encompasses the physical, mental, and emotional spheres. One who practices nonviolence does not cause pain to any living being at any time through the actions of one's mind, body, and speech. Here are some representative references to nonviolence from sacred texts. "When mind is firmly based on waves of ahimsa, all living beings cease their enmity in the presence of such a person" (Yoga Sutra, cited in Subramuniyaswami 1993, 204). Another example:

> Come together, Speak together, Let our minds be in harmony, Common be our prayer, common be our end, common be our purpose, common be our deliberations, common be our desires, united be our hearts, united be our intentions, perfect be the union among us. (*Rig Veda* 1973, vol. X, hymn 191, verses 2–4)

In this passage, what appears to be a call to unity of peoples, the ancient scriptures encourage us to think of our shared destiny and purpose, which, if realized, contribute to peace and harmony between peoples. Another aspect of nonviolence may be seen in how the scriptures regard animals, birds, and vegetation in general. In the Yajur Veda it is noted that: "no person should kill animals and birds [which are] helpful to all" (Yajur Veda XIII, 47, cited in Smith-Christopher 2007, 67). Thus, animals, plants, and all other living and inanimate beings are often regarded as deities, infused with the divine, hence deserving of reverence rather than harm. This prevents human groups from succumbing to the desire to kill and consume without consideration (Smith-Christopher 2007, 67–68).

The *Upanishads* teach that the "sense of duality or separateness is the root cause of hatred and violence." We must see ourselves in everything and everything in ourselves. When we love others we love ourselves and when we hurt others we hurt ourselves because we partake in the same divinity (Smith-Christopher 2007, 61–62). Similarly, there are scores of injunctions against violence and injury to others in the *Bhagavad Gita*, which is a sermon by Lord Krishna to Arjuna on the battle field of Kurukshetra. The Gita forms part of the Mahabharata epic and practically contains the essence of Hinduism. The following passage could be considered as the ideal definition of the practice of nonviolence.

> Non-violence in thought, words and deeds, truthfulness and geniality of speech, absence of anger even on provocation, tranquillity of mind, refraining from malicious gossip, kindness to all creatures, absence of attachment to the objects of senses, mildness, sense of shame in doing things not sanctioned by the scriptures, abstaining from idle pursuits, sublimity, forgiveness, fortitude, external purity, absence of

malice, absence of feeling of self-importance, these are the marks of one who is naturally endowed with divine virtues, O descendent of Bharata. (The Gita 16, 2–3, cited in Sharma 2000, vol. III, 92)

Hinduism's Response to Violence

In Vedic literature, a violent struggle is permitted if one is faced with violent forces, and if harm is imminent. *The Bhagavad Gita* considers war as one of the solutions to rid society of corrupt and "impure" elements. Since purification is a major goal of Hindu worship and rituals, it also figures prominently in social justice and moral aspects of its worldview. One may question why, when the message of non-violence is important in the Gita, is war considered as a solution to solve social ills? The discussion of the necessity of war – which forms the bulk of the discussion in the Gita – culminates in Lord Krishna's advice to Arjuna not to be hesitant in going into the battlefield and fighting, even if it meant that Arjuna would be killing his own cousins. This was a war to fight against the injustice done to the Pandava brothers by the Kaurava brothers. It is better to fight than to be a coward. This was justifiable violence.

The *Mahabharata* describes an 18-day war. All the kings of Bharata (ancient name for what is India today) were involved in this war. Thousands of heroes, kings, soldiers, elephants, and horses were killed within 18 days. When Arjuna, the war hero, appeared to be reluctant to fight and implored Lord Krishna to stop the war, he was advised to perform his duty as a warrior because there cannot be ultimate peace without war.

Permissible violence and restrictions

Nonviolence is very subtle, both as an idea and in practice. It cannot always mean refraining from fighting or from hurting or even killing someone. Krishna advises Arjuna in the Gita, to fight and to kill his enemies. When the armies of the Pandavas and Kauravas faced each other at Kurukshetra, Arjuna had his chari-oteer, Lord Krishna, drive him out before his army to survey the opposing army led by his cousins and elders. Arjuna asked whether he should simply allow him-self to be killed rather than kill family members for the sake of a mere kingdom. Krishna's reply was that he should do his duty as a warrior and fight; if he refrained from fighting he would bring disgrace to himself and disorder to society.

To say that the Gita teaches violence or justifies war because of this advice to kill was given on a particular occasion is as wrong as to say that violence is the law of life because a certain amount of it is inevitable in daily life. To anyone who understands the spirit of the Gita, it becomes evident that it teaches the secret of nonviolence, the secret of realizing the self through the physical body and spirit. In the epic story, Duryodhana and his party (Kauravas) represent the lower impulses

Figure 6.1   Krishna and Arjuna. Source: © Philippe Lissac/Godong/Corbis

of humanity, and Arjuna and his party (Pandavas) are the higher impulses. The field of battle is our own body. An eternal battle is going on between the lower and higher impulses. He who fears, who saves his kin, who yields to his passions, must fight the physical battle. Violence will go on eternally in this strange world. The Gita shows that rather than cowardice it is heroic to kill or be killed in battle (Gandhi 1994, 77).

The important point to be made here is that the higher aspirations of human beings are not fulfilled unless they engage in struggles with their lower nature. Therefore, metaphors of battle, struggle, and fighting are practically universal and even spiritual in nature; the *Bhagavad Gita* provides one of the best examples of this struggle (Ravindra 2002). However, a professional soldier may kill an opponent in battle because of the duty to defend one's country or people against aggression. Therefore, while the "conception of *ahimsa* is universal, but its application is practical. Hindu nonviolence historically includes morally justifiable violence" (Smith-Christopher 2007, 69).

One may question how Hinduism could advocate nonviolence when so many gods and goddesses carry weapons, in two or more hands. It is generally understood that the Hindu tradition has always maintained a balanced view of war and nonviolence. Whenever there was a rise of evil in society and peaceful methods to remove it failed, people resorted to the path of war to cleanse society. War against evil is considered one's *dharma* (duty). It would be considered cowardice if a person became a mute witness to evil and injustice.

Animal sacrifice as violence

A common understanding of Hinduism suggests that animals and all living beings are considered safe from harm and killing for any reason. Even though some Hindus consume meat and are less careful about harming other living beings, generally speaking, Hindus have avoided even professions that involve handling of animal products and byproducts, such as leather and ivory. Some scholars of Hinduism argue that such reverence for animals was not always part of Hindu practice and that in history animal sacrifices were common. Other scholars suggest that, while there were a few Hindu sects that engaged in such practices, it was not a widespread phenomenon. In fact, one can find many ancient texts attesting to the challenge of violence in the form of killing of animals. The *Sama Veda* and the Upanishadic sages, some commentators of the *Dharmasastras*, the Mahabharata and the *Puranas* all are full of criticism of such practices.

During the Vedantic period, the killing of animals and other living beings came to be regarded as a "great sin" and vegetarianism became the norm (Smith-Christopher 2007, 67). Priests (Brahmins) and other religious classes did not consume meat. Critics of the animal sacrifice believed that it was the result of ignorance about the nature of self (Smith-Christopher 2007, 66). In the words of the Mahabharata: "The meat of other animals is like flesh of one's son. That foolish person, stupefied by folly, who eats meat is regarded as the vilest of human beings" (XIII.114.11, cited in Smith-Christopher 2007, 67). Over time, this practice eroded at least in the dominant, upper classes, who had a bigger stake in maintaining their control of the discourse on what it means to be a Hindu. Other classes and groups that fall below the caste hierarchy in ancient Hindu strata may have continued to believe in and even practice animal sacrifices.

Traditional Methods of Conflict Resolution

There have been many methods of peacemaking and conflict resolution in the Hindu tradition. One can also find violence in the sacred stories of Hinduism. Hindu warriors fought battles when there was conflict between groups. At the same time, there are many examples of acceptance of apparently opposite points of view with an effort to discover common ground, so that resolution could be brought about by mutual understanding. The following are some of the more established nonviolent methods of conflict resolutions that have been practiced in India for quite some time.

The panchayat or local council

Prior to India's domination by Western powers, life was organized on the basis of local self-sufficiency in economic matters. Most of the conflicts that arose in villages were settled by means of local and regional councils. The term most universally used in India in this connection was "panchayat" (council of five). The village or the caste panchayats were autonomous local bodies subject to the supreme authority of the king. In the course of time the panchayats became harsher in their methods of resolving conflicts. Therefore, the rural inhabitants of India themselves tried to settle internal, local conflicts successfully without the help of the panchayat (Sinha 1972).

Dharna

In ancient India, another tradition of conflict resolution existed, which was rooted in the Hindu religious system. Fasting and penances, and other forms of hardship were undertaken by devotees in order to please the gods. Such an attitude has given rise to special procedures for securing justice in India. It is well-known practice in India that a debtor who cannot release his/her dues from a creditor may sit at the door of the latter's house and go on a fast. This is the suffering for a cause which he believes to be just. This traditional process is known as "*dharna*." The most powerful exponent of peace and nonviolence, Gautama Buddha, a Hindu reformer born in India around 2500 years ago was explicit with regard to how to end disputes and conflicts. "Hatred does not cease by hatred at any time; hatred ceases by love; this is the old rule" (Mohanty and Raja 2011, 31).

Gandhi's satyagraha

After experimenting with peaceful methods from various Eastern and Western traditions, M. K. Gandhi ("Gandhi-ji") developed a method he called *satyagraha*. This Gandhian method was a continuation of one of the comparatively important traditions produced by Indian civilization based on truth and nonviolence. The word satyagraha in Sanskrit means insistence or holding on to truth. Gandhi-ji said that "truth and nonviolence are two sides of the same coin; nonviolence is the means and truth is the end. Truth can be achieved through nonviolence. If we take care of the means we are bound to reach the end at the right time" (Sharma 2000, vol. 2, 158). Gandhi-ji developed his technique of satyagraha to resolve political, social, religious, and economic conflicts. One of his first nonviolent campaigns was to abolish the practice of untouchability, which he regarded as a blot on Hinduism and a negation of the Hindu doctrine of *ahimsa* (noninjury). In order to understand satyagraha it is important to know Gandhi's early life, and his experiments with this method while he was still in South Africa.

Mohandas K. Gandhi and the Satyagraha Movement

Gandhi was born at Porbandar, Gujarat state, India, on October 2, 1869. His father, Karamchand (Kaba) Gandhi, and mother, Putli Bai, were known to be religious and disciplined. His father and grandfather served as first prime ministers of the princely states indirectly controlled by the British. Gandhi passed his childhood in Porbandar as an average boy with what he called in his autobiography a sluggish intellect and raw memory. Gandhi's marriage was arranged by his parents when he was only 13 to a girl of the same age called Kasturi Bai. He once read in a booklet about lifelong truthfulness to the wife and that remained permanently imprinted on his heart. Until she was 18, Kasturi Bai lived with her parents because child couples were not encouraged to live together. Mohandas went to England at the age of 18 to study law. It was during his time in England that he had a religious awakening.

As a young lawyer at the age of 23, Gandhi set sail for Pretoria, South Africa, in 1893. He had to assist a Muslim-owned company in a legal dispute. During his stay there Gandhi observed that there was a huge Indian population there. Many Indians had come to Natal with a promise of labor-related jobs in British-owned companies. However, the Indians faced severe discrimination under British rule. Gandhi personally had a humiliating experience of racism when he was traveling in the first class compartment with an appropriate and legitimately purchased ticket from Durban to Pretoria. He was thrown out of the train by officials with his luggage in Martizburg Station on a cold winter night on June 7, 1893 (Das 2008, 6). It was made clear to him that the authorities wanted to maintain the strict practice of segregation of races. Later when he was traveling in the stage coach, the coachman ordered him to sit on the footboard, and when he refused he was beaten. He realized that his humiliation reflected a deep disease of color prejudice, injustice, and exploitation. These two incidents sowed the seeds of nonviolent resistance in Gandhi. He observed that immense injustice was being experienced by people of Indian origin, other Asians, and also natives of South Africa. They were all being deprived of their basic rights. Gandhi began publishing a newspaper *Indian Opinion* in 1903, and was involved in starting several organizations to give voice to the victims of injustice. He taught about satyagraha and asked people to use it to fight against injustice nonviolently. Between 1907 and 1914, satyagraha took several forms: organizing protest meetings, boycotts, picketing and strikes, civil disobedience, ceremonial marches, courting arrest, negotiations, prayer for self-purification, formation of political groups, and establishing solidarity among satyagrahis. As a result the South African government passed the Indian Relief Act of 1914, which affirmed the value of satyagraha as a credible way of solving social and political conflicts. After returning to India in 1914, Gandhi organized more satyagraha campaigns such as in Champaran, Bihar, where the farmers, virtual serfs to the British and laborers were in dire conditions and wanted the employers to do something about it. The satyagraha movement brought about social and political awakening among farmers. Some other examples of the satyagraha movement are:

1. Ahemadabad Satyagraha (1918) by the mill workers was continued with Kheda Satyagraha, and Rowlatt Act Satyagraha.
2. The nonviolent Non-cooperation Movement began on August 1, 1920 against the Department of Revenue.

Figure 6.2   Gandhi on the salt march. Source: Reproduced by permission of the Navjivan Trust

3. The Salt Satyagraha March began on March 12, 1930, and lasted until March 4, 1931, in which 78 members from Ahmedabad Sabarmati Ashram marched to Dandi on the Indian Ocean, gathering hundreds of marchers along the 230-mile trip. The two main objectives of this satyagraha were: (1) the demand for the repeal of "Salt Act," which resulted in great hardship for the poor; and (2) the demand for total "self-rule" for India by Indians. On April 6, 1930, Gandhi and thousands of others broke the Salt Law by lifting salt from the sea The Salt Satyagraha was a distinct moral victory as people developed trust in this method. Several other important satyagraha campaigns followed, leading up to the Quit India Movement in 1942.

Gandhi travelled to different parts of the country to strengthen relations and build communal harmony until the year of India's independence on August 15, 1947. He fasted on that day because of the painful reality of the partition of India into two nations, India and Pakistan. Gandhi was opposed to the partition plan, but was not able to prevent it. In January of 1948, he was assassinated by a Hindu fanatic apparently for his fair mindedness toward non-Hindus.

Gandhi read the *Bhagavad Gita* and other scriptures quite regularly in his life. He was deeply impressed by the *Bhagavad Gita* and used it as his "Spiritual dictionary," and referred to it in times of doubt and despair. Gandhi was also influenced by Edwin Arnold's famous work *The Light of Asia* about the life of

Gautama Buddha. Gandhi read both the New Testament and the Hebrew Bible. He was deeply impacted by the Sermon on the Mount and by Christ's words asking his followers to return evil with good; give more than asked for or give until it hurts.

Gandhi had seen a crucifix in Rome and was deeply moved (Gandhi 1931). Jesus' act of self-suffering for others resonated with the Hindu virtue of *tapasya* or self-suffering.

Practices and Disciplines that Contribute to Peacemaking

The attainment of spiritual peace is considered to be the highest goal of human existence. Spiritual peace can be achieved through giving up a sense of separateness and identifying one's own self with all living beings in the universe (Ishawasya Upanishad 6–7). The Hindu tradition teaches that we should aspire for peace in all beings. Human existence consists of human fulfilment, right living, enlightenment, salvation, etc. These can be achieved through austerities in body, speech, and mind.

Yogas

People can contribute to peacemaking if they practice all the four yogas. The Sanskrit word "yoga" means union. The four yogas are: Karma yoga, Bhakti yoga, Gnana yoga, and Raja yoga. A brief description of these is as follows:

1. Karma yoga: Karma means action. Therefore Karma yoga is union with God through action in the form of selfless service.
2. Bhakti yoga: Bhakti means devotion. Therefore, Bhakti yoga means union with God through devotion. Bhakti yoga is the practice of devotional disciplines, worship, prayer, and chanting and singing with the aim of awakening love and opening oneself to God's grace.
3. Gnana yoga: Gnana means knowledge and wisdom. Therefore Gnana yoga is union with God through knowledge and spiritual practices. It describes the spiritual practices of a fully enlightened person.
4. Raja yoga: Raja means king. Therefore, Raja yoga is the king of all yogas. The system of Raja yoga consists of scientifically worked out techniques for the attainment of higher spiritual perceptions about the nature of man and the universe. Raja yoga, the science of religion is applied to our internal life.

A person is considered to be truly divine if he or she can achieve the virtues of the four yogas in their life.

Yamas

Certain disciplines have to be practiced for right living and peacemaking. The *yamas* and *niyamas* are the essential foundation of all spiritual progress. The yamas can be defined as ethical restraints and the *niyamas* as religious practices. Both are important virtues.

1. Ahimsa: "Noninjury." Not harming others by thought, word, or deed.
2. Satya: "Truthfulness." Refraining from lying and betraying promises.
3. Asteya: "Nonstealing." Not stealing, or coveting, or entering into debt.
4. Brahmacharya: "Divine conduct." Controlling lust by remaining celibate when single, leading to faithfulness in marriage.
5. Kshama: "Patience."
6. Dhriti: "Steadfastness."
7. Daya: "Compassion."
8. Mitahara: "Moderate appetite." Not eating too much or consuming meat, fish, fowl, or eggs.

Niyamas

1. Remorse: Being modest and showing remorse for wrongdoing.
2. Santhosha: Contentment or seeking joy and serenity in life.
3. Dana: Giving generously without thought of reward.
4. Faith and worship of God: Believing in guru and the path of enlightenment through studying, listening, and teaching of the scriptures.
5. Performing penance and sacrificing physical comforts.

Hindu Peace Groups and Organizations

Many Hindu organizations are continuing to work to build an egalitarian society. Below are three of the many organizations that have played an important role in peacemaking.

The Vivekananda Kendra (center)

This organization was founded by Eknathji Ranade at Kanyakumari and is a spiritually oriented service mission that reflects Swami Vivekananda's vision of a glorious India in action. This center has inspired many youths who have committed their lives to serving others. The center has over 200 branches spread over 17 states of India to work for all strata of society. To achieve this, life-workers, full-time workers, and the local workers carry out various service activities classified under rural development, education, and development of natural resources, community organizing, and publication. All their activities are rooted in the teachings of Swami Vivekananda (Subramanyan 2006, 103).

Aurobindo Ashram

This ashram at Pondicherry was founded in 1926 and has grown from a small group of 10 disciples into a large diversified community with about 1500 members including the students at the Center of Education and the devotees who live nearby. The dynamic character of the community reflects the life-affirming aim of Sri Aurobindo's yoga. Work as an offering to the divine is an essential aspect of yoga, and the residents of the ashram undertake useful physical work every day to serve various needs.

The Sarvodaya and Gandhian Ashrams

These community ashrams manifested Gandhi's revolutionary program of social change, including land for peasants, an end to the caste system, and an end to poverty. Nonviolent struggle continues in many forms in India as part of the practice of Hinduism. Some of these struggles have been channeled through innovative and peaceful means. Below I describe four such innovative peacemaking practices.

Innovative and Emerging Peacemaking Practices

The Chipko movement

Nature has been protecting and preserving living beings for thousands of years. A truly spiritual person will always love and respect nature. Loving nature is equal to loving God. At present nature has suffered immensely because human beings have been very harsh to nature. The "Chipko" movement began in 1971 as a result of the efforts of Sunderlal Bahuguna to counter the harsh treatment of nature in the name of development. The word *chipko* is a Hindi word meaning "to cling." The movement received its name when men and women of some villages in the sub-Himalayan region took to clinging to the trees, challenging the efforts of others who wished to clear their forest. The Chipko movement was inspired by the perception that the people must organize themselves to save trees, water, and the environment from degradation. It is argued that the destruction of forests in the Himalayan region is a leading cause of recurring droughts and devastating floods, which have also led to reduced crop yields in the hills and in the plains. Love toward nature and love toward human beings are interrelated (Oza 1991).

Anandavan

Baba Amte's movement at Anandavan in the state of Maharashtra began as a campaign to help those who suffered from the dreaded disease of leprosy, to rehabilitate them, and to remove the horror and stigma that society attaches to this disease. The movement is no longer confined to the problem of leprosy but has acquired many other dimensions. The ancient Vedic literature has mentioned leprosy. The description of this disease and its treatment has been given in *Sushruta Samhita*, a medical treatise written around 400 B.C.E. It was believed that the disease was contracted as a result of past actions, therefore it was considered a curse with no cure. Thus persons having such a disease were segregated, ostracized, and socially rejected. Leprosy, if untreated, very often disables and disfigures the patient; it is a frightening sight. Though leprosy can be cured today, the stigma and the practice of casting out the patient persists. Baba Amte's resolve was to challenge this problem. In 1950, he founded the "Maharogi Seva Samiti" for the care of leprosy patients. This was the beginning of Anandavan ("the forest of joy") with the fundamental belief that life must be full of joy and hope. He made them learn many life skills, such as mat weaving, use of the handloom, woodwork, decorative arts, etc. Baba Amte has helped to bring joy and hope to the lives of countless people since the start of this movement.

The Art of Living Foundation

Love for nature and love for other human beings cannot occur unless we love ourselves and find peace within ourselves. The Art of Living Foundation was started by Sri Sri Ravi Shankar in 1982, where he began to teach the "sudarsankriya," a simple yet powerful breathing technique that eliminates stress and brings one completely to the present moment. This is taught around the world as a part of the Art of Living Course. Many people have experienced physical and emotional healing as a result of the various programs offered by the Art of Living Foundation. This foundation is a nonprofit, educational, and humanitarian organization committed to creating peace at the level of the individual and fostering human values within the global community in over 140 countries.

The practice of "sudarsankriya," which is the heart of a course taught at the Foundation is a powerful exercise designed to cleanse deep-rooted emotional stresses and toxins; it brings the mind and body into synchronicity with natural rhythms. Serenity, concentration, better health, greater joy, and enthusiasm for life and more harmonious relationships are some of the positive results of this practice (Shankar 2007, 203).

The Jana Satyagraha movement

Love for ourselves, nature, and other human beings cannot be complete unless there is a movement to fight nonviolently for the rights and entitlements of disadvantaged communities. One such movement is Jana Satyagraha, which began under the leadership of P. V. Rajagopal (a Gandhian) of an organization known as Ekta Parishad. This movement has spread to numerous cities and villages across India. Ekta Parishad – in alliance with over 1000 other independent organizations – continues to engage in motivating underprivileged communities, minority and tribal groups, agricultural workers, fisherman groups, nomads, urban poor, and marginal farmers to wage a nonviolent struggle for the rights over land, water, and forests. The Jana Satyagraha movement aspires to establish a society that is free from hunger, fear, and corruption.

In October 2012, over 10 000 people from all over India, especially the tribal, grassroots-level workers, activists, academics, and justice-loving individuals from all over the world, (including the author) participated in a foot march from Gwalior to Agra, which lasted for 10 days. Their aim was to gain the attention of the politicians and the ruling establishment, and to start a dialogue with government officials that would address the issue of rights of these underprivileged groups. The march did produce results and the Parliament of India acted in passing a comprehensive national land reforms act. The "foot march" was like a mobile training program on nonviolence to deliver justice to the rural society. The sacrifice of those who walked included walking in the hot sun for an average of 15 km per day, sleeping on the road, and living on little and simple food.

Hindu Saints and Seminal Thinkers

There are many reformers and saintly figures in the Hindu tradition. Below I have included some exemplary religious figures who command reverence and following among Hindus.

Ramakrishna Paramahamsa (d. 1886)

Ramakrishna was one of the greatest sages of the Hindu tradition who lived in British India, during the period when many Indians were attracted to British culture and to Christianity. Ramakrishna was an ascetic of the highest order. He considered his wife as the "divine mother" and, instead of living with her as a husband, he worshipped her and sought spiritual discipline from her. Ramakrishna was the pioneer of the modern renaissance of Hinduism. After practicing many religions like Islam and Christianity, Ramakrishna discovered that all were traveling toward the same God but the paths chosen were diverse. He realized and declared that all religions were part and parcel of one eternal religion. Ramakrishna had many disciples including Swami Vivekananda, who established the Ramakrishna Mission, which engaged in serving the community and in spiritual awakening of the masses.

Swami Vivekanada (d. 1902)

Vivekananda was born in Kolkata in 1863 and lived a very useful life of only 40 years. He had a mystic touch from Sri Ramakrishna Paramahamsa and became the world-renowned monk who roused the slumbering fire of religion in millions of hearts in the East and the West. Swami Vivekananda urged that all national activities in India should be organized round the spiritual ideal. Politics, social reform, and education would be successful in India only if these pointed to a higher spiritual life. It was during the meditation on the Rock in Kanyakumari that Vivekananda received many insights. He dedicated himself to the service of India, particularly to the service of those who are starved, oppressed, and rejected by society.

Sri Ramana Maharishi (d. 1950)

Sri Ramana was born in Madurai, Tamil Nadu and practiced Jnana yoga from childhood. Through his unique language of supreme silence, he spread the teachings of love meditation, self-realization, and the practice of asking "who I am?" He established an ashram at Thiruvannamalai, Tamil Nadu state. He taught that self-realization through self-enquiry is the most important pursuit for a human being.

Ram Mohan Roy (d. 1833)

Ram Mohan Roy was the founder of the Brahmo Samaj, which sought to initiate reforms in the Hindu tradition. He was the pioneer in abolishing the cruel system of "sati" (wives sacrificing their lives on the funeral pyre of their husbands). It was on the strength of the highest Hindu scriptures that he gave his verdict against idol worship and sacrifices. He had read the Hindu scriptures thoroughly and argued that the best means of securing bliss is pure spiritual contemplation. Worship of the rites and idol worship are intended only for persons of limited capacity. Ram Mohan Roy tried to conserve the best practices and remained faithful to the Hindu way of life.

Swami Dayananda (d. 1883)

Dayananda founded the Arya Samaj in 1875, which is still a thriving organization in India. His main emphasis was on the infallibility of the Vedas and the rebirth of the soul. He has played an important role in the revival of Hinduism through educational as well as religious reforms.

Saint Ramalingar (d. 1874)

Ramalingar, also known as Vallalar, belongs to the age of the Siddhas. His mission in life was to spread universal love and compassion. He was born on October 5, 1823, at Marathoor, a village in the South Arcot district of Tamil Nadu. According to Saint Ramalingam, God is formless but he is seen as *jyoti* (light). His experience and experiments with different religious traditions of South India resulted in the formation of Samsara Suddha Sanmargam, which is inclusive of diverse disciplines and practices. One of the chants or "maha mantra" (sacred chant) of Saint Ramalinga is: "Vast grace – light, Vast grace – light. Supreme Compassion, Vast grace – light."

Rabindranath Tagore (d. 1941)

Tagore was born in 1861 in Bengal and had an extraordinary veracity as a poet, composer, educator, philosopher, painter, and prophet. Probably no modern Indian has imbibed the spirit of the Upanishads so well as Tagore. His message of nonviolence is understood to perceive the unity of all things in God and that the emancipation of human beings requires absolute self-surrender in service and love. He viewed all the religions of the world as parts of one whole.

Vinoba Bhave (d. 1982)

Vinoba-ji was born in September 1895 at Maharashtra. He was a bright student but gave up his studies because he did not want to engage in the usual way of making a living through earning money. He went to Varanasi to study Sanskrit and philosophy and to live a life of contemplation and self-discipline. He learnt the Qur'an in Arabic and also the Bible along with the Hindu scriptures (Bhave 2007, 3). "Vinoba literature," the collection of his writings and speeches, deals mostly with philosophy and the theory and practice of nonviolence. Most significant in Vinoba's life has been the theory and practice of *satyagraha* beyond the stage where Gandhi left them. He was among the first to join Gandhi's Sabarmati Ashram, in Ahmadabad. He was the pioneer of the Bhoodan Movement in India (the movement of gifting land to the landless), the first attempt in history to bring about a social revolution and reconstruction by the means of love.

Aurobindo Ghosh (d. 1950)

Sri Aurobindo was a prolific Bengali writer and poet, philosopher and mystic. He saw the modern global crisis as marking a period of transition from a dark age to a more enlightened one, in which Hinduism will play a preponderant role. He founded the Auroville Community in Pondicherry for the practice of "integral yoga." The message of Sri Aurobindo and the ashram is that:

> If a single body is touched, all other bodies can be touched, for there is only one Matter and one body. If Matter changes at one, it can change al all points. ...One pure little cell in a single corner of matter, this is what can change the world. (Satprem 1977, 188, 338).

Pandurang Shastri Athavale (d. 2003)

Pandurang Shastri Athavale was one of India's greatest social reformers. He led a campaign for a program of "village uplift," one of Gandhi's greatest programs, to overcome elements of structural violence of his country: poverty, poor health, malnutrition, and illiteracy. Athavale wrote many books, and he and his fellow workers visited 100 000 villages and had several million followers.

Apart from the above there are some women saints who according to legends selflessly devoted themselves without expecting anything in return. There were apparently many such figures over the centuries but their names and lives escaped history books, partly because they were selfless and reclusive and partly because they were women whose achievements may not have been deemed as important as those of men. Three names are worth mentioning here: Tadagi, Vandi, and Andal. It can be argued that their self-devotion to God is an aspect of nonviolence and peacemaking, since by virtue of their acts they achieved peace and radiated it to those around them. Tadagi (sixth century C.E.) is known for her piety, which made the Lord bend his head down to her to accept a garland around his neck. Similarly Vadi (seventh century C.E.) and Andal (eighth century C.E.) charmed the divine in ways that seemed to defy the laws governing divine–human hierarchy. Although these are not mainstream saints, they are remembered nevertheless by many for their spiritual devotion and achievements (Sashital 2004, 274–285).

Conclusion

Sanatana Dharma or "eternal religion," the ancient name for the Hindu tradition, is an appropriate description of Hinduism. This tradition has survived thousands of years of change and yet it has retained a degree of continuity into the present. Hinduism in its many varieties has welcomed and assimilated peoples and groups from various parts of the world. They have become part of India. The notion that the entire world is one single family was originally expressed in the Sanskrit language as *vasudhaiva kutumbakam*. It suggests embracing and accepting all faiths and paths as "one."[2] Many people have been reading and internalizing the Hindu sacred texts as they are reflected in the Indian cultures and civilization. Not all of them are Hindus. Despite the variety of deities, gods, and goddesses worshipped in the Hindu tradition, the ancient Hindu system sustains the idea that there is only one, all-pervasive Supreme Being.

From the basic belief that all life is sacred we obtain principles such as equating nonviolence with truth. As Gandhi termed it, truth and nonviolence are two sides of the same coin. The Hindu tradition has justified violence and war to fight against injustice and evil forces. Gandhi and other saints and leaders were inspired by the examples of nonviolence shown by teachers like the Buddha, Mahavira (founder of Jainism), and Jesus Christ.

The challenge before us is how to implement the teachings of these exemplary predecessors today. Hindu fundamentalists are on the rise. In 1992, a fundamentalist–nationalist party (the Bharatiya Janata Party, BJP) campaigned on the slogan that India is a Hindu state and won general elections.[3] Their victory came partly as an aftermath of the inter-community tensions resulting in the destruction a five-century-old mosque (the Babri mosque) at the hands of Hindu militants. The destruction of the mosque was followed by communal riots in several cities of

India in which several hundred Muslims were killed. Despite their political interpretation of religion, the Hindu fundamentalists have failed to revive the true spirit of the Hindu tradition, which can only be achieved and sustained with the help of the Indian-style secularism that accepts all religions as equal partners in their struggle against violence and bigotry. The question facing us now is how can we stem the tide of violence in our societies, and how can we implement nonviolence as a principal method to resolve conflicts?

Many individuals and organizations noted in this chapter are working to establish peaceful societies and communities. There is an urgent need to support these organizations by word, deed, and prayers. Such a unity of religions, where each religion continues to maintain its distinct identity and practices while jointly contributing to the work of peace and justice is the noblest of objectives in our time.

Questions for Discussion

1. What do you find most insightful about Hinduism?
2. According to its teachings how committed to nonviolence is Hinduism?
3. What justifies war?
4. What are some of the responses to violence from a Hindu perspective?
5. Where do you think Gandhi stood on war?
6. Do you think that movements guided by satyagraha and ahimsa are likely to be successful? In your view, are these terms relevant today? Why or why not?
7. In what senses was Gandhi a reformer?
8. In what ways can the practices and disciplines of Hinduism be useful to promote peace in the present context?

Notes

1 Mohandas Gandhi called them "harijans" (children of God) who must be respected equally by the people of other castes. The term "harijan" is considered pejorative in India. Many of these communities have since organized themselves as "Dalits."
2 The original verse to this effect is found in *Mahaupanishad* (vol. VI, 71–73).
3 The BJP is again ascendant, winning the last general elections in summer 2014 defeating the long-running Congress party.

References

Bhave, Vinoba. 2007. *Talks on the Gita*. Paunar: Paramdham Prakashan.
Das, Varsha *et al.* 2008. *The Story of Satyagraha*. New Delhi: National Gandhi Museum.
Gandhi, M. K. 1994. *What is Hinduism?* New Delhi: Navajivan Trust.
Gandhi, M. K. 1931. *Young India*. New Delhi: Navajivan Trust.

Mée, Jean Le. 1995. *Hymns from the Rig Veda*. London: Jonathan Cape.

Mohanty, Kalpana and Raja. L. 2011. *Conflicts and Conflict Resolution in India*. New Delhi: Sonali Publications.

Oza, D. K. 1991. *Voluntary Action and Gandhian Approach*. New Delhi: National Book Trust.

Ravindra, Ravi. 2002. *Science and the Sacred: Eternal Wisdom in a Changing World*. Chennai: Quest Books.

Rgveda (Rig Veda). 1973. Trans. R. T. H. Griffith. Delhi: Motilal Banarsidas.

Satprem. 1977. *Mother: The Divine Materialism*. Madras: Macmillan India Press.

Sarma, D. S. 2007. *Hinduism through the Ages*, Mumbai: Bharatiya Vidya Bhavan.

Sashital, Meera S. 2004. *Rosary of Saints*, Mumbai: Bharathiya Vidya Bhavan.

Shankar, Ravi. 2007. *Celebrating Silence*. Mumbai: Jaico Publishing House.

Sharma, S. R. (ed.) 2000. *International Encyclopedia of Non-violence*. Vols II and III. New Delhi: Cosmo Publications.

Sinha, Surajit. (ed.) 1972. *Aspects of Indian Culture and Society; Essays in Felicitation of Professor Nirmal Kumar Bose*. Calcutta: Indian Anthropological Society.

Smith-Christopher, Daniel L. (ed.) 2007. *Subverting Hatred: The Challenge of Nonviolence in Religious Traditions*. Maryknoll, NY: Orbis Books.

Subramanyan K. 2006. *Value Education*. Chennai: Vivekananda Kendra Prakashan Trust.

Subramuniyaswami, Sivaya. 1993. *Dancing with Śiva: Hinduism's Contemporary Catechism*.Concord, CA: Himalayan Academy.

Vasudev. 1990. *Doctrine of Ahimsa*. New Delhi: Wasduhir Foundation.

Further Reading

Chinmaya Mission. 2013. *Hinduism – Frequently Asked Questions*. Mumbai: Central Chinmaya Mission Trust. This book provides concise and precise answers to basic questions about Hinduism, unfolding the foundation on which Hindu culture rests.

Iyengar, B. K. S. 2011. *Light on the Yoga Sutras of Patanjali*. London: Harper Collins Publishers. This is one of best treatments of the theory and practice of yoga. It provides detailed interpretation and application of the sutras.

Krupanandam, N. 2013. *Religious Thought of Modern India*. New Delhi: Readworthy Publications. A good discussion of the views of various Hindu reformers, Raja Ram Mohan Roy, Swami Vivekananda, Mohandas Gandhi, and Dr S. Radhakrishnan.

Mohapatra, A. R. 2011. *Philosophy of Peace*. New Delhi: Readworthy Publications. Contains some thought-provoking philosophical articles on aspects of peace and the means toward realization of peace.

Ranade, R. D. 2003. *Spiritual Awaking in Gandhi and other Indian Saints*. Varanasi: Sarva Seva Sangh publishers. This book provides insights into Mohandas Gandhi's spiritual life not found in other biographies of Gandhi.

Shankar, Sri Sri Ravi. 2008. *Wisdom for the New Millennium*. Bangalore: Sri Sri Publications. A collection of teachings on human distortions: anger, jealousy, lust, greed, arrogance, and delusion, and how one can move from these distortions to the state of pure love.

Sullivan, Bruce M. 2003. *The A to Z of Hinduism*. New Delhi: Vision Books Pvt. Ltd. This is an accessible and basic introduction to the teachings of Hinduism.

Vallés, Carlos G. 2012. *Gandhi – The Alternative to Violence*. Ahmadabad: Navajivan Publishing House. Originaly written in Gujarati, this book shows how to cultivate the path of nonviolence within us.

Hindu Peace Organizations

Bombay Sarvodaya Mandal: This group organizes social programs, seminars, workshops, meetings, and youth camps in the spirit of the teachings of Gandhi, Vinoba, and Jayaprakash Narayan. www.mkgandhi.org and www.mkgandhi-sarvodaya.org.

Center of Study of Society and Secularism: The aims and objectives of the center include promotion of the spirit of secularism (freedom of religion) and interreligious and inter-ethnic harmony. The center sponsors research and studies on the merits of secularism and pluralism and organizes interfaith dialogues in various cities in India.

Gandhi Peace Foundation: Publishes books on peace and non-violence, and *Gandhi Marg*, a quarterly journal on research in nonviolence and Gandhian studies. It holds youth camps on peace issues and serves as a resource center for peace workers and scholars.

Gandhi Museum, Madurai: This museum serves to propagate the ideals of Mohandas Gandhi through exhibitions, seminars, study circles, meetings, summer camps for students, and classes on yogasana. The museum also conducts educational programs for college and high school students. www.gandhimmm.org.

National Foundation for Communal Harmony: The National Foundation for Communal Harmony has been operating since 1992 with the main objective of providing assistance for the physical and psychological rehabilitation of the child victims of communal (religious) riots and caste, ethnic, or terrorist violence, with a special focus on education and training of the victims.

Ramakrishna Mission: Ramakrishna Mission is a philanthropic voluntary organization founded by Ramakrishna's disciple, Vivekananda, in 1897. The mission bases its works on the principle of karma yoga and conducts extensive work in health care, disaster relief, rural management, tribal welfare, education, and a variety of cultural programs.

Glossary

atman: the soul or the true self, pure consciousness, eternal.
avatar: an incarnation of the divine.
bhakti: devotion, spiritual and religious devotion to a deity, expressed through offerings, singing praises, and *darshan*.
Brahman: Supreme or Ultimate Reality.

Brahmin: male member of the priestly caste, highest among the four traditional castes.

darshan: viewing of the deity, being in the presence of the deity.

Guru: a spiritual teacher or guide.

karma: means action; also the name of the path or yoga that focuses upon one's actions; the path of moral action.

Krishna: one of the many incarnations (avatar) of God Vishnu. Krishna is worshipped and is one of the deities at the center of the Bhakti tradition.

moksha: liberation from the bondage of *samsara,* the cycle of birth, death, and rebirth.

Om: the sound or symbol from which all of creation came into being.

samsara: the flow or cycle of birth, death, and rebirth that each soul experiences before realizing liberation.

sutra: basic texts to understand the philosophical system of thought.

Vedanta: the end of the Vedic period, marked by schools of thought that gave rise to the Upanishads (texts).

Yoga: spiritual discipline that may lead to the realization of liberation; has many forms and styles.

6.1

A Christian Response

Michael K. Duffey

Religions are human institutions. As such they are enmeshed in cultures. But religions also offer the possibility of being countercultural, of criticizing culture. Hinduism's teachings on peacemaking and nonviolence have the power to overcome dehumanizing forms of discrimination such as caste and gender relations. It is fascinating to observe the drama of war in religious texts. To only understand the literal descriptions of ancient war making of Hindus, is not to have gotten to their depth. To read them literally is usually to miss their rich meaning.

The search for peace is the search for experiencing the divine. As Kalpana Mohanty put it, Gandhi helped Christians see how a good Christian should behave. *Satyagraha* (truth force), *ahimsa* (nonviolence), *tapasya* (self-suffering), and *moksha* (liberation) are surely in the teachings and example of Jesus. Gandhi put them into practice in a compelling way that would influence generations to come. Having read her chapter, I would like to raise three questions that specifically relate to the understanding of the morality of war in the Hindu tradition.

First, in the Bhagavad Gita Lord Krishna's counsel to Arjuna on the eve of battle, that it was permitted to fight and kill – even one's own relatives in that story – seems to be at odds with what Lord Krishna says is the goal of human life; that is, harmony with others through taming of the ego. How do the two co-exist? Why should this account be taken as normative? Why not?

Second, the Vedic literature permits war against "wicked" persons, evil forces, and untruth as a form of purification. Killing persons for the purpose of purification seems to me to be a potentially dangerous reason for war making. Don't the wicked need to be reformed in order for there to be peace? What does purification in this context mean?

My third question arises from having learned from Mohanty that there are at least 18 sacred texts of various lengths in Hinduism (I know that the Bhagavad Gita contains over 700 verses). Is it the case that there are different moral interpretations of war within or between these various texts?

Peacemaking and the Challenge of Violence in World Religions, First Edition.
Edited by Irfan A. Omar and Michael K. Duffey.
© 2015 John Wiley & Sons, Ltd. Published 2015 by John Wiley & Sons, Ltd.

Of the many things I learned from Mohanty, I would mention three. First, she described many saints in the Hindu tradition ranging from the first to the twentieth centuries. Some were poets, others spiritual seekers, others activists. What they all have in common was a dedication to a nonviolent life as the way to divine realization. Second, there are certainly many organizations inspired by Hinduism to work for justice and peace. Third, I realized the depth of her arguments when I came to know that Dr Mohanty's own life is a testimony to seeking active justice and nonviolent peacemaking from the perspective of her own faith tradition. She has engaged with both the theory and praxis, and that is the hallmark of a true seeker of peace.

6.2

A Muslim Response

Irfan A. Omar

Kalpana Mohanty lays out the historical background in which to understand the Hindu tradition, which speaks of itself in universalistic terms as "the inheritance of the whole of humankind." I very much appreciated her elaboration of various sacred texts that are central to the Hindu tradition. She speaks of the Bhagavad Gita as the most important of all, and dear to the heart of Hindus. The immense popularity of the Gita is primarily linked with the fact its central message is rooted in ethics. The Gita emphasizes the reality and necessity of respecting and observing the golden rule. This is a point that I believe connects all of the world's religions. At the heart of each tradition lies this core message, which is fundamentally about right relationships: relationship with the ultimate reality (God/Allah/Creator/Brahman/Nirvana/Self). This "vertical" relationship is built via our relationships with other people and other members of creation – i.e. the "neighbor."

Mohanty's summary of beliefs in the Hindu tradition was particularly helpful as it dispels more than one stereotype about Hinduism, the first of which is that Hindus practice "polytheism." The words from the first of the nine beliefs are that there is but "one, all-pervasive Supreme Being who is both immanent and transcendent, both creator and unmanifest reality." Here, a question that came to mind is whether to regard this worldview as "monotheistic" or whether there is another way more suited to this description. I am aware that some scholars have considered "the one, all-pervasive" as referring to a "monistic" reality from which all emanates. Regardless of whether the Hindu tradition considers this as "monotheism" or "monism" or refers to it by some other name, I thought that this discussion of the divine in Hinduism presents numerous possibilities for inter-religious conversation.

A Hindu might say that worshipping more than one deity is not possible, or at least it is no more possible than say, one human being claiming to love more than one person, in the same way, at the same time with absolute certainty and honesty.

Peacemaking and the Challenge of Violence in World Religions, First Edition.
Edited by Irfan A. Omar and Michael K. Duffey.
© 2015 John Wiley & Sons, Ltd. Published 2015 by John Wiley & Sons, Ltd.

I say this because often Hindu love for the deity is viewed as the devotee's love for the divine through the manifest deity. Like human beings deities can be a bit jealous.

In the past century, Hindu teachers and visionaries have contributed immensely to the development of religious notions of peace and nonviolence. Through their uncompromising teachings on nonviolence, Hinduism (and especially Jainism, which has considerable common ground with Hinduism) exemplifies ways of practicing peace even as it describes war and its consequences. Mohanty's description of war in the epic tale, the Mahabharata, was a good way to highlight Hinduism's aversion to war. Similarly, the Vedic texts implore their reader to cultivate nonviolence as it benefits both the self and all others. The chapter also contains several passages from the Upanishads that provide food for thought regarding *ahimsa* or noninjury. However, the most important passage regarding war and peace is in the Bhagavad Gita, which as she points out may be compared to the Christian "Sermon on the Mount." Outwardly it appears to be promoting war for the sake of justice. In spirit, however, it is referring to the war within. In my chapter on Islam, I tried to argue that the quranic view of jihad is quite similar in emphasizing the importance of war with oneself, with one's own conscience. Gandhi himself was convinced by what he read in the Qur'an, which may have prompted the following comment on jihad:

> where is the unerring General to order Jihad? Where is the suffering and love and purification that must precede the very idea of drawing the sword? We are too imperfect and impure and selfish to resort to an armed conflict in the name of God. (Gandhi 1922, 847)

It would have been appropriate and beneficial to the reader to also include here Gandhi's interpretation of the passage in the Gita in which Lord Krishna gives a sermon to promote war, which Gandhi read as a message of nonviolence.

In reading through some of Mohanty's analysis I realized the bold manner in which Hinduism forces us to think about life as an ever-changing continuum rather than as constant and permanent, even though it may appear to be that if viewed in a momentary reality. Therefore, one must try and live in every moment – fully, and yet be aware of the long journey towards *moksha* (liberation of *atman*), which may take as long as millions of lifetimes or just the twinkling of an eye. But this continuum is not thrust upon us without a mechanism for steering our lives into a direction of our choosing (*karma*). Every individual is potentially charged with being his/her own agent of change. The change in the "right" direction – above all else – requires one to follow a moral path. This boldness of Hinduism is visible in the words of Gandhi: "I believe in the Vedas, Upanishads, the Puranas and the writings left by the holy reformers. ... [However] I reject everything that contradicts the fundamental principles of morality" (Gandhi 1926, 356).

I am back where I started; the fundamental purpose of all religions is to persuade the believer to follow the moral path; sometimes the persuasion requires enticement through the promise of a reward, and at other times it uses the fear of punishment, but for a mature and reflective seeker (*transformed from being a mere believer*), it is no longer about reward and punishment but about peace – which according to Islam is one of the names of God – al-Salam. We may start on the path due to the incentives but we stay till the end only when there is a realization of the longing for this peace.

From the scripture passages Mohanty cites in her chapter and the evidence she has gathered, it is apparent that the path of morality and nonviolence is the path to inner peace; this is what we as human beings ultimately seek from the core of our inner being. Hinduism calls this "realization of the atman" or moksha. Mohanty also provides a good discussion of the seemingly contradictory elements in Hinduism. For example, she explains the weapons carried by some of the deities such as Kali: symbols of war and destruction are an indication that the forces of good and evil are both present in our world and each individual must choose the side of the good. When the force of evil seems to overtake evil, divine intervention is made and the balance is restored sometimes even through violence. She further points out that the

> Hindu tradition has always maintained a balanced view about war and nonviolence. … When … methods of peaceful means to resolve … failed … the path of war to purify society [may be taken]. … The Bhagavad Gita considered war as one of the solutions to purify society.

The Gandhian methods to achieve nonviolence in the face of the fast-paced and technologically driven society that Mohanty describes need further discussion. One question I have for Mohanty is how to appeal to the younger generation of today? Perhaps a discussion of traditional methods of conflict resolution may be expanded to include practices and disciplines that lead to peacemaking.

I see several layers of practices and more than one way of seeing what peacemaking is and how it works:

- The theoretical level: how it is defined in the tradition.
- The practical level: how it may be practiced today and its potential future benefits.
- The empathetic level: moving beyond the realm of the self and being part of the social movement for justice; contributing to peace for all.

What is most heartening about this chapter is that it emerges from not only erudite research and engagement with the sources, but also from her personal journey of practicing nonviolence and peacemaking over the years. Mohanty has truly lived a life in pursuit of peacemaking and nonviolence. Her participation in the peace march in 2012 did make a difference; through the concentrated media focus, Indian government officials and lawmakers took notice and were compelled to take action by passing the "comprehensive national land reform act." Mohanty writes that this act of walking together for several days achieved much more than just helping to move the wheels of bureaucracy, and the passing of the law. It provided a real-time workshop for the participants in learning how the process of trying to *right the wrong* works without resorting to violence; the secret lies in our willingness to sacrifice our own self-interest for a time and to collaborate with others no matter how "other" they might be in other respects:

> The "foot march" was like a mobile training program on nonviolence to deliver jus-
> tice to the rural society. The sacrifice of those who walked included walking in the
> hot sun for an average of 15 km per day, sleeping on the road, and living on little and
> simple food.

This is the power of nonviolence for spiritual growth and physical peace through the strength in unity, seeking good for all, putting aside differences, and remaining faithful to the golden rule.

References

Gandhi, M. K. 1922. *Speeches and Writings of M. K. Gandhi*. Madras: G. A. Natesan & Co.
Gandhi, M. K. 1926. *Young India*, October 14, 1926. New Delhi: Navajivan Trust.

7

The Irrelevance of euro-christian Dichotomies for Indigenous Peoples
Beyond Nonviolence to a Vision of Cosmic Balance

Tink Tinker

The idea of Indians as members of a "martial race," although not among the initial perceptions of native people articulated by [e]uropean colonists, is older than the United States itself.

Tom Holm

[As] to pre-Columbian warfare we know almost nothing, and what little we do know suggests that where wars took place, they were infrequent, short, and mild: in fact "war" … seems a misnomer for the kinds of [fighting that took] place, in which some act of bravery or retribution rather than death, say, or territory, would have been the object, and two "war parties" might skirmish without [lethal] effect on either one and none at all on home villages. Early European settlers often made a mockery of Indian warfare … John Underhill wrote of the Pequots that their wars were more for pastime than to conquer and subdue their enemies, and Henry Spelman, who lived among the Powhatans, said that "they might fight seven years and not kill seven men…" Organized violence, in short, was not an attribute of traditional Indian societies, certainly not as compared with their [e]uropean contemporaries, and on the basis of this imperfect record what is most remarkable about them is their apparent lack of conflict and discord.

Kirkpatrick Sale

Each morning these days I take my 5-year-old granddaughter out for an early morning walk to give her grandma a few minutes longer to sleep. "Good morning, cousin," she calls out to a rabbit. *wichozpa* walks (or navigates her scooter) very

Peacemaking and the Challenge of Violence in World Religions, First Edition.
Edited by Irfan A. Omar and Michael K. Duffey.
© 2015 John Wiley & Sons, Ltd. Published 2015 by John Wiley & Sons, Ltd.

carefully down the sidewalks, every now and then asking me to carefully circum-vent an ant or roly-poly bug. She would not want her granddad to hurt any of our relatives. In learning to relate to the world around her in this way, our little Osage *wichozpa* is learning and internalizing values that course through indigenous cultures on every continent.[1] At the same time, as we will discover later in this essay, traditional Indian folk find it a logical impossibility to affirm the philosophical position of nonviolence simply because eating a meal requires certain acts of violence against our relatives, whether four-legged or vegetative.

Religion

In terms of this volume it is important first of all to note that American Indian cultural traditions have never been included in euro-christian category of "world religions," for racialized reasons that assigned all Native Peoples to the realm of the primitive, savage, and uncivilized. In one important sense, excluding Native traditions from the category of world religions is actually correct, since whatever it is Indian Peoples do traditionally is inherently both local and cosmic in orientation rather than globally or universally metacosmic – to use Aloysius Pieris' distinction (Cruz 2004). Pieris, a sri lankan jesuit scholar, uses the term metacosmic to name so-called "world" religions as religions that are not rooted in specific locals or places but, rather, have inherently globalizing aspirations.[2] By local and cosmic, we mean to say that Indian folk experience their own place as the center of a cosmic whole, but that their experience of the cosmos is not an experience they would be in any way tempted to impose on peoples who experience the cosmos in other local places. To that extent, Indian communities were never evangelistic or proselytizing.

It will also be helpful to acknowledge from the outset that American Indian religious traditions have never fitted into and dare not be retroactively reduced to the more general modern euro-christian category called *religion*, never mind that more discrete category of world religions. Indeed traditional elders in all Indian communities have been clear over many generations now that our communities never had a traditional category called religion at all (see my entry in the *Encyclopedia of the American Indian* from a couple of decades ago).[3] In other words, the category itself is a colonialist imposition that cannot work with any accuracy for Indian folk in the final analysis.

We can say this much: The phenomena collectively called American Indian religious traditions encompass a wide variety of culturally discrete customs, behaviors, and practices that derive from the particularity of different national communities. While there certainly are deep structure similarities, the surface structure expressions can vary widely from one community to another. Plains Indian traditions are quite different from those of the new mexican Pueblos. And the traditions of the northeast are equally distinct from both, as again are the traditions of the northwest or the southeast. The first thing all of these have in

Figure 7.1   Native American dancers. Source: Osage News. Photo by Benny Polacca

common, of course, is that each is indigenous to the land, that is, to a particular geographical place, something that provides a sharp distinction between American Indians and the nomadic euro-christian commodification of land. But what does it mean to suggest a rootedness in place as a common denominator among such different American Indian communities? How does "place" serve as some deep structure connectivity?

The ultimate difference between American Indians and our euro-christian conquerors is one that can be classified as worldview, a notion to which we will return later in this essay. The American Indian framing of life around issues of place or spatiality is just the opposite of the euro-christian emphasis on framing life around issues of time and temporality and the broad-based temporal/progress oriented value system embraced by these colonial invaders. We should remember here that theological notions of redemption and eschatology are certainly temporal concerns. Thus, abandoning one's homeland in favor of invading and occupying another land is framed at its earliest in terms of a new temporal elite, that is, in terms of a new "chosen people" conquering a new "promised land" under divine guidance.[4] In contrast, the most life-affirming metaphors in all Indian communities are images of relationship, and particularly relationship to place, where place is not merely geographical location but is relational in terms of personhood and personality.

So then we might immediately enquire as to what other cognitive experiences these Indian traditions do have in common. One of the first identifiers that comes to mind is the pervasive notion of cosmic/holistic harmony and balance as the ultimate ideal or goal of all human activity – rather than an ideal of competitive achievement (which presumes various kinds of violence) at one end of the euro-christian spectrum, or notions of combating violence with nonviolence at the other end. Moreover, balance requires a community-ist relational perspective rather than the individualist ideology of euro-christian cultures. Balance is the key goal, for instance, rather than some notion of personal salvation or redemption. This notion is pervasive in Indian cultures, in the traditional stories people tell, in the very memory of human beginnings.

Balance is conceived in ways that pertain to each person, each family, each clan, whole villages, and ultimately to the cosmos surrounding a people. It is community-ist in the sense that personal balance can only be constituted in the relational context of the community whole. The balance of the community and the person's relationship to the community whole has to be the foundational concern of every person. More than that, a community's balance is predicated on the cosmic balance of our relatives in the cosmic whole around us.

Both as an ongoing daily personal practice and as a larger community-wide special event, ceremony is an important means for maintaining and restoring balance. Ceremony requires dedicated time, thought, and intentionality. Each day was marked by numerous personal ceremonial acts, beginning, for instance, with the personal song recited by each Osage upon arising in the morning. At the community level, some Osage ceremonies took several days to complete. Thus, ceremony was an important category for all Native Peoples in north America, yet we need to insist that ceremony is not a category of religion, per se, and especially not a category that can be simplistically reduced to euro-christian notions of worship and doctrine.[5]

Rather, ceremony is about structured ways of building and maintaining relationships, particularly those relationships we might classify as cosmic relationships. That is, we are maintaining and restoring relationships of balance with all our relations, including human and other-than-human relatives and those relatives that live in that other plane of existence we loosely call (in English) the spirit world (Hat 2012). Ceremony can involve action at the personal level as well as the whole community. Some are mandated by one's place in the community: among the two divisions of an Osage village, for instance, *hunka* (earth folk) are required to privilege right-sidedness; *tzisho* (sky folk), to the contrary, sleep on the left side and dress left-side first, putting on the left moccasin before the right. These are ceremonial acts that remind Osage folk of their place in a relationship to the cosmic whole. If *hunka* sleep on their right side, they are facing their *tzisho* relatives from opposite sides of the east–west road that divides the village; thus the two hold themselves in unity even as they are divided by a road. Sky and earth are thus held in a balance of reciprocal dualism even within the physical architectural structure of the village. In many other cases, personal ceremony was mandated solely for the person by virtue of some vision or dream. Others would never think to criticize or naively copy someone else's response to spiritual communication from the other side. At the same time in a traditional community context, everyone would understand implicitly that even their personal ceremonies function "so that the People might live."

Balance as Reciprocal Dualism

The collective worldview of American Indians across the continent, then, is one of reciprocal dualism, a dualism that is very different from the euro-christian oppositional/manichaean dualism of good versus evil. If we do not identify the enemy as evil, it is much harder to wipe them out, to kill them indiscriminately. Yet, our histories and traditions, even our stories, have been "euro-formed" by scholars and missionaries, to use Seneca scholar Barbara Mann's useful phrase, so that the colonized reflect back to the colonizer precisely the colonizers' own christian worldview of good vs. evil (Mann 1998). Since this struggle of good vs. evil was always perceived as a universal by euro-christian invaders, they reasoned that Indians must have divided the world likewise. Thus, the invaders proceeded to impose their perception of reality willy-nilly on each Indian nation they encountered. So the Iroquoian twins, key figures in the Seneca (*et al.*) creation stories, have been persistently cast in euro-christian interpretation as one good and one evil (Mann 2004).

Mann insists to the contrary that the twins represent something far more balanced than the tensive opposites of good and evil. Rather, they represent male creator personalities (balanced in prior stories by two female creator figures) who try, on the part of one, to make the world easy and comfortable for the two-leggeds; and for the other (the so-called *evil* twin in the euro-christian interpretation) to provide natural challenges to give people reasons for living. So mountains, tornadoes, earthquakes, storms, floods, and so on, are not created by an "evil" twin, but are simply created by the other twin as challenges to make life interesting and to balance the comfort and ease created by his brother. In this way, balance is marked as a crucial value from the very beginning of life.

This never-ending quest for establishing and maintaining balance in the cosmos then affected the particularities of the responsibilities of each of our clans. Each had its own discrete part to play in maintaining the whole. Just one example: while my immediate family is eagle clan, I have two sons who are also adopted members of the buffalo bull clan, a clan that also includes my granddaughter. So close to our buffalo siblings are members of this clan that they are proscribed from eating buffalo meat, since their spiritual responsibility is to protect the sacred relationship between the buffalo nation and the whole of the Osage community who historically have relied on buffalo meat for protein.

Warfare

In order to make my case for traditional Indian ideologies of harmony and balance, we will need to diffuse and refute some long-standing colonialist euro-formed misconceptions about Indian Peoples of this continent that surface persistently in colonialist historical rhetoric. White euro-christian scholars, along with other colonialist voices (missionaries, government functionaries, etc.), have done a great injustice to

Indian people in their interpretations of what they perceive to be Indian war-making habits. Indians are, to name the stereotypes, war-like, bloodthirsty, barbaric savages who have no respect for human life. So deeply embedded are these colonialist misconceptions, from Hollywood portrayals to university classrooms, that it is clear to most fourth graders on this continent yet today that Indian people were savages who live, even now, as warrior cultures. Little white lies, except there is nothing trivial or benign about these tenaciously determined and demeaning prevarications, no matter how "professional" they might seem in academic texts – with all their claim to "objectivity." While this lie about Indian Peoples is utterly self-serving on the part of the christian conqueror, it is so tightly imbricated with the psychological and theological need to justify and validate their own violent history of murder and land theft that the lie has become the well-rehearsed, common-sense truth on this continent, a deeply embedded part of the american narrative.[6]

We should never forget, for instance, that just as the euro-christian word-smithing and military machinery began its invasion of north America (Episcopalians, pilgrims, Puritans), christian folk on the european continent (and in England) were killing each other by the millions (1618–1648) to determine which particular interpretation of the salvific death of Jesus would rule the continent. In the light of the euro-christian history of warring and violence, we should *ipso facto* resist any euro-christian historical description of people native to north America as warlike, savage, or hostile. All descriptions of Indians in terms of bad Indians and good Indians, hostiles and nonhostiles, serve explicitly to legitimize euro-christian intentions to steal Native lands – even as they implicitly depict the invading euro-christian hordes as righteous and innocent.[7]

Given this euro-christian colonialist landscape – in academia and in the public imaginary, fueled by Hollywood representations and television – we need to deal forthrightly with this imputed American Indian proclivity for violence. On the contrary, it seems actually self-evident that Indian Peoples across the continent valued a peaceful and balanced state of being, even as they kept up skills and a ready vigilance for protecting their communities.[8] We get a hint of this truth in the research already reported by American Indian scholars. *Ojibwa-Cree* author, D'Arcy McNickle, demonstrated nearly eight decades ago (1936) that at least 70% of pre-contact Indian societies practiced no form of warfare (Halsey 1992). And my own work would suggest that even this surprising number is a very low estimate, arguing that even those that have been purported to have words for war actually do not. At least there was no word for "war" until colonialist missionaries and government functionaries came along and picked a word in each language to function in ways that made sense to their own euro-christian war-making/warrior culture sensibilities. From our Native perspective, the euro-christian warrior cultures and their persistent war-making savagery has left the whole world in radical imbalance for more than five centuries.

Francis La Flesche, an Omaha ethnographer engaged in research among the Osage, reported that defensive military action was always honored much more highly among the Osage than offensive battle. The highest tribal honors were always reserved for those who demonstrated heroism in the defense of an Osage town and of women and children in particular. In a wonderful chapter in his monograph on American Indian veterans of the US war against Vietnam, Cherokee scholar Tom Holm (himself a Vietnam veteran) demonstrates the dramatic differences between tribal peoples' practice of "war" and the massively destructive forms of warfare that have emerged in the euro-west (1996). In the course of his description, he reiterates the relatively nonviolent nature of Indian warfare. Warfare in north America showed little interest in conquest, the total destruction of an enemy, or even the subjugation of an enemy prior to the invasion of european peoples. In fact, he refers to traditional Indian warfare as "relatively bloodless encounters" (Holm 1996). Armed conflict in Indian cultures was nearly always limited to skirmishes over territorial boundaries and was limited in its perpetration of violence. If a single member of a military contingent was lost in a battle, it caused considerable uproar in an Osage town.

Likewise, the numbers of those killed in battle in Sioux history prior to the devastating military outbreak of war with the United States was very minimal indeed. One or two deaths every three to four years, with frequent ambiguity as to the cause of death, are the sorts of numbers recorded in the winter counts. Thus, the euro-western war-making with its thousands of deaths (e.g., Roman, Goth, Vandal conflicts) and then millions of deaths (from the 30 Years War to World War I and World War II) is mind-boggling and appalling to Indian folk. Yet it seems that euro-western folk are left somewhat insensate to war death, numbed by the historical numbers.

While early conflicts between Indian communities almost always involved hunting territories, the resulting casualties were extremely low until euro-christian conquest pressed Indian communities to respond in ways that were counterintuitive to their traditional cultural values. Extant Lakota winter-counts, for example, recall minuscule numbers of military deaths or campaigns prior to the 1854 aggression of the US military in killing an important *wazhazhe* Lakota leader.[9] In the century prior to 1854 the number of people killed is almost always countable on one hand and usually with one finger. After the Euro-Christian murder of *wazhazhe* headman Conquering Bear, all bets were off. The *wazhazhe* were forced in an act of self-defense to kill the entire platoon of 29 men commanded by a rash, utterly racist, and inexcusably over-confident lieutenant intent on punishing this Lakota band for killing a lame, abandoned cow for food. In retaliation for Lt Grattan's death a year later, William Harney, an army colonel called "Woman Killer" by the Lakota, led US army troops to slaughter an entirely different band of Lakota People (*Brule Sicangu* people who were uninvolved at the murder of Conquering Bear) at the massacre of Bluewater Creek, murdering and abducting an inordinate number of women and children. About 40% of Little Thunder's band were killed in this vicious and premeditated pre-emptive attack.

While La Flesche reminds us that defensive commitments dominated traditional Osage military involvement, his recording of the actual ceremony is most instructive. The so-called Osage "war" ceremony (like other Indian languages, the Osage language has no word for war, per se) bore the less assuming name *washábe athi^n watsi* (the making charcoal dance). It was performed in preparation for the military defense of a village and was in all its aspects identical to the ceremony performed before hunting buffalo. Both ceremonies, then, were very complex and all-encompassing. The Osage Council of Elders (*nó^{n}ho^{n}zhi^{n}ga*) had to make a carefully considered decision that military action was called for in the situation at hand. A decision to engage in military defense called for a lengthy and costly resource-consuming community ceremony of preparation. In every case one of these elders needed to step forward and agree to become the spiritual leader of the military contingent, requiring that elder to engage in serious fasting before and even during the arduous journey with the military contingent (La Flesche 1939). For this defense of the village ceremony to continue toward fruition, we should also remember that the ceremony required that the designated *nó^{n}ho^{n}zhi^{n}ga* from each clan had to be in attendance with the appropriate ceremonial components in order for the ceremony to proceed. This complex necessity was insurance that the consensus of the whole was intact before the military action was irreversibly engaged.

Even after such serious and costly ceremonial preparation, conflicts were quite often resolved without loss of life on either side. On the other hand, any Osage loss of life required a careful explanation to the Council of Elders when the military contingent returned to the village. That is, the utter gravity of warfare for Osage peoples can be seen in their ceremonial reaction to the loss of a single combatant's life. Any Osage combat unit that returns home having lost one of their members is not allowed to reenter the village or the special ceremonial house of *wako^n* until the elders ascertain responsibility for the loss of life and certain ceremonies have been conducted by those elders (La Flesche 1939). That is to say, the loss of one human life was considered a terrible price to pay for having engaged in battle with an enemy, however necessary that battle may have been.

At the same time any enemy loss of life became a time for the Osage People to gather with respect for that fallen enemy. First of all, the killing of an enemy required Osages to engage in a soul-releasing ceremony on behalf of that enemy casualty upon return to the village. Second, crying for the fallen enemy became also an important part of the ceremony to end the cycle of violence. Even while still in the field, an Osage military battalion was called upon to shed tears for those they had killed in battle. As J. O. Dorsey reports:

> After mourning over their own dead, they will mourn for the foe just as if he was a friend. At certain intervals (answering to every two or three hours, as we reckon time), the standard bearers tell the captains to command the warriors to mourn. (Dorsey 1884).

When the military excursion was of the "mourning" variety, there was a much lengthier ceremony that needed to be completed in order to mark the community's return to peace and balance. It includes a much more remarkable act of mourning for the slain enemy. The ceremonial (spiritual) leader of the mourning combat brigade is constrained to shed tears in a formal manner for the enemy who was killed. More importantly, he is obligated to make the same rite of vigil for the slain enemy that he had made before the military excursion for an Osage who had died and had been the initial cause of the military outing. That is, the ceremonial leader (the aforementioned elder) would immediately leave the village behind to engage in a wilderness fast for a period of seven days of crying, thirst, and hunger.[10]

These two acts, I want to argue, are certainly inconsistent with the sort of blood-thirst that euro-christian scholars (including an orthodox jewish historian) have projected back on these ancient Osages. Further, all of this was part of restoring the balance that had been necessarily disrupted with the resort to the military defense of the people. And I would be remiss by not recounting that what I have described here for the Osage People worked its way out in similar ceremonial structures in every north American Indian community. Ceremonial particularities would invariably be different; the underlying (deep structure) meanings would be very much the same.

Figure 7.2   Seal of the Osage Nation. Source: Reproduced by permission of the Licensing Agent, Osage Nation

Nonviolence as Incompatible

Nonviolence is a contemporary euro-christian cultural signifier that is too easily presumed by the "liberal colonizer" as some sort of universal that all people should automatically affirm. Indeed, given Osage and other Native Peoples' hesitancy to engage in reckless and wanton killing, one might think that affirming a philosophy of nonviolence might be almost automatic. Yet this is far from the reality. In actuality, in a traditional Indian context this language of nonviolence makes no sense and should not be used to describe the cultural practices of Indian Peoples. To begin with, nonviolence as the contemporary liberal/radical euro-christian/Gandhian (and increasingly global) ideal for achieving peace has always framed violence as something perpetrated by humans on other humans. That is, affirming this notion of nonviolence seems automatically to impose euro-christian notions of anthropocentrism on anyone using the category. Indian peoples could never limit the category of violence only to acts perpetrated on other human beings, which means that the category itself simply fails to compute within Indian culture. Nonviolence is a logical and, more importantly, practical impossibility.

We have already pointed to one aspect of the problem: We need to eat in order to live. In order to eat, we must necessarily perpetrate acts of violence against our close relatives. For instance, the traditional Osage village depended both on the "three sisters" (corn, beans, and squash) and on our sibling the buffalo for survival – which means taking their lives in the process and thus perpetrating violence against relatives and disturbing cosmic balance, constantly requiring ceremonial acts to restore balance. Whether it is our three sisters or our buffalo siblings or any other living thing that we take for our own subsistence, we are committing a violent act that must somehow be mitigated in order to bring the world back into balance. Among the Osage, this principle was manifest in the ceremony of "Mourning for the Slain Enemy" – something that could hardly be imagined occurring in the dominant euro-christian culture that so decidedly structures modern life. Similarly, while clear-cutting forests has been the status quo for industrialized euro-western societies, cutting a tree down for the (sacred) sun dance ceremony has never been a simple thing for Native Peoples. It has always involved its own complex ceremony accompanied by deep spiritual conversation with the tree relative whose life is to be taken and replete with (sacred) offerings given back to the "tree nation" for the life of this one tree relative.

Contemporary nonviolence theories and practices, always implying euro-christian modernity's notion of anthropocentrism as a concern for intra-human violence, focus invariably on the wellbeing of human persons involved in conflictive encounters with one another. Even in the contemporary call for environmental protection, the persistently expressed anxiety is whether the planet will be able to provide for the continuing existence of human beings. Or, as conservative Denver radio pundit Mike Rosen stated so succinctly:

> Call me human-centric if you like, but in the final analysis, the only reason to preserve the balance of nature is to sustain human life. In the absence of humans, what would it matter if the Earth existed?" (Rosen 2006)

In this light, nonviolence seems invariably intended to speak to intra-species, human-on-human violence, something that would immediately preclude an American Indian worldview perspective. I was asked a couple of years ago to speak on American Indian notions of nonviolence to a national gathering of the Christian Peacemaking Teams organization (CPT). After acknowledging CPT's highly respectable history of "peace" intervention, I began that talk by insisting that I have never been committed to a philosophy of nonviolence – and somewhat facetiously suggested that CPT (a classic non-violence activist organization) also lacked that philosophical commitment. I pointed to a long table in the back of the room that they had set up for our supper buffet at the completion of my talk and said, "If we are going to eat, none of us can really profess nonviolence, since our very eating is predicated on the perpetration of violence against our relatives."

For Indian people, the term relationship never signaled merely human relationships, but has always been inclusive of all "people," from humans to animals, birds, trees, mountains, and even rocks.[11] So when we pray, "For all my relatives" (e.g., the common Lakota prayer, *mitakuye ouyasin*), we mean to include all of life and not just next of kin within our own species.

Needless to say, then, an American Indian must approach the topic of violence from a very different perspective than most contemporary social justice writers. On the other hand, the notion of balance or harmony does fit all traditional Native communities. Instead of nonviolence, the American Indian goal is always and at all times to "restore" balance in the world and to disrupt it as little as is necessary. Indeed the ideal of cosmic balance is played out at levels from the personal to the community to the immediate world around us.

World Incommensurability: the Dissimilitude of Otherness

At this point it becomes imperative that I emphasize more explicitly the enormous and immutable worldview differences that impede any easy Indian appropriation of contemporary euro-christian (and Gandhian) notions of nonviolence. That is, the American Indian worldview is in most respects the polar opposite of the euro-christian worldview. This difference, argues Deloria, is the "fundamental factor that keeps Indians and non-Indians from communicating." They are, says

Deloria, "speaking about two entirely different perceptions of the world" (Deloria [1979] 2012). The worldview of these two disparate human communities, that is, the deep structure realities of euro-christian culture and American Indian cultures are inherently in opposition to one another. Or as Barbara Mann puts it in *Iroquois Women*, "[I]n the [e]uropean/Iroquoian instance, none of the metanarratives of the two cultures coincide," where metanarrative (a word that can function as a parallel to worldview) signals the fundamental underlying structures of thought that shape the way that a community of people think (Mann 2004). In other writings I have tried to highlight key worldview differences between these two cultures: radical individualism in the euro-christian west vs. communityism; manichaean monism vs. Indian reciprocal dualism;[12] foundational temporality (e.g., "time is money") vs. Indian foundational perceptions of spatiality, place, and land. And most notably I have pointed to the up–down image schema in the christian west resulting in clear hierarchies in all aspects of world perception vs. what I have described as the American Indian egalitarian–collateral image schema that results in a perception of the world that puts humans on the same plane as all other living nonhuman persons (Tinker 2013).

We have already noted the absence of the typical euro-christian notion of anthropocentrism in the Native worldview. In the list of metanarrative or worldview differences we might point to, this distinction is absolutely essential. While many liberal euro-christian folk today presume that they are challenging the deeply embedded anthropocentrism in their tradition, they still, almost necessarily, live anthropocentric lives. If there is a bug infestation problem in the house, they still exterminate – maybe looking for bug sprays that are less toxic for human beings (and their pets). Even those committed to environmental justice have a strong tendency in most cases to argue the survival of other species is important to the survival of the human species first of all. For Indian folk a view that we might call distinctly nonanthropocentric runs very deep in the basic traditional values of every community and comes to mind in nearly every moment. As any culturally intact Indian will be quick to recite, we are all relatives, human and nonhuman – or rather, other-than-human persons (Wildcat 2013).

Anthropocentric thinking, first of all, derives from the basic hierarchical structures of the euro-christian worldview, what I have called a foundational up–down image schema (following the lead of cognitive linguistic theorists). Euro-christian folk have long imagined themselves in a hierarchical relationship with all of creation and with all species categorized as "lower" than human – just as women and femininity have been structured traditionally in the christian west as lower on the human scale than men or masculinity. In the euro-christian worldview, the earth was created explicitly for human beings at the top of the creational hierarchy – who were empowered to name, classify, and categorize into taxonomies, before exercising their privilege and status to use up the rest of the world. We should note here that the more progressive euro-christian theological move to supplant the Hebrew Bible's notion of "dominion" (Genesis 1) with a more responsible notion of stewardship certainly fails to change the hierarchical relationship embedded in euro-christian thinking. This new theological perspective still has humans at the top exercising control (now responsibility) over lesser life forms. More to the point, hierarchy (the up–down image schema) always puts someone in authority to pass judgment on the worth of someone or even everyone else, and ultimately it is that judgment that allows for one people to exercise violence on another. Yet we must add that hierarchy and the up–down image schema – along with its collateral Manichaean division of the world into good and evil – is ultimately flat and uni-directional, almost limited to a two-direction dichotomy.

The American Indian egalitarian–collateral image schema expands those dimensions exponentially and significantly changes the conceptual terrain. When we talk about relatives (e.g., the invocation "For all my relatives"), our horizons are immediately expanded to include those persons other-than-human. Thus, "my relatives" include much more than my immediate family or even all two-legged folk of the world. Indeed it necessarily includes all of life on our planet: the four-legged persons; the flying persons (from birds to butterflies, and even flies); and all those people called the living-moving ones (that is, the mountains and rivers; the trees and the rocks; corn, beans, and squash; the fish in the lakes and the ocean. Only then can we begin to appreciate the moral ethic involved in concern for *all our relatives* – including especially those other-than-human relatives.[13] Ultimately our understanding of our relationship with all that lives in the world around us is an understanding of a shared earth. When Indian people take from the earth we always feel a need to return something of value back to the earth. So, for instance, we might need cedar leaves to use ceremonially as a medicine; we would use the smoke of the cedar to purify or might use a cedar tea for a variety of medicinal purposes. Yet before we can take these cedar leaves for our use, we would always offer something, perhaps tobacco, back to the cedar tree persons as a way thanking the cedar trees and doing our part to maintain harmony and balance. And yes, before picking the tobacco some offering would be made back to the tobacco plant persons to thank them for their gift.

Whatever we humans take requires some reciprocal act of giving back to our cosmic relatives in order to repair any disruption of cosmic balance. It becomes all the more important to remember how to perform those ceremonies needed, on a daily as well as a periodic basis, to restore balance in the cosmos and to maintain balance in our relationships with those other-than-human people around us. Thus in our balancing of the world around us there is much more at stake than just one's own village or a community's national wellbeing. If we act recklessly and thoughtlessly we could easily put the whole cosmos out of balance – for others as well as for ourselves.[14] In most Indian national communities there was an annual ceremony that functioned more generally to restore balance. Ceremonies like the Plains Indian sun dance or the southeastern Green Corn Dance were concerned for the renewed balance of the whole cosmos. In most Indian national community contexts, the killing of any one (human or other-than-human) was not allowed in the vicinity of the ceremony because of the nature of the ceremony itself.[15]

Relationship = Less Extraneous Violence

As Cherokee legal scholar Steve Russell reports, "According to our traditions, much human sickness comes from humans mistreating other animals. Therefore, we apologize when we kill for food, and express our gratitude" (Russell 2013). If we live with a sense that we cannot hurt any person (human or nonhuman) without both a clear purpose and some ceremonial act, if we cannot disturb medicine persons like sage or cedar or tobacco without ceremonial acts of giving back, then it should stand to reason that we certainly cannot recklessly hurt any other human person. Thus I must argue that we should be negotiating a massive shift away from the dominant euro-christian worldview with its implications of hierarchy, away from modern euro-christian cultures, toward a worldview of interrelationship. The mitigation of violence (not a commitment to nonviolence) that historically and traditionally characterized Native communities in north America ought to be very attractive to liberal euro-christian folk who share the traditional Indian revulsion with the history of euro-christian violence that has swallowed up our land and increasingly the whole world during the past 500 years, the history of christian violence that seems to be perpetuated in US foreign policy decisions even today.

Perhaps Barack Obama should have engaged in a 12- or 13-day ceremony before deploying any murderous drone attack in Afghanistan or Pakistan. Perhaps there is a ceremony we have not yet discovered to protect the earth from leaking crude oil from intercontinental pipelines, a ceremony known only to Keystone XL, Enbridge, or other pipeline mega-corporate structures – which are persons only by the spiritual magic of some invented and imaginary "rule of law." If Suncor Energy and other extractive mega-corporations functioning in the tar sands had performed religious ceremonies prior to clear-cutting Alberta's boreal forest, if they had spoken to the trees as relatives explaining why their death was necessary, and if they had returned something of value back to the forest, we might be constrained to be more lenient in our criticisms. Even this, of course, can never make right the devastation of the aboriginal peoples of those lands who have been thoroughly adversely affected and displaced – culturally as well as physically – not to mention their close relatives (fish, game, forests, etc.) who have been utterly destroyed. Instead, we have extraction industries that return hazardous waste to the environment in the form of naphthenic acid, trace metals such as methyl mercury and other pollutants into the watershed sickening human communities (e.g., increasing cancer death rates, poisoned food supplies) as well as destroying the habitats of so many of our other-than-human relatives. Here, both the earth and Indigenous Peoples are crying out for a cessation of violence to which nonviolence advocates certainly should respond!

My argument would suggest that American Indian Peoples, the aboriginal *owners* of north America,[16] have much to teach the colonial-christian settlers who have conquered our lands. We might all begin with personal commitments to balance and the mitigation of violence in our everyday lives. While it seems strange to think of doing ceremony before buying a pound of ground hamburger (there is no hunting ceremony for that!), perhaps we could at least learn to make a small food offering (a personal ceremonial act) to the ancestral spirits to include them in our lives. *wichozpa* (my granddaughter) makes a small plate before every meal, taking some of everything prepared for the meal, to offer it and to invite our relatives in the spirit world to share with us – always remembering the spirits of those plants and animals that provide for us in that meal.

If we can begin to recognize our appropriate place in the world in a concern for all our relatives in the cosmos, human and other-than-human, then notions of justice and peace would flow naturally from that spiritual center. If I know empirically that I am related to all these persons in the world, then it becomes more difficult for me to hurt any one of these persons, human or other-than-human. It becomes more difficult to engage in any war to destroy one's enemy when we understand the enemy as our relatives. Then eventually living in balance becomes a real possibility for the social/political whole.

Questions for Discussion

1. How can peoples with conflicting worldviews begin to communicate with one another without one perpetrating violence on the other? This question is especially acute when one people exercises an almost complete hegemony (read hierarchy again) over the other.
2. How can folk who are culturally euro-christian begin to grapple with the indigenous cultural other on this continent in ways that might change the hierarchical nature of the relationship between these two groups of people: euro-christian colonizer/conqueror and the conquered aboriginal *owners* of the land? The concept of "owning," of course, is already a violent cultural imposition on the worldview of Indigenous Peoples.
3. If euro-christian culture were to begin to correct the anthropocentrism in its cultural foundation, how would euro-christian folk then begin to change its relationship to the rest of creation?
4. Nonviolence is a great idea, perhaps a great starting point. But how do we account for the daily perpetration of violence inherently involved with eating lunch? What happens when euro-christian folk expand their notion of nonviolence to include other-than-human persons?
5. How would an ideal of balance and harmony affect notions of violence and nonviolence? How might a deeply and culturally embedded ideal of balance offer different kinds of solutions within US foreign policy? And how might it change the behaviors of young people on the streets of our cities?
6. How is the Indigenous understanding of the land different from the euro-christian conqueror's understanding?

Notes

1 The Osage Nation, or *wazhazhe*, once resided in a territory that included the modern state of Missouri and small bits of Kansas, Oklahoma and Arkansas. After the political and legal subterfuges of the US government, the Osages were removed from their homes to a small corner of their traditional territory in what is today northeastern Oklahoma. Since *wazhazhe* was always an oral language, I resist imposing any further englishizing colonial spelling conventions on the language. Hence, words at the beginning of a sentence remain uncapitalized.

2 My use of the lower case for such adjectives as "euro," "christian," "jesuit," "sri lankan," etc., is intentional. While nouns naming religious groups might be capitalized out of respect for each Christian – as for each Muslim or Buddhist – using the lower case "christian" or "european" for adjectives allows readers to avoid unnecessary normativizing or universalizing of the principal institutional religious and political quotients of the euro-west. Likewise, I avoid capitalizing such national or regional adjectives as american, amer-european, european, euro-western, etc. I also refer to north America. It is important to my argument that people recognize the historical artificiality of modern regional and nation-state social constructions. For instance, who decides where the "continent" of Europe ends and that of Asia begins? Similarly, who designates the western half of north America as a separate continent clearly divided by the Mississippi River, or alternatively the Rocky Mountains? My initial reasoning extends to other adjectival categories and even some nominal categories, such as euro, and political designations like the right and the left and regional designations like the west. Quite paradoxically, I know, I insist on capitalizing White (adjective or noun) to indicate a clear cultural pattern invested in Whiteness that is all too often overlooked or even denied by american Whites. Moreover, this brings parity to the insistence of African Americans on the capitalization of the word Black in reference to their own community (in contra-distinction to the *New York Times* usage). Likewise, I always capitalize Indian, American Indian, and Native American.

3 See Tinker (1996).

4 See the fine analytical treatment in terms of cognitive linguistics by Steve Newcomb in his groundbreaking legal text: *Savages in the Promised Land: Decoding the Doctrine of Christian Discovery* (Newcomb 2008); in particular, see chapter 3, "The Conqueror Model," pp. 23ff. And here too one should read Robert Warrior's 1989 essay, "Canaanites, Cowboys, and Indians: Deliverance, Conquest, and liberation in Theology Today." reprinted in several anthologies (Warrior [1989] 1995).

5 Since we are discussing characteristically oral cultures, there are also no "texts" or sacred texts to consider. Indeed, most of what is written about these Native traditions is not very helpful for understanding the actualities of what takes place in any community.

6 Mel Gibson's movie "Apocalypto" (2006). A full-blown racist imagination embodying a catholic version of the american narrative.

7 For the appellation of righteousness, we should note the title of Martin Marty's text, *Righteous Empire: The Protestant Experience in America* (Dial Press, 1970). In the case of the Osage People, a classic example of such a self-serving euro-christian colonialist history is the pernicious volume by Gilbert C. Din and Abraham Phineas Nasatir, *The Imperial Osages: Spanish-Indian Diplomacy in the Mississippi Valley* (University of Oklahoma Press, 1983).

8   The comment of Cherokee legal scholar Steve Russell (2013) is to the point: "Traditionally, we separated war leadership from peace leadership because we believed that the skillsets for governing a free people differ from those for making successful war." And we will leave open here what the Cherokee word translated as war actually means.

9   For an accessible Sioux winter count, see the detailed example of the "No Ears" winter count included in Walker (1982). For the first 94 years of the No Ears winter count (up to 1854), there appears to have been a stunningly low rate of combat related fatalities for this *sicangu lakota* band.
    The terrorist murder of wazhazhe chief Conquering Bear is usually spoken of in euro-christian historical accounts as the Grattan Affair, named after the offending US Army lieutenant who brashly led his platoon into Conquering Bear's village issuing threats and eventually killing the chief.

10 La Flesche describes the intensity of the ceremonial requirement:

> The difficulty of complying with this requirement was not so much in the physical hardship it entailed on the ceremonial mourner as in the mental effort he must make in order to bring himself into sympathetic touch with the slain strangers. When mourning for the deceased member of the tribe he had shed tears of heart-felt sorrow, having brought himself into close sympathy with the chief mourner by meditating upon the cause of his grief, upon the kindly deeds of the deceased that had won for him the affection of his people, and upon those tribal ties that unite all the people and make them as one; whereas between himself and the strangers whom he was credited with slaying there existed no personal intimacy, no common ties of sentiment that could stir his heart, there was nothing but the naked, common bond of human sympathy that could save him from making a mockery of this final ceremony; nevertheless, the man, without any show of reluctance, always went forth again to fast and to suffer the pangs of hunger and thirst for a period of seven days during the ceremony of Mourning for the Slain Enemy. (War Ceremony and Peace Ceremony, 138–139)

11 See my essay (Tinker 2004), where I argue an Indian understanding of the consciousness of rocks, rocks as relatives. Also, Vine Deloria, Jr (1999).

12 As Barbara Mann argues in *Iroquoian Women*, the number one is dysfunctional. See also Mann (2010, 2011) and Tinker 2013, pp. 167–179.

13 Here we can begin to see that interrelationship has to do with something much more important than allowing or inviting White New Age relatives to invade the private intimacy of our ceremonies.

14 This, of course, is precisely what we are experiencing globally today in this eco-crisis of global warming. For an example of an American Indian sense of disrupting and restoring cosmic balance, see Leslie Silko's remarkable novel, *Ceremony* (Penguin), 1977.

15 Food was prepared, of course, to feed nonfasting community participants, but the harvesting acts had to be performed off-site unless it was integral to the ceremony itself. Three times in four days at one Lakota sun dance I attended a stray rattle snake crept up out of the canyon next to the arbor and entered the arbor itself. At the first instance, some White visitors ran to get something to use to kill the snake and had to be restrained and told that they were acting inappropriately. Each time two fire keepers

carefully carried the snake out of the arbor and down to the bottom of the canyon and left it there with offerings of tobacco and gentle words asking the snake to stay away until the ceremony was over. At another sun dance the cooks had to be asked to remove the flypaper they had posted to catch flies and keep the flies out of their food preparation. Killing flies was not an option; rather, they had to be tolerated and allowed to take their share of the food.

16 Ownership, of course, is an inherently euro-christian word and finds no counterpart in any Native American Indian language. I use it here merely as a cross-cultural metaphor, one that ultimately fails. Rather than owners of the land, Indian peoples are those who have historically had a close *relationship* to the lands of north America. Cross-cultural communication is inherently problematic, especially in colonial relationships of imbalance.

References

Cruz, Robert, Marshal Fernando and Asanga Tilakaratna. 2005. "Encounters with the Word: Essays to Honor Aloysisu Pieris, S.J." *East Asian Pastoral Review* 42: 4.

Deloria, Jr, Vine. 1999. *Spirit and Reason: The Vine Deloria, Jr, Reader*. Edited by Barbara Deloria and Sam Scinta. Golden, CO: Fulcrum Publishing.

Deloria Jr, Vine. [1979] 2012. *The Metaphysics of Modern Existence*. Golden, CO: Fulcrum Publishing.

Din, Gilbert C. and Abraham Phineas Nasatir. 1983. *The imperial Osages: Spanish-Indian Diplomacy in the Mississippi Valley*. Norman, OK: University of Oklahoma Press.

Dorsey, James Owen. 1884. "An Account of the War Customs of the Osage." *American Naturalist* 18: 126–127.

Halsey, Theresa and M. Annette Jaimes. 1992. "American Indian Women: At the Center of Indigenous Resistance in Contemporary Native America." In *The State of Native America: Genocide, Colonization, and Resistance*. Edited by M. Annette Jaimes, 315. Boston, MA: South End Press.

Hat, Albert White. 2012. *Life's Journey-Zuya: Oral Teachings from Rosebud*. Salt Lake City, UT: University of Utah Press.

Holm, Tom. 1996. *Strong Hearts, Wounded Souls: Native American Veterans of the Vietnam War*. Austin, TX: University of Texas.

La Flesche, Francis. 1939. "War Ceremony and Peace Ceremony of the Osage Indians." *Bureau of American Ethnology* Bulletin 101.

Mann, Barbara. 1998. "Epilogue: Euro-forming the Data." In *Debating Democracy: Native American Legacy of Freedom*. Edited by Bruce Johansen, 160–190. Santa Fe, CA: Clear Light.

Mann, Barbara. 2004. *Iroquoian Women: The Gantowisas*. New York: Peter Lang.

Mann, Barbara. 2010. "A Failure to Communicate: How Christian Missionary Assumptions Ignore Binary Patterns of Thinking within Native American Communities." In *Remembering Jamestown: Hard Questions about Christian Mission*. Edited by Barbara Brown Zikmund and Amos Yong, 29–48. Eugene, OR: Pickwick Publications

Mann, Barbara. 2011. "All My Relatives: The Binary Fractals of the Gift Economy." In *What Comes after Money?* Edited by Daniel Pinchbeck and Ken Jordan, 58–66. Berkeley, CA: Evolver Editions.

Marty, Martin. 1970. *Righteous Empire: The Protestant Experience in America*. New York: Dial Press.

Newcomb, S. 2008. *Savages in the Promised Land: Decoding the Doctrine of Christian Discovery*. Golden. CO: Fulcrum Publishing, 2008).

Rosen, Mike. 2006. "Warming 'Watermelons.'" *Rocky Mountain News*.

Russell, Steve. 2013. "What Baby Veronica's Adopters Should Know about Her Cherokee Roots." *Indian Country Today*, August 13. Accessed 11 December 2014. http://indiancountrytodaymedianetwork.com/2013/08/13/what-baby-veronicas-adopters-should-know-about-her-cherokee-roots.

Sale, Kirkpatrick. 1990. *The Conquest of Paradise: Christopher Columbus and the Columbian Legacy*. Alfred Knopf.

Silko, Leslie. 1977. *Ceremony*. London: Penguin.

Tinker, Tink. 2013. "American Indians and Ecotheology: Alterity and Worldview." In *Eco-Lutheranism*. Edited by Karla Bohmbach and Shauna Hannon, 69–83. Minneapolis, MN: Lutheran University Press.

Walker, J. R. 1982. *Lakota Society*. Edited by Raymond J. DeMallie, 125–157. Lincoln, NE: University of Nebraska.

Warrior, Robert. [1989] 1995. "Canaanites, Cowboys, and Indians: Deliverance, Conquest, and liberation in Theology Today." In *Voices from the Margins: Interpreting the Bible in the Third World*. Edited by R. S. Sugirtharahah, 277–285. Maryknoll, NY: Orbis Books.

Wildcat, Daniel R. 2013. "Just Creation: Enhancing Life in a World of Relatives." In *Buffalo Shout, Salmon Cry: Conversations on Creation, Land Justice, and Life Together*. Edited by Steven Heinrichs, 295–309. Kitchener: Herald Press.

Further Reading

Alfred, Taiaiake. 2005. *Wasáse: Indigenous Pathways of Action and Freedom*. Calgary: Broadview Press. This is a wide-ranging discussion of Native traditional values and worldview by a younger Mohawk scholar. It is very useful for capturing something of the flavor of the Indian world.

Deloria, Jr, Vine. 1999. *Spirit and Reason: The Vine Deloria, Jr, Reader*. Edited by Barbara Deloria and Sam Scinta. Golden, CO: Fulcrum Publishing. Barbara Deloria helped bring this fine collection of Deloria essays together. They cover a large waterfront of issues signaled early on in his work *God is Red*.

Deloria, Jr, Vine. 2003. *God is Red: A Native View of Religion*. 30th Anniversary Edition. Golden, CO: Fulcrum Publishing. Deloria's monumental piece makes an analytical comparison between the Indian worldview and with the worldview and values of the Euro-Christian colonizer. He revised it two decades after the original publication in 1973. It is still the gold standard among American Indian folk.

Holm, Tom. 1996. *Strong Hearts, Wounded Souls: Native American Veterans of the Vietnam War*. Austin, TX: University of Texas. Tom Holm is Muskogee and Cherokee and a veteran of US military service in Vietnam. His study of Indian veterans is nuanced and very useful for understanding Indian cultural issues around military conflict. He has one essay in particular on Indian war-making that is very useful for clarifying the difference between Indian and Euro-Christian values and understandings of violence.

Mann, Barbara. 2006. *Iroquois Women: The Gantowisas*. New York: Peter Lang. Euro-Christian war-making is inordinately gendered around maleness. Mann demonstrates the realities of Native matriarchal social structures that deal with war and violence very differently.

Tinker, Tink. 1996. "Religion." *The Encyclopedia of the North American Indian*. Edited by Frederick E. Hoxie, 537–541. Boston, MA: Houghton Mifflin. A short encyclopedia entry, this advances the argument that religion is a category entirely lacking in traditional Indian communities. Rather, Indian peoples have a way of life, a cultural whole that includes ceremonial structures that White observers persistently want to identify as religion.

Tinker, Tink. 2004. "'The Stones Shall Cry Out': Consciousness, Rocks and Indians." *Wicazo Sa Review* 19 (Fall): 105–125. This is an early Tinker essay that sets the stage for the more cognitive analytical approaches in his later essays. It underscores the interrelationship of all life where even stones are relatives.

Tinker, Tink. 2013. "American Indians and Ecotheology: Alterity and Worldview." In *Eco-Lutheranism*. Edited by Karla Bohmbach and Shauna Hannon, 69–83. Minneapolis, MN: Lutheran University Press. The interrelationship of all living things is under-scored in this essay around a clear articulation of Native worldview. The collateral-egalitarian social structure of the Native world, including all other life forms, means that violence is clearly boundaried around survival needs like eating.

Tinker, Tink. 2013. "Why I Don't Believe in a Creator." In *Buffalo Shout, Salmon Cry: Conversations on Creation, Land Justice, and Life Together*. Edited by Steve Heinrichs, 167–179. Kitchener: Herald Press. The attempt here is also to differentiate the Native collateral–egalitarian worldview from the hierarchical worldview of euro-christianity and its up–down image schema. Tinker uses a cognitive linguistic analysis to advance the argument.

White Hat, Albert. 2012. *Life's Journey – Zuya: Oral Teachings from Rosebud*. Salt Lake City, UT: University of Utah. Published just before White Hat's passing, *Zuya* is perhaps the clearest and richest articulation of a particular community's experience of the world.

Waziyatawin (Dakota). 2013. "A Serpent in the Garden: An Unholy Worldview on Sacred Land." In *Buffalo Shout, Salmon Cry: Conversations on Creation, Land Justice, and Life Together*. Edited by Steve Heinrichs, 210–224. Kitchener: Herald Press. Waziyatawin is a persistent post-colonialist Indian voice, arguing for a discrete understanding of Indian cultures and their worldview.

Wildcat, Daniel R. 2013. "Just Creation: Enhancing Life in a World of Relatives." In *Buffalo Shout, Salmon Cry: Conversations on Creation, Land Justice, and Life Together*. Edited by Steve Heinrichs, 295–309. Kitchener: Herald Press. Wildcat advances Deloria's distinction between space and time along with a coherent description of the Indian experience of the interrelationship of all life.

7.1

A Confucian Response

Sin Yee Chan

Tink Tinker's chapter portrays a fascinating worldview that is complex, enlightening, and refreshing. As he puts it so aptly, the American Indian worldview is beyond the dualism of violence and nonviolence and is anchored in cosmic harmony and equality. All creatures – including humans, animals, birds – are our relatives, and even trees, mountains, and rocks are also connected to sentient creatures. Actions that we take to ensure our own survival necessarily involve violence to something that is valuable and connected to us – the food that we eat, the natural resources that we use to keep us warm, hydrated, and sheltered, all involve acts of violence. In this way, violence is an inevitable part of this cosmic pattern and human existence, and it is the assumption of anthropocentrism that allows us to think mistakenly that humans can and should live a life of nonviolence. However, the inevitability of violence does not mean that harmony and peace cannot be attained. It only means that violence must be a part of the conception of harmony and peace, which is the thought embodied in the American Indian conception of "balance." Through the performance of ceremonies as well as actions that express concern, respect, and/or bring benefits to the "people" of the cosmos, we perform the "reciprocal act of giving back to our cosmic relatives in order to repair any disruption of cosmic balance." While acts of violence are inevitable, we also need to be responsible and be extremely wary in inflicting them. Hence "war" as a word is nonexistent in the American Indian language and we need to mourn for the enemy that we kill.

The American Indian vision of cosmic unity and equality is shared by the Chinese philosophical school of Taoism. Taoism also rejects anthropocentrism and sees humans as an insignificant part of nature as a whole. One expression of this idea can be seen in Chinese landscape painting, which reflects strong Taoist influence. Humans often only occupy a tiny part of the whole painting.

However, I see important differences between Taoism and the American Indian worldview. For example, Taoism believes that as long as humans follow their nature

Peacemaking and the Challenge of Violence in World Religions, First Edition.
Edited by Irfan A. Omar and Michael K. Duffey.
© 2015 John Wiley & Sons, Ltd. Published 2015 by John Wiley & Sons, Ltd.

instead of artificial desires and conceptions, they are following the *dao*, the cosmic principle that explains and supports the cosmic harmony. No action is required to restore balance because harmony already prevails in situations in which each creature follows its own natural desire to survive, enjoy, and live its life in a particular way. There is no "violence" and "nonviolence," for these are only man-made conceptions. The *dao* consists of incessant changes and transformation. Death, being eaten, and being used are a part of the natural change. As humans, we will eventually die and get transformed into some other form of existence and will take our turn to be eaten and used. Hence, whilst humans live, they just need to follow their nature and be free and happy wanderers following the *dao*.

Confucianism and Native American views share the following ideas: cosmic unity, harmony, and rituals. I shall briefly focus on the comparison of these three ideas and raise questions.

Cosmic Unity

Like American Indian culture, Confucianism speaks of cosmic unity: humans are unified with everything else in this world. "All the ten thousand things are there in me" (Mencius 7A:4). Moreover, the role of a deity is insignificant in the idea of cosmic unity of both traditions. On the other hand, there are two important differences between the Confucian idea and that of the American Indian culture. First, the Confucian cosmic unity has a moral nature. As I explain in my chapter, the flood-like *qi* (vapor energy) that is presumed to fill up between Heaven and Earth has a moral dimension. It can only be accumulated by a person who has virtue and not by someone who sporadically does a morally right act. Second, in talking about the trinity of Heaven, Earth and humans, Confucianism does subscribe to anthropocentrism. Within this trinity, a person should "revere what lies within his power and does not long for what lies with Heaven" (Xunzi 17:8). "How can glorifying Heaven and contemplating it, be as good as tending its creatures and regulating them? How can obeying Heaven and singing it hymns of praise be better than regulating what Heaven has mandated and using it?" (Xunzi 17:13). Humans can be seen as the "agent" of Heaven in that they actively tend, regulate, and use the animals and resources created by Heaven. It is by exercising the abilities naturally endowed by Heaven that humans can achieve an orderly government based on virtues; a distinctive accomplishment of humans.

In light of these two points about the moral dimension and the human-centeredness aspect of cosmic unity, I would like to raise the following questions for Tinker:

1. My first question concerns the roles of morality and virtues in the American Indian concept of cosmic unity, especially in the concept of balance. Does one need to be moral in order to achieve cosmic unity? Put differently, is "balance"

considered a moral good? Or is it just a natural good, or just something natural? What are the criteria for deciding whether a person is moral or not? Are those criteria related to the concept of balance, or some other values, such as filial piety, benevolence, loyalty, moral courage, etc.? How are the common human moral values such as loyalty, honesty, and so on related to the idea of balance? Can an amoral person, that is, someone who is not moved by moral or immoral motives, still attain personal balance?

2. My second question is this. I am wondering whether the American Indian worldview still expresses a form of anthropocentrism, though a very, very mild form. For example, according to the American Indian culture, are not a person's duties toward other humans such as his/her family and community still more stringent and more significant than his/her duties toward other nonhumans in the world? Tinker's chapter does seem to suggest that priority or more significant values are indeed accorded to humans. For example, he vividly and sensitively portrays how the American Indians mourn for the death of a human, even an enemy, and what a serious matter it is to launch a "war" and kill in a war. But I do not expect – nor is there any evidence – that American Indians are giving the exact same treatment to the animals that they kill and eat. The fact that we humans are consuming more food than is necessary for survival shows that self-defense is not an adequate ground to justify our current treatment of animals. Above all, if the idea of all equality is assumed, a gruesome and terrible implication will be that we can kill or treat another human in a violent way against his/her consent as long as we perform some ceremonies to express our respect and gratitude, just as we do to animals.

Harmony

The American Indian ideal of harmony can be seen as embodied in the idea of "balance." Tinker writes that "personal balance can only be constituted in the context of the community whole. … A community's balance is predicated on the cosmic balance of our relatives in the cosmic whole around us." Balance is achieved when things achieve a certain kind of coordination. Acts of violence, for example, need to be followed by ceremonies or acts with benefits that "restore the balance." The Confucian idea of harmony as I have explained in my chapter does not include the idea of balance. Instead, harmony is constituted by different things responding to and interacting with each other in a positive way that produces favorable results. Later Confucianism, which was developed after the classical period (i.e. after 220 B.C.E.), does have the idea of harmony as the balancing of the two cosmic forces of *yin* and *yang*. But the two forces take turns to become dominant so that the balance point between them is never static.

Three differences can be observed then, between the Confucian and the American Indian account of harmony. First, in both Confucian accounts of harmony, there is no suggestion of a "middle" position as the American Indian idea of "balance" seems to imply. Second, the American Indian notion of balance requires conscious efforts of reckoning and coordinating each act; something similar to the acts of balancing one's accounts. Such conscious acts are absent in Confucianism. Third, in Confucianism acts to restore a harmony consist of removing the disruptive force, as in the punitive expedition, rather than undertaking a compensatory act as suggested by the Native American notion of balance.

One interesting question that can be raised about the American Indian notion of harmony, then, is whether there is any difference between justifiable acts of violence, such as killing for food, and unjustifiable acts of violence, such as killing for greed, if both are seen as acts upsetting balance and requiring acts of restoration of balance. (This harks back to the earlier question of how morality is related to the idea of cosmic unity and also balance.) Another related question is whether the notion of balance is primarily about retribution or about compensation, or both, or neither. Is there some underlying principle or rationale behind the acts of balancing? If there is, is it similar to the Buddhist idea of *karma* in which one needs eventually to "repay" for the evil deeds that one has done previously? And is the repayment in the form of accumulating positive credits which can cancel out the negative liability, rather than repaying in the form of suffering, as in Buddhism?

Ceremonies/Rituals

Both Confucianism and Native American culture prize rituals and ceremonies. Confucianism believes that rituals can help to achieve social harmony as well as one's moral cultivation. American Indian culture relies heavily on ceremonies to restore balance. Both seem to value the function of rituals to express, channel, and nurture one's emotions and wills with regard to certain significant actions such as mourning and killing. In the Native American culture, ceremonies sometimes seem to be seen as having nonempirical efficacy. For example, in restoring cosmic balance, ceremonies are sometimes performed in the absence of other acts that have concrete compensatory effect.

My question is about the nature of ceremonies in the Native American culture. What are their functions and supposed effects? Do they help to achieve social harmony besides cosmic balance?

7.2

A Hindu Response

Kalpana Mohanty

I feel the power of nonviolence through the honesty, simplicity, and humility of the Native Americans. It is a matter of joy to know that a 5-year-old child calls out to a rabbit, "Good morning, cousin." This is a true example of a child learning to identify with the wider world around her. This is the first step toward nonviolence.

The pervasive notion of cosmic–holistic harmony and balance as the ultimate ideal or goal of all human activity is a crucial value from the very beginning of life, from the personal to the communal. It is similar to the Vedic thoughts in the Hindu Tradition. Ceremony and cosmic relationships with the cycle of nature and also with the spirit world are very similar to the religious practices in many tribal communities in India. The collective worldview of reciprocal dualism in which the Native Americans' refusal to consider their enemy as "evil" prohibits them from killing them is a true example of nonviolence. It is sad to know that the so-called civilized people considered Native Americans as "savages" and "warriors." In fact, the Euro-Christians' theft of native lands was an act of violence.

It is encouraging to know that 70% of Native American societies did not engage in any warfare, and preferred a peaceful and balanced state of being. It is very inspiring to know that the concept of a "relative" includes all living beings – from birds to butterflies and fish, the trees, and the rocks. This concept is similar to the teachings of Isha Upanishad in the Hindu tradition.

It was interesting to learn that Tink Tinker's granddaughter *wichozpa*, makes a small plate of food before every meal to offer relatives in the spirit world and also to plants and animals. This is very similar to the practice in the Hindu tradition of offering food to the crows before every meal. Hindus believe that ancestral spirits reside within the crows.

When the Osages killed an enemy, upon returning to the village they shed tears as part of a ceremony to end violence. The wilderness fast for a period of 7 days to mourn for the enemies they had killed is a true example of repenting for their sins. This can be considered a form of nonviolent practice because it is an attempt to

Peacemaking and the Challenge of Violence in World Religions, First Edition.
Edited by Irfan A. Omar and Michael K. Duffey.
© 2015 John Wiley & Sons, Ltd. Published 2015 by John Wiley & Sons, Ltd.

clear the conscience. Traditional Native Americans argue that in their need for survival, for food, they inflict violence against their close relatives: corn, beans, squash, and buffalos. Later on they mourn for them. Should we not ask ourselves whether we feel that we are effecting violence when we consume food?

Native Americans do not use the word nonviolence; however, they emphasize restoring balance in the world and disrupting as little as possible. The major challenge before us is to understand the subtle difference between nonviolence and restoring balance. I feel that restoring balance in the earth is not possible unless one commits to nonviolence.

Tinker has beautifully explained that the notions of justice and peace must flow naturally from the spiritual center if we think of our "enemy" – and everyone in the world – as a relative. He has truly pointed the way toward discovering the essence of all religions. I am reminded of the opening of a poem:

> After a while you learn the subtle difference
> Between holding a hand and chaining a soul,
> And you learn that love does not mean leaning
> And company doesn't always mean security.
> (from a poem "Comes the Dawn," by Veronica A. Shoffstall,
> cited in Sharilyn A. Ross 2012, *The Spirit of Camp*,
> Maitland, FL: Xulon Press, p. 166)

Conclusion

Irfan A. Omar and Michael K. Duffey

It may be a generalization at some level, nevertheless, it is true that wars have *generally* been organized and waged by men while peacemaking and humanitarian movements have *often* been initiated and managed by women. This seems to be true at least at the grassroots level, where efforts to make peace and seek justice begin without fancy office furniture, buildings, or bank balances. Often the violence impacts women with greater severity because in most places they still happen to be primary caregivers to children and the elderly. In many situations women bear the burden of working with meager economic resources and in dismal social conditions.

Even a cursory look at the hundreds of grassroots groups and communities across the world reveals a deep concern for the rise in violence. Depending on the country and region, these concerns are with violence in varying forms and intensity. Organizations seeking to address domestic violence in the United States are not *fundamentally* different from groups in the Maldives, for example, who show a sense of urgency in drawing attention to climate change. Each is concerned with preventing violence of one kind or another. Military generals are decorated with colorful medals for their ostensible bravery, while others, women and men, who spend their entire lives working and engaging in nonviolent activism for peace, often putting themselves in harm's way, receive little, if any, recognition. Although this book does not directly address the conditions and causes of societal violence a humble acknowledgement of these dynamics is helpful in clarifying the wider field within which this book locates itself.

We have mainly addressed violence committed in the name of religion and what religions say can be done to prevent it. The chapters have included hopeful discussions on various efforts to bring about peace and of growing commitment to nonviolence among people of faith. What is clear from the preceding chapters on the seven religious traditions is that religious teachings and practices offer numerous resources for the prevention and resolution of conflict as well as for peacemaking.

Peacemaking and the Challenge of Violence in World Religions, First Edition.
Edited by Irfan A. Omar and Michael K. Duffey.
© 2015 John Wiley & Sons, Ltd. Published 2015 by John Wiley & Sons, Ltd.

Many of the authors in addition to identifying the resources available for peace-making, also pointed to some of the difficulties in employing these sources in the service of peacemaking. One major obstacle seems to be the practice of insularity that pervades religious communities, not too different from the kind of "us" vs. "them" mentality found in ethnic and class groups. Religious communities are sometimes divided along ethnic lines as well (e.g. Christians and Muslims in Macedonia, Buddhists and Muslims in Indonesia), which makes the dichotomous divide even more prominent and seemingly impossible to overcome.

Hope for the future lies in the work of interfaith dialogue, which offers a promising path toward seeing the other in one's own image. Recognizing the humanity of the other is essential for a truly genuine and lasting peace to emerge. Interfaith dialogue offers the following: it allows one to learn about the other and about oneself through the other (Omar 2005). It helps reduce fear of the other within one's community by a sustained engagement with the aim to find common ground.[1] It gives everyone a chance to work for peace through and within the common moral framework shared by all the major religions of the world. Interfaith collaboration not only provides greater personal strength but also material strength by pooling of resources from different communities (e.g. it would be nice if different communities could use the same space for worship at different times – these multi-faith worship and meditation spaces are now fairly common at airports; this could help save enormous resources and bring communities together at the same time). Interfaith dialogue provides a unique opportunity to see oneself in perspective – that is, "how others see me." It offers a model – which transcends ethnicity, culture, and religion – to be known and emulated.

According to the World Health Organization's report on "Violence Prevention: The Evidence" (2010), over 1.5 million people are violently killed and many more suffer injuries each year. Our world is marked by violence that is not likely to disappear anytime soon. Terrorism is on the rise, some in the name of religion. The voices of exclusion and revenge are increasingly raising the bar of tolerance. In this climate, this book may not seem like it is making a huge difference, but every step, however small, is needed to call attention to existing resources that may help address the problem of violence. Today, communities around the world are more aware and rightly concerned about the increasing militarization of police forces as well as the rising levels of production and sale of weapons. This book makes the voices of peace and nonviolence heard. Thus it is a modest effort with universal aims: to assert the right of every individual to live in peace and to make those religious voices calling for the imperative of peace known, using whatever medium is at our disposal. We want to end with a story of hope.

On August 5, 2012, Wade Michael Page who was identified as a "white supremacist" shot and killed six members of the Sikh Temple in Oak Creek, WI. It was a major tragedy for the Sikh community and the news made national headlines. What followed was quite unprecedented: the entire community in the greater Milwaukee area and others from around the country and the world came together to mourn, remember, and honor those who were killed and to be with those who had survived the attack. They wanted to stand together in this tragedy with their Sikh brothers and sisters. It was dubbed an "American Tragedy" and by all accounts it *was* one (Singh 2012). This was primarily the result of how the Sikh community in Oak Creek had responded to the tragedy. Among the various responses from the relatives of the dead and injured and other members of the Temple, a consensus emerged calling for forgiveness and compassion. There was no desire to exact revenge on the relatives of the shooter (who had killed himself after confrontation with the police). In fact, when the community was arranging the funerals of the six community members, the leaders of the Sikh community wanted to include the seventh coffin (that of the shooter) in the procession along with the coffins of the victims. Their request was denied by the Oak Creek police chief citing security concerns. This was a nonviolent, compassionate response that reflected the teachings of their faith tradition. For days on end, and now two anniversaries later, one can still feel the extraordinary energy and community spirit that resulted from the ashes of that tragic day (Johnson 2013).[2] This was essentially the result of an act of faith – rooted in patience, compassion, and community spirit. The actions of the Sikh community that day showed what faith can do and how it can unite people across faith, color, and even country. It was an interfaith moment *par excellence* that galvanized many people, from various faith traditions and even those with no faith; it even moved the hearts of politicians, law enforcement personnel, media crew, and many others. We hope that practicing of one's faith in this way would help others see that religion can unite across faith lines with the same intensity that has sometimes been used to divide one from another.

Notes

1   Marc Gopin (2002, 57) remembers a hopeful comment by a Croatian diplomat in relation to religious tensions in the Balkans, "remove fear and everything else becomes possible."
2   For some of the photos of the gathering of hundreds who participated in the vigil published in the Milwaukee's leading newspaper, *The Journal Sentinel*, see http://www.jsonline.com/multimedia/photos/218459321.html (accessed December 11, 2014).

References

Gopin, Marc. 2002. *Holy War, Holy Peace: How Religion Can Bring Peace to the Middle East.* Oxford: Oxford University Press.

Johnson, Annysa. "Crowds mark date of Sikh Temple rampage." *The Journal Sentinel.* August 5, 2013. Accessed on December 11, 2014. http://www.jsonline.com/news/crime/sikh-temple-shooting-anniversary-vigil-b9968926z1-218383491.html.

Omar, Irfan A. 2005. "Submitting to the Will of God: Jews, Christians, and Muslims Learning from Each Other." In *Heirs of Abraham: The Future of Muslim, Jewish, and*

Christian Relations. Edited by Bradford E. Hinze and Irfan A. Omar. Maryknoll, NY: OrbisPress.

Singh, Naunihal. 2012. "An American Tragedy." *The New Yorker*, August 13, 2012. Accessed on December 11, 2014. http://www.newyorker.com/news/news-desk/an-american-tragedy.

World Health Organization. 2010. "Violence Prevention: The Evidence." Accessed December 11, 2014. http://www.who.int/violence_injury_prevention/violence/status_report/en/.

Index

Peacemaking and the Challenge of Violence in World Religions, First Edition.
Edited by Irfan A. Omar and Michael K. Duffey.
© 2015 John Wiley & Sons, Ltd. Published 2015 by John Wiley & Sons, Ltd.

Printed in the USA
CPSIA information can be obtained
at www.ICGtesting.com
JSHW012124171223
53894JS00010B/167